The Myth *of* Chinese Capitalism

The Myth of

Chinese Capitalism

The Worker, the Factory, and the Future of the World

Dexter Roberts

St. Martin's Press

New York

First published in the United States by St. Martin's Press,
an imprint of St. Martin's Publishing Group

www.stmartins.com

Designed by Donna Sinisgalli Noetzel
Map by Rhys Davies

Library of Congress Cataloging-in-Publication Data

Names: Roberts, Dexter, author.
Title: The myth of Chinese capitalism : the worker, the factory,
    and the future of the world / Dexter Roberts.
Description: First Edition. | New York : St. Martin's Press,
    2020. | Includes bibliographical references and index.
Identifiers: LCCN 2019043143 | ISBN 9781250089373
    (hardcover) | ISBN 9781250089380 (ebook)
Subjects: LCSH: Capitalism—China. | China—Economic
    policy—2000- | China—Social conditions—21st century. |
    Chinese—Foreign countries.
Classification: LCC HB501 .R573 2020 | DDC 330.951—dc23
LC record available at https://lccn.loc.gov/2019043143

Our books may be purchased in bulk for promotional,
educational, or business use. Please contact your local
bookseller or the Macmillan Corporate and Premium Sales
Department at 800-221-7945, extension 5442, or by email
at MacmillanSpecialMarkets@macmillan.com.

First Edition: March 2020

10 9 8 7 6 5 4 3 2 1

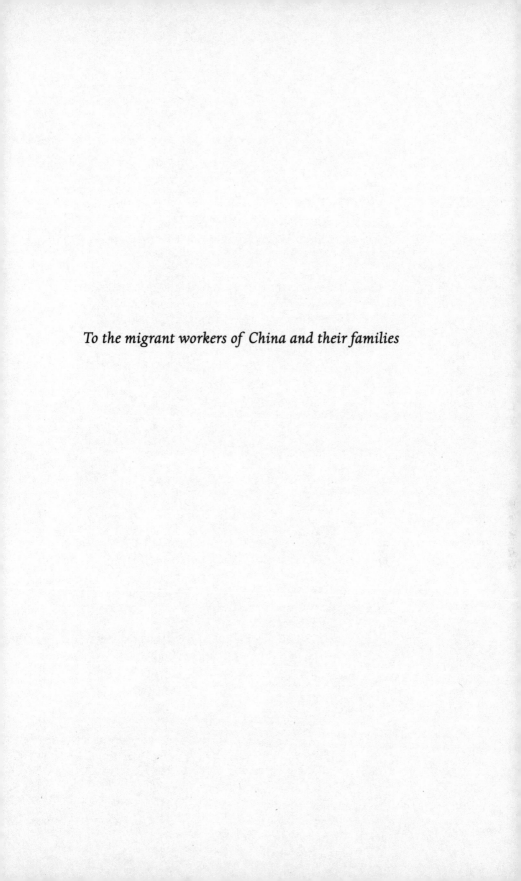

To the migrant workers of China and their families

Contents

Key People in Book

Barshefsky, Charlene: Former U.S. trade representative. Barshefsky helped negotiate China's entry into the World Trade Organization in 2001.

Deng Xiaoping (1904–1997): Long a key member of Mao Zedong's inner circle, Deng was later purged twice by Mao before launching reform and opening of the Chinese economy in late 1978, following Mao's death in 1976. Often called China's "paramount leader."

Dong Xiangzhu: Elderly farmer woman in "empty nest" village of Shangxule, Hebei.

Fang Hongbo: Chairman of Midea, China's largest white-goods appliance maker. Fang's company acquired German robot maker KUKA in 2016.

Fei Xiaotong (1910–2005): Prominent anthropologist and sociologist. Fei was an early advocate for rural land reform and establishing grassroots democracy in the Chinese countryside. After being purged during the Anti-Rightist Movement of 1957, Fei spent twenty years out of academia, at one point cleaning toilets for a living.

Feng Xingya: President of Guangzhou Automobile Group Co. Feng's company is branching into new-energy vehicles and is a large recipient of government Made in China 2025 funds.

Gou, Terry: Founder of Foxconn, Apple's largest supplier.

Gu, Andy: Midea deputy CEO who oversaw the acquisition of KUKA. Gu originally studied demography at Cornell University.

Han Dongfang: Prominent worker leader during the Tiananmen protests of 1989. Thrown in jail in China for a time after the crackdown, Han now runs a labor advocacy group from Hong Kong.

Hong Xiuquan (1814–1864): Leader of the millenarian Taiping Rebellion that seized control of much of southern China from 1850 to 1864. Hong was a utopian who believed in radical land reform and claimed to be the younger brother of Jesus Christ.

Hu Jintao (1942–): China's top leader from 2002 to 2012. Hu launched the New Socialist Countryside policy in 2005 in an effort to improve rural health care and education.

Jiang Zemin (1926–): China's top leader from 1989 to 2002. Jiang rose through the party ranks mainly while based in Shanghai. In 2000, Jiang launched the sweeping Develop the West plan to address the growing regional gap in China.

Lai Ruoyu (1910–1958): Head of the government-run All-China Federation of Trade Unions during huge Shanghai labor protests in 1957. Lai, a former soldier, broke with the official line that blamed workers for their "low-class consciousness" and instead criticized the unions for not aiding workers. He was purged by the party and died of liver cancer in 1958.

Lee, Dee: Founder of a small labor consultancy in Guangzhou. Lee's company consults for global brands and retailers operating in China.

Lenin, Vladimir I. (1870–1924): Russian revolutionary leader and Bolshevik theorist.

Li Keqiang: China's premier from 2012 to the present. Li has pushed for more rapid urbanization in China. The leader, who comes from the interior province of Anhui, has also championed a policy of encouraging "mass entrepreneurship and innovation," which aims to move China to a more sustainable model of growth.

Lin Zexu (1785–1850): Qing dynasty scholar and official known from youth as "unusually brilliant." Lin advocated for the revitalization of traditional Chinese thought. Posted in Guangdong as the imperial commissioner in 1829, he is heralded in China today for fighting to stop the opium trade.

Liu He: Gray-haired senior aide who is liked by many Chinese intellectuals. He is a proponent of the automation of Chinese factories.

Liu has served as Xi Jinping's top trade negotiator during the trade war with the United States.

Lou Daren: A Taiwanese businessman based in Dongguan, Guangdong, for more than twenty years; formerly served as the chairman of the Taiwan Businessmen Association. Lou once ran a bicycle-helmet factory in Superior, Montana.

Ma, Jack: Founder of Alibaba, China's largest e-commerce company.

Mao Zedong (1893–1976): Communist revolutionary and founder of the People's Republic of China in 1949.

Meng Han: A fifty-two-year-old former hospital guard turned labor activist who worked for Zeng Feiyang in Panyu, Guangdong. Meng was sentenced to twenty-one months in jail in late 2016 for "disturbing public order."

Miao Wei: Former president of Dongfeng Motor Company. Miao is now a key official in China's technology strategy.

Reuter, Till: KUKA's former CEO, who previously worked as an investment banker for many years. Reuter is pushed out of management by senior Chinese executives, after the German robot maker is acquired by Midea.

Stalin, Joseph (1878–1953): Leader of the Soviet Union from the mid-1920s to 1953.

Wang Kan: Professor of industrial relations in Beijing.

Wang Mang (45 BC–AD 23): The only emperor of China's Xin dynasty. Wang introduced radical land reform during his reign. He was killed by rebels who rose up to end his rule.

Wang Yang: While serving as Guangdong provincial party secretary from 2007 to 2012, Wang advocated a policy of adding robots and technology to factories, called "Emptying the cage and changing the bird." Now a senior official in Beijing.

Wen Jiabao: China's premier from 2002 to 2012. While his family is known to be spectacularly corrupt, Wen launched measures to try to alleviate rural poverty, including by ending the agricultural tax in 2006.

Woo, Louis: Former Apple executive; now serves as special assistant to Foxconn's Terry Gou.

Wu Guijun: Former migrant worker; he became a labor activist in

Shenzhen after being jailed for a year for participating in a strike in a furniture factory.

Xi Jinping: Took over as top leader of China in 2012 and quickly moved to amass sweeping power and reassert the role of the Communist Party across politics, the economy, and society.

Zeng Feiyang: Early labor activist from southern China.

Zhang Zhiru: Prominent labor activist in Shenzhen who has had to move his office and home repeatedly due to police harassment.

Zhu Rongji: Chinese premier from 1998 to 2002. Zhu pushed reforms through the Chinese economy, including overseeing massive state enterprise reform and China's entry into the World Trade Organization in 2001.

THE MOS FROM BINGHUACUN

Mo Bochun: A local party official. He hopes to see Binghuacun become a tourism destination, rather than end up an "empty nest" village.

Mo Meiquan: A cousin of Rubo's. Once a shy factory worker in Dongguan, she eventually returns to Guizhou to start a family.

Mo Rubo: A charismatic kid who dropped out of middle school. He worked in a succession of factories around China before finally starting his own business selling sports clothing. Rubo opted to stay in Dongguan, not far from one of the first factories he worked in.

Mo Ruchun: A onetime factory worker, he is now a serial entrepreneur but has never become the big success he aspires to be. Ruchun thinks he's finally going to make it by capitalizing on a rejuvenated Binghuacun that draws vacationers.

Mo Ruji: The eldest brother of Ruchun and Ruxuan. He works as an official in a township not far from Binghuacun.

Mo Ruxian: The father of Meiquan who never leaves Binghuacun

Mo Ruxuan: An ambitious local official. Ruxuan has risen through the party ranks and now is a manager in a showcase economic zone near Guizhou's capital, Guiyang.

Mo Wangqing: A migrant-worker returnee to Binghuacun. Wang-qing is now running a fish farm in the village that aims to cater to tourists.

Mo Wenke: The longtime party chief of Binghuacun who hoped foreign investment would transform his village. He is now retired and lives nearby.

Mo Wenzhi: One of the first to venture out from Binghuacun; he worked as a cook in a Dongguan factory. Wenzhi now is a manager in a lumber factory in the neighboring province of Guangxi.

Mo Yukai: A relative of Rubo's and Meiquan's. Yukai hates working in the city and hopes to someday return to the village.

Attachment to the soil is one of the characteristics of rural society. It is normal for farmers to settle in one spot for generations; it would be abnormal for them to migrate.

—FEI XIAOTONG, *FROM THE SOIL: THE FOUNDATIONS OF CHINESE SOCIETY*[1]

Introduction

When I arrived to live and work as a journalist in Beijing in early 1995, Deng Xiaoping, China's once-paramount leader then retired and reliably reported in ailing health, was still widely discussed by academics and businesspeople, cadres, and average Chinese folks alike. Years earlier he had already given up his last formal position, as head of the military forces, and his only remaining title was head of the China Bridge Association; he had been an avid player. But despite his precarious physical state, Deng's influence over everything from top party promotions to economic policy making was still hotly debated. Just hours after getting off the plane from New York City and emerging into the cold, dry January evening of Beijing, I listened as two foreign journalists discussed their plans to write obituaries for the tough, chain-smoking Sichuan native. As had happened before, rumors of his imminent demise had swept the capital; they would flare up every few months, sparking similar conversations, interspersed with more speculation about whether he was still strong enough to wield power from behind the scenes, until he died, just over two years later, at the age of ninety-two.

We were sitting in a restaurant serving *Maojiacai,* or "Mao family dishes." (Mao Zedong was born in the province of Hunan, next to Deng's Sichuan, both places known for peppery food and producing national leaders.) The pungent smell of the coal briquettes then still burned for heat was sharp in the night air as an American reporter chided her boyfriend, an Australian reporter, for not having started writing his obituary. Whenever Deng did die, any self-respecting journalist would have to be ready to push the SEND button on an expansive piece looking at the legacy of the leader who more than any other was credited with moving China away from its autocratic past and into the modern world. And that obituary inevitably would focus on Deng's seminal role in launching economic reforms.

In carrying out what Deng called *gaige kaifang,* or "reform and opening," the paramount leader had taken a decisive step away from Mao's radical egalitarianism and set China and its people on a path toward today: a country with a high-speed railway network that accounts for two-thirds of the world's total; cities with craning skyscrapers and roads jammed with new cars while below the ground ever more intricate webs of subway networks expand; a growing power in artificial intelligence and the world's second-largest producer of patents; and a country behind only the United States in producing billionaires with an ever more assertive leadership. At least two policies closely associated with Deng had been key: The first was ending the Mao-era communes and allowing China's hundreds of millions of farmers to begin to till their own agricultural plots or leave the land and work in manufacturing; the second was welcoming foreign investors, at first in the newly created special economic zones in Shenzhen, Xiamen, and other coastal cities, while at the same time encouraging the growth of private business.

The story of farmers abandoning the communes in particular has become central to the official narrative of China today. In it, we are told, the pragmatic nature of the Chinese Communist Party shines: it shows how top officials were capable of accepting crucial changes when necessary, even while maintaining their unassailable ruling position. Much the way they allowed entrepreneurial Chinese in cities to create their own private businesses, they, too, had shown tolerance when farmers began to take charge of the land, deciding what to plant and where to sell it, while at the same time boosting productivity and powering new economic growth. Similarly, when foreign investors were invited to set up factory operations, the business-minded party had provided them with labor; the excess rural workers freed up as the communes were dismantled could now travel to the coast and, earning much more in their new jobs as factory hands, build better lives for themselves and their children—thus setting off the biggest human migration in history.

It, too, was what I had learned while studying contemporary Chinese history at Stanford University some years earlier. China's transition from an autarchic Maoist state to a country led by new practical, reform-minded leaders seemed pretty much unquestioned, among academics and corporate heads alike. Awful tragedies like the June 4, 1989 massacre raised serious questions about the future of any significant political change. But the course toward an ever more open economy seemed certain. Uneven development would be inevitable in the process. As Deng himself had reportedly said, in his version of trickle-down economics, "Some must get rich first." But opportunities for all able Chinese, including hundreds of millions of farmers and migrants, were part of an implicit bargain: The people would not openly criticize the party or demand political and civil rights; the party would preside over a constantly evolving economic system, one that, above all, would ensure rising material welfare.

In the years following my arrival and long after Deng had died, the deal still seemed alive, at least in China's cities. In the fall of 1997, at the 15th National Congress of the Communist Party of China, the leadership formally announced that private business, once banned, henceforth was "an important part of the economy," a reflection of its already fast growth, with more and more Chinese making their fortunes outside the confines of the state. In 1999, the reform-minded premier Zhu Rongji, like Mao a native of Hunan but by contrast an advocate of loosening party control, had overseen the difficult market-opening concessions necessary to win entry into the World Trade Organization. China's leaders promised to welcome foreign companies into everything from the automobile and agricultural industries to banking, insurance, and tourism; that liberalization would later bring a flood of money from overseas, creating jobs and opportunities for tens of millions of Chinese. And in a sign touted as evidence that the new China was fast becoming a desirable place to do cutting-edge business, by the millennium an internet boom had seized the country, with then-hot web companies like Netease.com, Sohu.com, and China.com soaring in value after listing on Nasdaq. People in the know in the country's big cities started using a new initialism: "VC," for venture capital. And for the first time since the outmigration of Chinese students overseas had begun in the 1980s, Chinese students educated abroad started to return in large numbers, eager to get in on the action.

The new web boom, however, was of limited interest to me, even as news stories about deal making drew readers. When I had decided to study China, years earlier, my motivation had been to see how an ancient country with a very different culture from the West had gone through an agrarian revolution before becoming socialist and finally was changing to a market economy. Now, working in Beijing as a reporter for *Businessweek,* I wanted to see how the *laobaixing,* literally "old 100 names" or regular folks, were faring during the new reforms. As I explained to friends at the time, I hadn't come to China to write about Harvard-educated MBAs, former McKinsey consultants, tapping VC money to fund internet start-ups in China. That, in fact, completely bored me. (I was pleased when I discovered, many years later, that academics writing about rural China used "VCs" as shorthand for "village committees," the lowest level of government in the countryside.)

So while talk of hot new internet plays gripped Beijing, I headed south in the summer of 2000 to visit two parts of China then still largely untouched by the web craze: Guangdong, home to China's top export-manufacturing base, and Guizhou, its least developed and poorest province. The Pearl River Delta, which had won China the sobriquet "factory to the world," was already home to millions of migrant workers laboring in thousands of factories, including in Shenzhen, the country's first special economic zone, and just north of it in Dongguan, a rough-and-tumble string of factory towns, each distinguished by an industry, including shoes, toys, furniture, and lamps. Guizhou, meanwhile, had long been a frontier region of China, known for its beautiful plunging green karst mountains, among which lived a startling variety of ethnic minority groups with a history of rebelling against central control. Then, as before, it was known for a dearth of arable land and much poverty. And those conditions meant that most young people left for the coast to find factory or construction work. "No three days are clear, no three feet of land are level, and no one has three ounces of silver," as an old Guizhou saying put it.

My intention was to see how the party's grand bargain was working for the Other China, of workers and farmers from lagging interior provinces—not the relatively well-off residents of its showcase coastal cities, where signs of material success were becoming increasingly apparent. Earlier that year, policymakers had launched another major economic policy, whose name, the Develop the West plan, suggested that things were not going as smoothly in the hinterlands. The plan, the brainchild of President Jiang Zemin, the most urban of leaders—he had spent the bulk of his career in Shanghai—aimed to bring economic growth to China's inland provinces, including Guizhou, Guangxi, Sichuan, and Gansu, as well as Tibet and the sprawling city of Chongqing. Tax breaks and low-interest loans were to lure big Chinese and multinational companies into investing, combined with massive government spending on infrastructure, including roads, rail, and power projects. Officials in Beijing recognized that parts of the country were falling behind, as inequality between regions and urban and rural areas widened. Less openly expressed was that the new policy aimed to ensure that migrants, after years laboring in the factories, would eventually go home; that required some minimum level of prosperity in China's interior.

At the dawn of the twenty-first century, the electronics-manufacturing town of Changan was a top destination for migrants; indeed, with a population of almost six hundred thousand, it was the country's most populous *zhen,* or town. (With its huge population, China's government is split into five levels: the central government in Beijing; provinces; cities; counties; and townships, which sometimes can be home to hundreds of thousands of people, as Changan is. Villages, although not officially part of the administrative system, have their own village chief and party secretary.) Changan, like all the factory towns that together made up Dongguan, was spread along the 107 Guodao, the national highway that runs north to south across China, from the capital city of Beijing to the border with Hong Kong. Here, on the final stretch, the ugly inner workings of the country's export machine became apparent; for kilometer after kilometer, dust-stained two-story factories with bars on their windows jostled for space along this artery that led to the massive Yantian Port in Shenzhen. Occasionally glimpses of villas could be seen, the homes of Taiwanese and Hong Kong factory owners, hidden behind gray cement walls. Only when a typhoon swept over was Guangdong once again recognizable as a semitropical region, the lush green mountains reasserting their presence in the distance, as rain temporarily washed clean the industrial landscape.

Mo Meiquan was one of four migrants here hailing from the same small village in Guizhou. At eighteen years old, she was already on her second year of factory work in 2000. After dropping out of school at fifteen, making her one of the most educated in her village, she had helped her parents in the rice fields for two years before coming to Changan in 1998. Still dressed in her blue work smock, worn for the fourteen-hour shifts she put in every day checking videocassettes and audiocassettes for flaws, Meiquan seemed painfully shy. "There were no jobs at home, and our land was a very small plot. So I left home to find work," she said, carefully avoiding my gaze as we sat in a restaurant across the street from the Triton Electronics Factory. Her pay was only one yuan (twelve cents) an hour, she explained, staring at a spot on the table. And while a dormitory room was provided, it was sweltering in the summer and bone-chillingly cold in the winter, and she shared it with fourteen others.[1] "I think it's pitiful. I want to go back and start some small business, and never return to Dongguan," said her distant cousin Mo Yukai—twenty-four years old, a red streak of dye in his hair giving him a stylish flair—who had joined us for dinner.[2]

Later I met the other two migrants from the same Guizhou village. Thirty-two-year-old Mo Wenzhi had been the first to come to Changan, and now worked as a cook in a Taiwanese-owned electronics factory, but fretted about his wife and five-year-old daughter, back in the countryside, whom he got to see only once a year. Twenty-five-year-old Mo Rubo, who worked as a welder in the same factory, had an easy confidence about him rare among the migrants, and was determined to stay in Dongguan. Sitting in the dank dormitory room he shared with ten others, he marveled at how easy it was to buy everything from toothpaste and music cassettes to the many different varieties of food available in the many small shops and restaurants that lined the street outside the factory; in his village, one had to wait for the weekly market. At the foot of the bunk bed Rubo slept in lay two barbells he used every evening after his long shifts. On a nearby scuffed small desk was a simple model of a motorcycle; one day he hoped to get a real one, he said. The self-assured Rubo had a pretty girlfriend his age, who worked in a nearby factory, and came from a farming family in Henan, far north of Guangdong and Guizhou. Later that night he introduced us when I met them on the bustling nearby street, with tiny eateries catering to the migrants from all over China.[3]

Having seen where the Mos worked, later in the fall I traveled to their remote hometown of Binghuacun, a village of less than a thousand people, almost all Buyi ethnic minority, in southeast Guizhou. ("*Cun*" means "village.") To get there I took a three-hour plane flight from Beijing to Guiyang, a five-hour train ride to a county seat, followed by two hours in a bus. There I met a young, up-and-coming official named Mo Ruxuan, who came from the village but now worked in a nearby town, and who escorted me for the final stretch. That involved more than an hour riding on a horse cart through the mountainous terrain. (For Meiquan, back for a brief stay from Dongguan, the trip had involved a twenty-nine-hour train ride.) The final approach required crossing the narrow and slippery top of a crumbling concrete dam, water rushing about one's feet, before reaching ramshackle wooden houses clinging to a steep green slope. Narrow cobblestone paths wound through the village, chickens scratching in the rare flat patches of land; water buffalo lowed and pigs snorted from inside the dark stables that comprised the first floor of each dwelling, with the family's living quarters one floor above. Bathrooms were attached outhouses, while cooking was done over wood-burning hearths. The nearest hospital and middle school were hours away. There was no phone service.

"The bad roads are a big obstacle to our village's development," the fifty-some-year-old village party secretary Mo Wenke told me gravely, as we sat in the shadows of a darkened room (electricity was available for only a few hours a day), the orange glow of his burning cigarette casting a pin of light. But that was about to change with the launch of big new infrastructure projects under the auspices of Develop the West, officials from the township government that oversaw Binghuacun had assured Wenke and the other villagers. In particular, the muddy horse track was to be paved and made double-lane, connecting the village to the nearby township, which in turn would connect in to other yet-to-be-built roads that went to the provincial capital, some 222 kilometers distant. China's expected entry into the World Trade Organization a year-plus later was sure to open up new markets for the village's agricultural products, too, they were told. And the new opportunities, they hoped, would lure back some of the young adults who had left, thus helping Binghuacun avoid becoming a home for only the elderly and children. Already the villagers were planning to stop growing only corn and rice and add more valuable crops like chili peppers, rapeseed, and fruit. And the construction of a small factory to process the new crops would be key to his village's success, the party secretary said.[4]

Meiquan was a changed person here far from the factories, her shyness gone, smiling, and eager to show me around the village, as we went from house to house meeting her relatives. Villagers dressed in muted shades of blue—either in the proletarian canvas outfits common across China since Mao days or the darker blue homespun cloth traditionally worn by the Buyi—kept coming up to us, curious to see a foreign visitor, but also eager to quiz Meiquan about life in the faroff city. How much did she earn in the factory? What did she eat? What were the city people like? They asked, feeling the plush of her new red vest with farm-roughened hands. "I would like to study more first if I had enough money," Meiquan later told me. "Then after the roads are completed, I want to open a business and do something useful for my village."[5]

Meiquan had come back to help her parents harvest rice for the fall. But an equally important reason was to replace her expired identity card. Otherwise, she risked being picked up by the police in Dongguan. Migrants, who usually were forced to hand over their IDs to factory managers when they started working, were often put into the feared "black jails," or arbitrary detention centers, where they were held against their will and sometimes beaten up by police, for not carrying identification. A shakedown payment of one hundred yuan to their captors, a large sum for most workers, around a week's pay, could win one's freedom. A distant relative of Meiquan's had been held in a detention center for three months in Huizhou, a nearby city in the Pearl River Delta; following his release he had fled home to Binghuacun, abandoning his job in a local toy factory, and now was afraid to return.

"It's preposterous that almost one-tenth the country's citizens are illegal aliens in their own homeland. Fixing this situation by granting existing internal immigrants legal status is the only way to stop the shakedowns, jailing, and even torture that many undergo when picked up by local police simply for not having the right ID," *Businessweek* editorialized in a commentary that same year, referring to the household registration system, or *hukou,* restricting where one is supposed to live. "The longer [the party] delays, the greater the chances that the social discontent among farmers, workers, and their floating offspring will boil over into disorder of a sort that even China's fearsome security apparatus cannot handle."[6]

For the next decade and a half, I did not return to Binghuacun, but went dozens of times to Dongguan and other factory towns and villages across China to interview workers and farmers. While their lives were arduous, with the *hukou* system relegating them to second-class citizens, things seemed to be slowly getting better. The era of outright sweatshops began to fade as worker wages and bargaining power went up in the first decade of the twenty-first century. Workers became more assertive of their rights, encouraged by the passage of a labor-contract law in 2003, even as the official union remained largely toothless. Meanwhile, a series of tragedies involving the left-behind children of workers, many of them occurring in Guizhou, had triggered a national debate on the treatment of migrant families, with calls to address the problems, including making it easier for migrant offspring to attend urban schools. A series of small reforms that aimed to strengthen farmers' rights to their land were launched, including at key party meetings in 2008 and 2013.

Then, in the summer of 2016, I finally went back to Binghuacun but none of the Mos I had met in Dongguan were there. As manufacturing costs inexorably went up and some factories shut or moved abroad, some factory workers had started to return to the countryside, seeking employment in service industries, including tourism. Thousands of new kilometers of roads and rail tracks had been built in western China. But while an expressway extended south from the provincial capital Guiyang, shortening the driving time by half, the village was still waiting for the new double-lane, paved road to connect them with the nearby county township. In preparation for what local officials assumed would be a flood of tourists following the road's eventual completion, work had begun on restoring many of the rustic wooden farmhouses to serve as bed-and-breakfasts; most of the villagers now lived in three-story, often half-finished concrete farmhouses, across the river and at the base of another hill. A steady supply of electricity was now the norm and every adult villager had his own mobile phone, but life still seemed tough, with women washing clothes by hand in the river and most families cooking over woodstoves.

It took coming back to Binghuacun a half a year later during the Lunar New Year Festival, the traditional time for people to return to their hometowns, for me to finally see one of them. Mo Rubo, the former youthful factory welder, now slightly pudgy from middle age, had the same lively look in his eyes when I met him on a street corner in the nearby township of Jialiang. After my driver and I had gotten hopelessly lost on the country roads, Rubo had offered to drive to the nearest town to meet us. We followed his little red Honda along the bumpy one-lane road that straddled a mountain before dropping precipitously into the valley where Binghuacun lay; the Honda had come after the motorcycle that he had coveted as a young factory worker and that had been his first motorized vehicle. He had made the fifteen-hour drive from Dongguan to the village to see his aging parents just days earlier. Although happy to no longer work long hours in a factory, he said he was barely scraping by in his new business, selling sports clothes online from the living room of a small rented apartment in Changan town, where he and his former girlfriend, now wife—the same one I had met many years earlier—lived with their five-year-old daughter. As for returning to Binghuacun for good, it was out of the question. He was determined that his daughter go to school in Dongguan, which had better teachers than schools in the countryside, he explained later that evening as we sat around the small wood brazier in the combined living-room and farm-tool-storage-area that made up the first floor of his parents' big but largely empty cement four-story farmhouse. But it wasn't going to be easy to pay the high tuition fees at the private institutions that migrant children must attend, barred as they are in most cases from city public schools. That amounted to a minimum of six thousand yuan, or almost a thousand dollars, per term at the private establishments, for what were often poorly taught classes in run-down classrooms, he said.

The next day I woke to a village with a festive feel. Locals, including those back temporarily from work in factories, construction sites, and elsewhere, were getting ready for the evening's banquet to be held in celebration of *chusan,* or the third night of Lunar New Year. A group of men were slaughtering two pigs on a well-used cement platform in the open air, and a small rivulet of bright red blood had become a twisting stream down the roadside, with yellow, wiry-haired small village dogs lapping at it in the sun. Later, at a low-lying long table outside, two dozen men sat on little plastic stools and quickly dismembered the carcasses, the sound of cleavers thunking as they hit flesh. Fish had been netted from the river, and elderly women were preparing the local specialty, cubes of hard white tofu, with a ball of pork and chopped leek inside. Later that night, *mijiu,* locally made rice wine, was brought out in tall thermoses, and drunk from enamel bowls over multiple toasts. Any attempt to bow out of the drinking was met with an argument that went something like this: "You must drink with me; next time you come, I will be not be here, but once again far off sweating for money. What a rare chance the New Year gives us to celebrate together!"

China is now at a critical turning point. Years of investment-led

growth have saddled local governments and companies with excessive debt and banks with bad loans. Factories in cities like Dongguan
that once relied on paying dirt-cheap wages to turn a profit now can't
find enough workers, and many struggle to survive. Farmers in the
countryside still till tiny plots, the legacy of a system that restricts
their ability to sell or rent their land; local governments, meanwhile,
are addicted to the revenues they earn from seizing that same land
and converting it to commercial uses. The high-speed rail and impressive expressways, too, in part are reliant on that same system,
which favors the state over individuals, allowing governments to take
land from people at little cost, but which is sparking social resentment. Top officials are well aware that the growth model of previous
years is no longer sustainable and that the country must shift to an
economy more reliant on service industries and the spending power
of the people. To do that, it must ensure that hundreds of millions of
rural Chinese and migrant workers, accounting for about one-half the
population, begin to earn enough to join city dwellers, as part of a
swelling middle class that Mckinsey & Company estimated to be 256
million strong in 2012.[7]

For the first time in decades, the flow of people into cities ap-
pears to be ending. Demography, combined with the discriminatory
policies migrants continue to face in urban China, explains this mo-
mentous shift. Workers are getting older, are less willing to do back-
breaking work for low pay, and have families to think about. Many
cities are cracking down on the private schools catering to migrant
children and are putting up barriers to workers getting treated in hospitals. At the same time, their aging parents in the countryside need
more care. Seven million people returned to their villages in the first
half of 2017, China's agriculture minister Han Changfu said in the
fall of that year. The reverse migration fits nicely with policymakers'
plans. More than three decades after farmers first started to leave the
land for the cities, China's economic planners now want most of them
to go home, to settle down in villages and those small cities that have
been anointed by authorities for population growth. In their neat formula, the returnees will revitalize lagging local economies in poorer
parts of China, through launching their own small businesses, in ag-

riculture and services, and buying up the vacant apartments left from years of overbuilding. For those migrants who remain in the cities, officials have set a high bar. It expects them to be well educated and skilled and work in new higher-value-added service industries, like writing mobile apps and developing e-commerce businesses.

For manufacturing, authorities envision a future where its factories are largely automated, with few people employed. Under yet another grand national plan, "Made in China 2025," which aims to bring high technology to manufacturing, Beijing has ordered provinces and cities to push five-year industrial-upgrading action plans, with targets set on robot adoption. Local governments are offering subsidies to factories to encourage more rapid automation. Top officials see a cautionary example in the hollowing out of manufacturing in Japan, another country with a rapidly aging population, and want China to avoid its fate and become a global innovative power while preserving its role as factory to the world. While manufacturers have been struggling to find workers at the low wages they have long paid, the new strategy allows them to stop worrying about improving worker conditions, wages, and workplaces, and instead focus on automation.

All this is supposed to help China achieve its desired standing as a global superpower. Not surprisingly, its ambitions are frightening to many, including governments in Washington, Tokyo, and Berlin. U.S. president Trump has attacked China repeatedly for harming American companies and workers, and on a visit to Asia in September 2017 Commerce Secretary Wilbur Ross said the country's robot and other manufacturing subsidies were undermining global industry. China's leaders realize that successfully developing a stronger consumer market and starting to import more goods will reduce the massive trade surplus it holds with the U.S. and other countries. They know, too, that that would help curb resistance to their state-led model of economic growth.

There are serious obstacles to realizing this vision. Government funding for technological improvements and social-welfare programs could easily dry up as China's economy slows. Officials have done much to improve education and health services in its interior and have rolled out a minimum guaranteed income, or *dibao,* for

China's poorest, spending hundreds of millions of dollars over the last decade-plus. But huge disparities in social services and income between city and countryside remain. That helps explain why less than one-quarter of rural youth complete high school, and life expectancy in the interior still is shorter than on the coast. Income inequality continues to swell and already exceeds the U.S. in its unfairness. "The system has failed to tackle the fundamental inequalities of the old society, so that it redistributes income primarily among the comparatively well-off urban population," wrote University of California, San Diego economist Barry Naughton. "Social services for rural residents have improved significantly, but they remain far below those enjoyed by urban residents."[8] That gap has curbed consumption, with workers nervous about future costs afraid to spend much.

If returnees can become part of a new entrepreneurial economy flourishing in the country's interior, as optimistic policymakers hope, China could become the powerhouse economy the world is counting on. But workers aren't guaranteed to find the employment they want, while other migrants have no interest in going back. Not surprisingly, most of the jobs taken by former factory workers aren't ending up being higher-skilled ones, but instead low-end and often dangerous trades like motorcycle express delivery. Falling productivity in both agriculture and industry worrisomely suggests that China's economy is already stalling and runs the risk of getting snared in what development economists call the middle-income trap, unable to compete any longer in industries built on low-cost labor, but without the technological sophistication to transition to a higher-value-added economy. Today rural Chinese incomes are still only a little over $2,100 a year, just over a third of those earned by urbanites.

Ultimately, ensuring that migrants integrate into China's middle class requires ending the rigid Mao-era policies of household registration and the collective-ownership system for rural land, allowing them to live and work where they wish while truly benefiting from the land they hold. The question is whether the Communist Party, once touted as deeply pragmatic but now reverting to a "politics in command" ideology, will accept today's crucial changes. Rather than policies that loosen the restrictions that have long held back the lives of Chinese outside cities, under party general secretary Xi Jinping's rule the preference has been for top-down, state-directed policies like Made in China 2025, for automating manufacturing, and strengthening the role of village collectives run by party members to "modernize" agriculture. Similarly, a national campaign to end poverty has focused on pumping money into building new schools and hospitals, as well as, controversially, relocating entire poor villages, rather than giving power to individuals to choose where to live and work. Guangdong, under a plan called the Greater Bay Area, is supposed to be linked more tightly with the economies of Hong Kong and Macau, a domestic version of Xi's massive infrastructure plan to build railways, roads, ports, and power grids in other countries, the One Belt, One Road strategy. And Guiyang has been anointed a base for the Big Data industry, a decision seemingly more about national vanity than economic practicality, with enormous subsidies used to lure investors to Guizhou's still relatively remote capital, including Apple, which in mid-2017 agreed to invest $1 billion. Where people fit into the capital-intensive visions of economic grandeur are unexplained.

It is clear what the workers want. After years of hard labor in factories and on construction sites, their hope is that the party will finally ensure that their living standards rise to match those of the urban minority. They want less arduous jobs, perhaps starting their own businesses, either as residents with full rights in the cities, or back in the countryside but with control of their land. And they are not the docile labor force that once attracted global investors to China. They are more educated and web-savvy, and demanding of what they see as their proper due. In recent years, protests by workers upset about unpaid wages and farmers angry at arbitrary land seizures have grown in number, even as the government has overseen a sweeping crackdown on civil society, including labor activists, rights lawyers, and feminists. Xi, busy amassing more power than any leader since Mao, seems particularly unsuited for the inevitably complicated and chaotic transition that would come with a more open society. But without the party loosening controls over the half of the population still composed of farmers and workers, China will never make the transition to a more sustainable consumer-driven economy, and could instead face serious social instability.

The myth China wants the world to believe is something different. It says that the country is on an inexorable path toward a vastly expanded middle class at home, with cutting-edge technology and powerful companies dominating markets abroad. Fueled by continued economic growth, a much stronger and less brittle China is supposed to emerge. The myth says that China's development path and authoritarian system will become a model for countries around the world and perhaps replace the already battered Western one of freer markets and individual rights. This book looks at why all this is unlikely to prove true and how instead China's growth could seriously slow, shattering the expectations of millions of Chinese, very possibly leading to social unrest. That, of course, is a dangerous challenge to China's leaders, ending the bargain of continued economic growth in return for political acquiescence that has served them for several decades now. How China faces its challenges has huge implications for the future of its own people and those of the world.

1

The Factory

I thought there was a whole world out there that must be very different from the village. And I decided leaving was the only way to improve myself.

—MO MEIQUAN

I had never heard of factories where it's impossible for workers to make any money! This one really is a "blood and sweat factory."

—MIGRANT WORKER

By the time he turned thirteen, Mo Rubo was ready to get out of school. The teachers in the run-down elementary institution in Jialiang Township, some two hours over a twisting one-lane mud road from Binghuacun, had already decided which students had a shot at high school, and he wasn't one of them. Rubo, a cocky kid who had always chafed at the routine of village life, sat bored at the back of the drafty, old classroom and thought about what it must be like in the coastal provinces of Guangdong and Zhejiang. He had heard you could earn up to three hundred yuan (then thirty-six dollars) a month—an unimaginable sum for a kid from a farming family that measured a good year by whether there was an extra pig to sell. So, like many other rural youth before him, he dropped out. Rubo stayed another year in the village, occasionally helping out his mother and father in the rice fields, but kept daydreaming about life on the coast. He also started hanging out with a gang of youth layabouts, who had a propensity for getting in trouble, fighting with kids from other towns. "I was becoming a bad boy. It wasn't looking like a good future for me in Binghuacun," Rubo recalls.[1]

While an older cousin, Mo Wenzhi, one of the first teenagers to leave the village back in 1989, was already working in Dongguan, Guangdong, Rubo, with an independent streak since his toddler years, didn't like the idea of following in his footsteps. He had heard there was lots of work in electronics factories in the booming Yangtze River Delta, the watery artery that feeds into the big cities of Shanghai and Ningbo and their ports. So in the summer of 1993, Rubo finally left home. Arriving after a thirty-plus-hour train ride, his first ever, Rubo emerged from the station disoriented by the city outside and unsure how he was going to find his first job. Three ruffians surrounded Rubo, and demanded he hand over his money, the equivalent of twenty bucks, originally intended to tide him over before he found work. Rubo fought back but to no avail. He ended up bleeding badly from the face where they had punched him, sitting by the road in front of the station, without any money, and unsure where to go or what to do. As an unregistered migrant, he knew that going to the police would be no help; indeed, they might lock him up for being in Ningbo without a temporary residency permit, required for all migrant workers and something one could get only after finding employment.

He still marvels over what happened next. A couple came up to him, asked what had happened, then offered him a job in a factory they owned that made pot lids, to help him get himself on his feet. "They took me back to their factory and gave me a job. They gave me a place to shower, shampoo, and a towel to get the blood off," he recalls, nodding his head in disbelief. "At important times, strangers have treated me like a friend. I've so been so lucky. You know we migrant workers are not usually welcomed in the cities." Years later he returned to Ningbo eager to find and thank them, but his benefactors and their factory were gone.

Nothing defines the lives of China's other half—the hundreds of millions of farmers, many now turned migrant workers, and their families—more than the *hukou*, or household registration, policy. The *hukou*, physically a small red passbook that records where each family is officially registered and determines what kinds of benefits as citizens they receive,[2] is why China's vast numbers of migrant workers—or *nongmingong*, literally "farmer-workers"—are treated as second-class citizens and live such precarious lives. It's why much of the country's factory, construction, and service-industry workforce spends years laboring in cities, but ultimately cannot settle down. It is why they receive far lower-quality health care. It is why their children usually grow up in the countryside separated from their parents, and drop out of school at a rate far higher than their urban counterparts.

At the same time, the *hukou* ensures that China's cities, including Beijing and Shanghai but also dozens of smaller urban centers, are free of the slums commonplace in Africa, South America, and much of the rest of Asia. It explains how authorities are able to suddenly and forcibly sweep whole neighborhoods of migrant workers from the cities, with little concern or attention from city dwellers. As a result of the policy, urban kids attend smaller classes, with better teachers, and more-professional doctors treat their parents. It helps explain why the average life span of a person from Shanghai is a full five years more than one born in Guizhou Province. It, more than anything else, explains how China has ended up with today's imbalanced, deeply unequal society.

The policy's origins go back before the founding of the People's Republic. Indeed, China, like South Korea, Taiwan, and other Asian societies, has had a system of registering its households for hundreds of years. It was used mainly for taxation and conscription and less frequently for controlling population movements during wars and other times of upheaval. And it was not until after 1949, when Mao decided to model China's development path on the so-called Big Push of Stalin's Soviet Union, focusing it on industrialization rather than agriculture or consumption, that a more draconian system to keep the huge rural population from moving to the cities became necessary, according to University of Washington geographer Kam Wing Chan.[3]

As China's officials grabbed rural land from landlords and set up communes in the countryside, while instituting a pricing system that kept agricultural products artificially cheap, waves of peasants started leaving for the cities. When famines hit China in the late 1950s, during the Great Leap Forward, the numbers grew far larger. That internal migration was derisively labeled *mangliu,* or "blind drift," by party officials, who believed it must be stopped. A new, more stringently enforced *hukou* policy was officially launched in 1958, ending most migration while ensuring that peasants survived "at a bare subsistence and siphoned off resources from the countryside to push industrialization," says Chan. That also meant funneling the best education, health care, and pensions to an elite of urban workers, amounting to only 15 percent of the population in 1955, leaving the countryside with substandard social services. "It is the same program, *propiska* [internal passport system], that Stalin used in the late twenties and thirties in the Soviet Union and that influenced China's first five-year plan, from 1953 to 1957. Soviet experts in China—there were thousands of them—helped set that up," the University of Washington geographer says.[4] The policy allowed China to rapidly industrialize without becoming urbanized, a rare combination throughout history.

That was to change in the late 1970s as China dismantled its communes and underwent the wrenching transformation from a command to a more market economy. As millions of farmers who had previously worked in the communes found themselves without a means of livelihood, they once more started flooding the cities. While that contravened *hukou* policy, officials first tolerated then welcomed the flow. Deng Xiaoping's reform and opening policy was not just about liberalizing the rural economy, it also included freeing up manufacturing and welcoming in foreign factory owners, who were eager to find cheap labor, something the rural migrants provided.

But even as the population of migrants grew from a few million in the early 1980s to surpass 250 million by 2014, they were never granted the same social benefits or privileges accorded to *hukou*-holding city dwellers. So while China first stood out as a country where urbanization didn't follow industrialization, it later proved equally idiosyncratic in featuring a new form of urbanization that has seen city populations swell, but one where huge numbers of the new residents have been discriminated against as second-class citizens. As Chan has neatly put it:

"During Mao's era, this strategy was to prevent peasants from entering cities, and resulted in China's low level of urbanization compared to its industrialization level, leading to the phenomenon of 'under-urbanization.' In the reform era, the strategy of 'incomplete urbanization' has taken on a different form. Controls preventing physical movements have been lifted, resulting in a rapid expansion of rural-urban migration, but urban social and economic benefits have not been extended to most migrants from the countryside. Many of the de facto urban residents are deemed only as 'temporary' and denied urban citizenship and benefits that typically come with migration."[5]

For the policymakers who took over running China's now rapidly marketizing economy, this was a desirable result. By ensuring that migrants remained an underclass in the cities, the *hukou* also guaranteed that there would be no end to China's pliable, low-cost labor force; with little recourse, legal or otherwise, most migrants accepted, albeit unhappily, the meager wages and poor working conditions. That in turn was to underpin the rapid GDP growth China experienced over the last several decades. As Chan wrote, the policy "is perhaps China's best-kept secret behind its unprecedented economic growth."[6] And so a policy that sacrificed the living standards of rural workers to ensure cheap raw materials for industry and food for elite urbanites, once central for industrialization, now had a new role: ensuring that China had the labor force necessary for the current era. Excessively long work hours and harried workers under the yoke of the *hukou* would support the rise of China's export-oriented economy.

The demand for cheap labor was to soar after 2001 when China opened its once-autarchic industries to foreign investment with entry into the World Trade Organization. This crucial next chapter in the development of China's economy—one that helped bring us to today's fractious trade battles and growing global fears of an ascendant power poised to dominate global technology and manufacturing industries—did not come about without a fight. An old guard of party elders, including former premier Li Peng—known as "the Butcher of

Beijing" for his role in bloodily suppressing the student and worker protests during the June 1989 Tiananmen Square movement—were opposed to introducing real competition to China's backbone industries, thus weakening party control. Meanwhile, economic reformers like paramount leader Deng, along with his successor Jiang Zemin and premier Zhu Rongji, saw the influx of foreign money and expertise as critical to building more modern industries, while raising people's living standards.

In the tough years after 1989, when many international companies stopped their operations for a time following the Tiananmen tragedy, Li Peng and his supporters argued that China should revert to a more closed and controlled economic state, and rely less on fickle foreigners. To counter them, Deng set out on his famous 1992 Southern Tour, or *nanxun,* where he traveled to Guangdong's Shenzhen, Zhongshan, and Foshan, the cities that first welcomed foreign investment after being designated special economic zones in the early 1980s. Following his death, in 1997, Zhu—like Deng and Mao, also a native of Southwest China, known for its spicy food and leaders with volatile temperaments—took on the role of hard-nosed advocate for the controversial economic reforms and later became a key player in the battle over China's entry into the World Trade Organization. Under Jiang's watch, Zhu pushed through a painful and much-resisted restructuring of China's state sector in the late 1990s, shuttering tens of thousands of companies, with some thirty million urban workers losing their jobs. At the same time, he launched the privatization of city housing, as the apartments once owned by state enterprises and provided free or at low cost to urban workers were sold off at nominal rates to their tenants. This later would lead to the widening wealth gap between urban and rural Chinese, as real-estate markets in the cities took off, benefiting property owners.

The battle over whether to continue opening the economy came to a head over the prospect of China entering the global trading association. For Zhu and other reformers, the WTO would not only bring needed hard currency, it would also pull in foreign expertise and technology, as international firms would be required to form joint ventures with Chinese companies as the price of entry. At the same time, the influx of new companies and products would raise competition, shaking up coddled industries, forcing the weakest local players to close and encouraging the better ones to up their game. WTO would also be cover for ongoing reforms: Zhu and his supporters would tell skeptical Chinese that allowing more competition was the nonnegotiable price for China's entry.

The reality however, was that the reformers were in a very tough spot. On the one hand they wanted to strike a deal soon, allowing the restructuring of China's ailing state economy to begin. At the same time, they wanted to get the best deal possible for China's industries, while not appearing to have sold out to the capitalist West, not long before viewed as enemy number one. Any sign that they were giving in too easily to international negotiators would not only bring public opprobrium down upon them but also lower the odds of China ultimately successfully entering the WTO. And more than with any other country, the outcome of negotiations with the United States would be key to the success or failure. (China was required to do bilateral deals with multiple countries before finally entering the trading organization; the deal with the U.S. was one of the last and most important.)

In the spring of 1999, the feisty premier made a trip to Washington as negotiations with the U.S. showed signs of stalling. Particularly difficult had been convincing Chinese trade skeptics to agree to open economically important but deeply uncompetitive industries such as agriculture, automobiles, and telecommunications. What first appeared a potential breakthrough was to backfire. When the Office of the U.S. Trade Representative surprised China by posting Zhu's surprisingly generous terms on the internet, growing public concern that the leaders were giving away the country's crown jewels flared. What the U.S.-led NATO insisted was an accidental bombing of the Chinese embassy in Belgrade that happened shortly afterward in May turned the worries into a conflagration. "Concerns about sovereignty and national dignity are now linked to economic nationalism," Wang Yong, an associate professor and expert on U.S.-China trade relations at Peking University, told me at the time.[7]

The China negotiators were facing a formidable opponent. The U.S.

negotiating team was headed by forty-eight-year-old Charlene Barshefsky, a U.S. trade representative, raised in a Jewish-Polish immigrant family on the North Side of Chicago, and known as a tough and savvy broker. Skilled negotiators must always remember, she liked to say, that only an unequivocal no was a deal-breaker. "The only word for no is 'no,'" Barshefsky would later explain. "The phrase 'That's impossible!' is not no. It just means find a different way. The phrase 'I'll lose my job if I agree to that'—that may be a shame, but it isn't no. The phrase 'I've never been this insulted in my life' just means ask for the same thing but do it in a better tone," she said to *The Wall Street Journal* in 2015.[8]

By summer, rumors were flying that Zhu, whose successful career until then had been distinguished by his pugnacious confidence, might actually end up losing his job. His visit to the U.S. was roundly criticized as a sellout to the foreigners, and the premier was absent as talks continued, even as they seemed to be going nowhere. Then, on November 6, Jiang, who not only saw China's WTO entry as key to driving ongoing economic reforms but also viewed it as a chance to strengthen the country's global standing and sway over archrival Taiwan, had a lengthy phone call with U.S. president Bill Clinton. Shortly afterward, Barshefsky flew to Beijing in an effort to save the talks. After last-minute tightrope tactics—at one point during the six days of final negotiations, Barshefsky's team packed their suitcases and threatened to leave on the next plane out of Beijing—China and the U.S. emerged with an agreement. Barshefsky and China's then trade minister Shi Guangsheng signed the multipage accession document and then toasted it with champagne, before a gaggle of foreign and Chinese journalists, in the trade ministry. Barshefsky and her team were then whisked off to Zhongnanhai, the elite leadership compound that hugged a lake at the center of Beijing, to meet China's president. A beaming and clearly delighted Jiang welcomed the U.S. delegates into the Purple Light Pavilion, and exuberantly called out in English, "Everyone!," meaning that he wanted to shake each American's hand. "Good, good, good," he said as he led the delegation into the hall that for centuries has been used to host foreign government dignitaries. Despite Zhu missing the signing ceremony and triumphant reception, it was obvious to all that the tough Chinese negotiator from Hunan had prevailed.[9]

WTO, which the country would formally join at the end of 2001, would inflict pain on many of China's companies, driving those least prepared for competition out of business. At the same time, a flood of money would enter China's manufacturing sector, tens of thousands of new factories would open, and globally competitive industries including electronics and machine tools would be created. Foreign investment into China jumped from $47 billion in 2001 to $124 billion a decade later. Established export industries in countries including Mexico and Thailand would be shaken by the rise of China. At the same time, there was much idealism about how China's economic integration with the world would inevitably lead to further political changes, an argument used by leaders like President Clinton to sell the deal to their own citizens. In a speech at Johns Hopkins University School of Advanced International Studies in March 2000, the year before China's entry, Clinton was eloquent on this prospect: "By joining the WTO, China is not simply agreeing to import more of our products, it is agreeing to import one of democracy's most cherished values, economic freedom," said Clinton. "When individuals have the power not just to dream, but to realize their dreams, they will demand a greater say."[10]

Whether China's entry has on balance led to more opening or repression has become the subject of contentious global debate. One thing it unquestionably did was transform China's economy, and clearly so in the cities of the Pearl River and Yangtze River deltas. As Chinese tariffs came down on everything from semiconductor chips to plastics and international taxes were lowered on Chinese-produced toys, textiles, and electronics, setting up new manufacturing expressly for export was a no-brainer. The cities along China's coast and near its biggest ports were the obvious choices for production and vast new factory zones grew up, including the country's consummate factory town of Dongguan, just up the Pearl River from Shenzhen. Guangdong's

Pearl River Delta would see many of the last stands of rice fields and palm trees come down, replaced with quickly assembled, tile-walled factories, with their dismal worker dormitories, while nearby gated villa communities for overseas Chinese factory bosses sprung up. (It would mean much less for the little settlement of Binghuacun, however, as the hoped-for chili-pepper-processing factory never got built.)

At the turn of the millennium, Dongguan was widely perceived as a place without history. Rather than as a municipality that had organically developed over years—it wasn't officially formed until 1985—it was seen as a collection of factory clusters that had seemingly erupted overnight. Each town in Dongguan had its own specialty—toys, electronics, shoes, or furniture—and together they formed the city, an agglomeration of more than seventeen thousand square kilometers stretching up the delta from Shenzhen, in the south, to the provincial capital Guangzhou, to the north; from Huizhou, in the northeast, to the Yangtze River, to the west. The Taiwan-born and Hong Kong–born factory owners, with a particular reputation for loucheness, were seen as a necessary but temporary evil; the huge ranks of migrant workers—more than three times the number of permanent residents—were also viewed as interlopers, albeit with far fewer rights than the manufacturing bosses. Both groups were expected to leave at some undefined point in the future, after the region had become wealthy and self-sufficient enough to do without them anymore.

The reality was different. Before the factories first came, in the early 1980s, the subtropical region of rolling hills and lush fields had been mainly agricultural, producing bananas, lychees, and the lychees' cousin the *longan*, or dragon eye, fruit. And while it may be known for its transience today, Dongguan is a place with ancient roots. It is home to the Baogang shell mound, with its pottery fragments and bones said to be the remains of a five-thousand-year-old settlement, the earliest in the Pearl River Delta. A town in Dongguan had a cameo at a critical moment in China's more recent history: the start of the Opium Wars of the mid-nineteenth century. Humen—literally, "Tiger Gate," so named because of a nearby island said to resemble a crouching tiger with paws stretched forward—today is one of the country's biggest electronics producers and has played a key role in the country's rise to become a leading global exporter. But that economic history is not taught to young Chinese. Instead every elementary-school student learns about how it was in Humen that a national hero first stood up to the British, and launched the national resistance to the scourge of opium the imperialists had brought with them.

In 1839, white-bearded Qing dynasty scholar-official Lin Zexu, known from youth as "unusually brilliant" and an advocate for the revitalization of traditional Chinese thought, arrived in Guangdong as the newly appointed imperial commissioner. His mandate, direct from the Daoguang Emperor, whom he had personally met an unusual nineteen times, was clear: finding a way to rid China of its opium curse. By 1838, some forty thousand chests of opium, each weighing about 140 pounds, were imported into China every year, in exchange for Chinese tea, silk, and porcelain. Just two years later, there were an estimated ten million addicts in China.[11] Lin first tried moral suasion, then forcibly seized 2.6 million pounds of opium from the English traders. After it was mixed with lime and salt, it was dumped into the bay of Humen, a task that took five hundred men working for twenty-three days. Lin, always the scholar and gentleman, composed "an ode of apology to the god of the sea for defiling his ocean with confiscated opium."[12]

This early victory by Lin was to end badly for China. Britain reacted angrily to the blow to its opium traders and set about attacking China's coastal cities. Ultimately what had begun with Lin's brave gesture against the opium trade led to China kowtowing to Britain's overwhelming force and ceding Hong Kong to the Crown in 1842. Lin, first celebrated for his forceful move against the opium trade, was made a fall guy for what was seen as a national disaster and deep blow to imperial pride. He was banished briefly to Xinjiang, now known for the party's brutal suppression of its Muslim Uighur people. Lin was later rehabilitated and is still remembered today for his forceful stand against foreign ruthlessness, expressed in an open letter he wrote to Queen Victoria:

We find that your country is sixty or seventy thousand *li* from China. Yet there are barbarian ships that strive to come here for trade for the purpose of making a great profit. The wealth of China is used to profit the barbarians. That is to say, the great profit made by barbarians is all taken from the right-ful share of China. By what right do they then in return use the poisonous drug to injure the Chinese people? Even though the barbarians may not necessarily intend to do us harm, yet in coveting profit to an extreme, they have no regard for injuring others. Let us ask, where is your conscience?

—LIN ZEXU, OPEN LETTER ADDRESSED TO THE SOVEREIGN
OF ENGLAND AND PUBLISHED IN CANTON (1839)[13]

Today a statue of Lin stands not just at the Opium War Museum in Humen, Dongguan, but also in Chinatown's Chatham Square in New York City; SAY NO TO DRUGS, reads the inscription in English and Chinese on the red granite base of the eighteen-foot-five-inch-tall statue of Lin, erected in 1997 and paid for mainly by Chinese business associations from Fujian Province, where he was born.

While drugs no longer play a major role in Dongguan, another vice has taken center stage, earning Dongguan the nickname "Chi-na's sex capital." Today Dongguan is known for its rampant prostitu-tion industry, fueled mainly by its Taiwanese factory bosses, most of whom have come without their wives, who live across the Taiwan Strait in cities including Taipei and Taichung. The hundreds of saunas—on offer is one variety of massage, where young women use their breasts to lather oil over the customer's body—are the risqué side of a vast infrastructure that has grown up to cater to the Tai-wanese community, estimated to number some half a million. The thousands of women and sometimes girls who work in this miser-able trade, are themselves migrants from across China. Dongguan has its own international school for those Taiwanese who have brought their families (allowed until Xi's reign to use Taiwan-issued textbooks, rather than the party-propaganda versions mandatory in Chinese classrooms), its own hospital, and its own "Little Taipei" food street. Restaurants down both sides of a narrow road sell Taiwan favorites, including bubble tea and beef noodles, and the sidewalks have the occasional little glass stand ubiquitous in Taiwan, where betel nuts with a lather of limestone paste are sold as a chewable stimulant. Splotches of bloodred expectorations dot the sidewalks from previous customers.

In Dongcheng District, home to pricey boutiques and the closest thing to Dongguan's city center, towers the Taiwan Businessmen Association Tower, a 68-floor, 289-meter skyscraper. Its construction began in 2008, but completion was stalled for years after the global financial crisis hit Dongguan's export factories. When it was finally finished, in 2013, the TBA Tower was more than triple the height of the next-tallest building. The sixth and seventh floors house the offices of the business association and an open-air Chinese garden; a traditional circular-shaped entrance opens onto a long pool of water stocked with goldfish, with a bamboo grove at the end.

I'm here one morning to see an old friend, Lou Daren—English name "Hayes," chosen when he lived during the 1980s in the tiny town of Superior, Montana, helping a friend run a bicycle-helmet factory. His years in the Rocky Mountains, before he moved, along with the factory, to settle in Dongguan in the early 1990s, were challenging, he says with a rueful smile. (The connection to the state I also happen to come from will make us "old friends from Montana" in his telling, even though we never actually met there.) The six-foot-three-inch-tall Hayes's first test was dealing with racist locals who assumed he was Native American until they heard his fluent but Chinese-accented English. Another trial followed after his ill-advised decision to buy a pink-tinted parka to weather the Montana winter. That immediately invited derision, he says, but with his big frame he quickly convinced his abusers to stand down.

Hayes is president emeritus of the association and one of the longest-resident Taiwanese in Dongguan; he is unofficially recognized as an éminence grise of the local community and now serves as editor of the monthly magazine for the association. As he finished up a meeting before we had lunch in a nearby restaurant, I was ushered into the association's "museum," a room full of photos of past directors of the group, each meeting with visiting government dignitaries, as well as a multitude of delicate porcelain vases and plaques given to the association to herald the financial contributions it has brought to Dongguan.

The TBA museum, I later realize, could be seen as the ornamental face of the closely entwined relationship between the Taiwanese business community and local officialdom. This bond is expressed in ways at times elaborate, as in the ceremonies awarding the ornamental vases, followed by long banquets with bird's nest soup, shark fin, and multiple dainty seafood dishes, and other times seedy—the visits to saunas and karaoke parlors that usually follow later in the evening. (A visit to a karaoke will start with the ritual of numbered women parading out, to be chosen by the all-male guests as companions in singing, drinking, and sometimes more.) The exchange, however, is simple: the Taiwanese or overseas Chinese from Hong Kong or Macau are here to make money, having seen their factories priced out of whatever place they came from, by rising wages and new environmental regulations; the officials, too, want to profit, whether it is from the factories paying a portion of their revenues into local tax coffers, or, more directly, from the overseas Chinese bribing an individual cadre who can facilitate a factory expansion or will turn a blind eye to labor violations.

This reciprocal relationship more than anything else was dependent on a never-ending supply of pliant migrant workers. The lure of low-wage labor was the most important single thing to attract the Taiwanese and other overseas Chinese to the Pearl River Delta, something cadres knew all too well. When the local employment bureau was ordered to implement a new labor contract law in 2003, officials seemed nonplussed: of course they hoped migrants earned enough to get by, but paying workers extra for overtime hours or on weekends, as now required, was going to damage the businessman-official alliance, built up over the course of many years. Most migrants earned just a few dozen dollars a month, worked twelve or more hours a day, and often went for weeks without taking time off, and that was exactly how the managers wanted it. "We must ensure that our guests can continue to staff their factories and not have to pay an exorbitant amount for wages," one smiling female labor official, a native of Dongguan, told me during an interview. "We have to be reasonable in what we ask of them."[14]

Chun Si Enterprise Handbag Co., whose leather wallets and purses were sold in Walmart, had been producing for a decade in Macau before rising labor prices finally convinced its owners to close shop in 1990 and shift operations to the mainland. In making that move, they were joining tens of thousands of other overseas Chinese factory owners in Macau, Hong Kong, and Taiwan, who, confronted by rising wages, were all relocating to China, many settling in the Pearl River Delta. Chun Si Enterprise chose the western side of Guangdong's largest river, opposite Shenzhen and Dongguan, to open two factories, one in Zhuhai, just across the strait from the former Portuguese colony now turned global gambling mecca and money laundering center, and the second in nearby Zhongshan, some forty-five minutes from the pleasant, palm-tree-lined city's downtown.

The decision to relocate was the right one, as Chun Si tapped into the rapidly expanding supply chain of leather producers, tanneries, and buckle makers that were also setting up shop nearby, all the while taking advantage of the far lower labor costs. For a low-end bag maker like Chun Si, cutting corners was an imperative for survival—and finding ways to reduce the wages paid to the vulnerable migrant workers was a simple matter. So like many other export-producing companies then operating in China, Chun Si developed their own system of fees, withholdings, and penalties levied on its workers, all aimed at reducing the company's wage bill while whittling away at the migrants' already meager take-home pay.[15]

From day one, each successful applicant for a job had to pay a hundred-yuan (twelve-dollar), nonrefundable registration fee. During traditional hiring seasons, like right after Lunar New Year, Chun Si intentionally overhired, using the registration fee as a cash cow. The workforce grew so large that the migrants were forced to sleep two to a bed, and the factory lines couldn't fit all the hires; when eventually the excess workers resigned, as the company all along intended, management simply pocketed the fees, one former worker told me. A new worker, too, was required to pay in advance the first two months of food and board, amounting to another three hundred yuan or so, and had his or her first salary payment delayed (putatively to reduce high worker turnover). Those who left in the first sixty days simply forfeited the unused board and food fee, often getting no payment or only partial payment for the work they had done.

And if a worker decided to stay, there were penalties ranging from a few dollars to more than ten for a host of factory infractions. Going to the bathroom too many times in a shift, talking to another co-worker, forgetting to wear one's work badge, or, worst of all, leaving the factory grounds without permission—all were breaches of factory rules that were punished with wage deductions. With factory guards and managers able to pocket a portion of the levies for infractions they reported—sometimes amounting to 30 percent of their own take-home salary—the incentives to tattle soared. Paid on the piece rate and earning only a few pennies for each handbag they worked on, most Chun Si workers struggled to earn more than subsistence, even as they put in long days on the factory line. "We usually worked until eleven or twelve at night," says one migrant worker, a short, dark-skinned man who previously worked in the Zhongshan factory but has now left for more strenuous but higher-paying construction-site work. "The first month they don't give you your salary and you have to pay up front the cost of a couple months for the dormitory and for your food. With most of us getting maybe only ninety to a hundred yuan per month for piecemeal work, it's only by the third month that one actually gets paid anything, and that's maybe just three or four yuan," he explained angrily. "Then you have the factory's penalty system, which is really extreme. Before Chun Si, I had never heard of factories where it's impossible for workers to make any money! This one really is a *xuehan gongchang* [literally, "blood and sweat factory"]," he said, his black hair with glittering white strands damp in the heat.[16] Later sitting in her small office at the factory in Zhongshan, Chun Si's export manager Selina Qing, the nervous thirty-something daughter of the company boss, defended their practices: "The workers are always going to the bathroom, they talk too much, and we sometimes discover we have a complainer. We are very frustrated. We train the workers and then they leave. According to the labor law of China, if they want to go, we can't make them stay."[17]

This was the harsh environment in which China's migrants found their first jobs. And in a power relationship already deeply skewed to favor management over labor, local cadres were focused foremost on satisfying factory managers. Also disturbing was how many officials saw the vulnerable migrants as an additional source of their own revenue. Public-security officers would stop workers on the street, demanding to see their identity cards as well as temporary residency permits. If they did not have them—and usually they didn't, as managers would demand they hand them over for the duration of their employment to ensure they would not stray far from the factories— the migrants would end up in detention centers better known as "black jails." It was a form of shakedown. There they would be held until one of their fellow factory workers or a manager came to pay what was usually a substantial fine to get out—sometimes as much as a couple of months of a worker's salary. That's what had happened to the Mos' unfortunate cousin, who left Dongguan after his release from one black jail and now was afraid to return to Guangdong.

"Periodically, the police carry out raids to round up those who do not possess a permit. Those caught are harassed, humiliated, and mistreated, thrown into detention centers where the conditions are sometimes worse than state prisons, and then sent back to the countryside. . . . The permit system controls them in a similar way to the passbook system under apartheid," wrote Professor Anita Chan of Australian National University.[18]

The fear of vanishing into China's black jails is what sent Mo Meiquan back to her village in 2000, for the first time in two years. Her identity card had expired and the prospect of being picked up by the police was so frightening that she quit her job, returning to Binghua-cun to get a new one. When Meiquan had first left the Guizhou countryside, at the age of fifteen, she had been nervous but excited for the future. The example of Rubo—Meiquan's cousin, who had worked a series of factory jobs in Zhejiang Province, then in Shanghai, before settling into his latest as a welder in Dongguan—helped the shy fifteen-year-old get up the courage to leave the mountainous village of Binghuacun. (Rubo had told few people in his village about being mugged in Ningbo, and Meiquan did not know about it.) On a clear morning in June 1998, she boarded her first-ever bus, and settled in for the thirty-hour ride to Dongguan. "I thought there was a whole world out there that must be very different from the village. And I decided leaving was the only way to improve myself," Meiquan said. "She left right after we had started to plant the rice sprouts," said her father, Mo Ruxian. "I thought if my child can go out to find work, of course it's good news. It is so hard to make money from the land."[19]

Indeed, the world outside the village was completely different, but not in all the ways she had hoped. Meiquan's first job was in a Hong Kong–owned factory in Humen, making belt buckles. Her task was to polish metal molds for twelve-hour days, a finger-numbing exercise that earned her only some thirty dollars a month, depending on how many she completed. Later, when the factory boss got a particularly large order for belts, he ordered the migrants to keep working until the contract was finished. After forty-eight hours with few breaks, Meiquan, along with a quarter of the factory's four-hundred-some workers, quit in protest. "I was so angry. I thought I'm still young and money isn't that important. I walked directly from the line to the office and told them I was done," she said.[20]

When I talked to China's migrants, it sometimes seemed as if their lives revolved around an elusive quest to find the rare factory that actually cared about their well-being. As I sat in one Dongguan restaurant with a few of the workers from Binghuacun, I pointed to a flyer on the wall advertising work in another electronics factory. Across it someone had scrawled *"pianren de difang,"* or "place of liars." "They will trick you. The factories that put those notices up will charge you a hundred yuan just to apply then afterward won't give you a job," said thirty-two-year-old Mo Wenzhi, the first Binghuacun native to have come to Dongguan. "And if they do give you a job, the living conditions won't be anywhere as good as promised," he added dismissively. But Wenzhi, after years of suffering under a succession of uncaring bosses, felt that he had finally found the right factory. He now worked as the cook at the Shiqing Hardware Machinery Equipment Factory, a producer of the molds and machines used in metal sheeting manufacturing, and was paid the hefty sum of a thousand yuan a month. Shiqing was owned by a Taiwanese businessman and run by a general manager from Hunan Province; both seemed to really care whether the workers were happy, Wenzhi said.

Later he and Rubo, who worked there as a welder, would take me to the factory complex. Across the street was an opulent compound of apartments for factory bosses and rich locals. From the street and over the wall, one could just make out balconies with ornate metal grilles hanging off of new apartment buildings; a guard at the gate stood ready to keep the riffraff out. While from the outside Shiqing, comprising several three-story, white-tiled buildings with neatly painted blue trim, looked well cared for, that impression dissipated as one entered the compound. The factory floor was dimly lit while the whir of machines beat out a steady racket. Line workers in blue uniforms with large wrenches moved about, stopping occasionally to tighten bolts on the green plating machines being produced; with one end higher that then sloped gently down, the factory's products from a distance looked like bulky psychiatrist couches.

The stuffy, hot rooms of the sleeping quarters each had six sets of bunk beds, housing twelve, and had no toilets or running water; those were provided down the hall in a common bathroom, pungent with the smell of human waste. Drying washcloths and T-shirts hung from clothes lines that had been strung between dormitory bunk beds; the occasional lower bed had a sheet draped over a line run between the outside bunk posts, creating a modicum of privacy. A single fan mounted on the ceiling slowly rotated, momentarily providing a feeble breeze as it swept over each bed in the room. Only the occasional worker splurged and bought his own fan, and it would inevitably be locked into place, directing its wind at whatever bunk the big spender slept in. It seemed remarkable that anyone sleeping here could believe this factory took special care of its workers, but that was how Wenzhi felt. The quiet-spoken Guizhou native explained that comfort and privacy were not high on his list of concerns. "I'm from a poor region and I am not looking for a woman. Every night after work, I just go to sleep."

A visit to the cafeteria, however, showed signs of a more caring boss. This room was nicer. The state of factory dining halls and particularly the food served in them were key to satisfying Chinese workers. (Alternately, they often are a source of worker instability; bland, low-quality, or meatless meals are often the reason for strikes and work stoppages.) A room with a series of benches at long tables, the dining hall had a twenty-one-inch Panasonic TV mounted on the end wall for singing karaoke songs together in the evenings, a popular pastime for workers (a much tamer version than in the karaoke parlors frequented by the factory bosses of Dongguan). Fans were mounted at regular intervals from the ceiling to fight the heat. A banner on the wall at the head of the room read SHIQING IS OUR HOME; CLEANLINESS DEPENDS ON EVERYONE next to a painting of red flowers with sweeping Chinese script reading *"xiangjia de rizi,"* or "homesick days."

The work domain of Wenzhi was the attached kitchen. Although poorly lit, with walls slick with old cooking grease, it was rich with the smell of chicken cooking in a wok, evidence that this factory provided a higher caliber of food to its workers; the number of times meat was served a week was a common measure of how good or not the meals in a factory were. Chopped garlic and chilies were piled on a cutting board ready to be added, while a rice cooker steamed nearby, Stacks of metal plates sat beside porcelain cups of soy sauce. A calico cat slinked by with her kitten following her, as Wenzhi, in gray pants, with a dirty white apron tied over a yellow shirt, stirred the chicken broth.

"Yes, conditions are quite poor, but Wenzhi still works very hard," factory manager Lei later explained as he led me on a tour of the sweltering factory, palm trees waving in the heat outside; spray-painted in red across one workroom wall were the words "2000 Merry Christmas," featuring white snowflakes for good measure. Within his first six months at the factory, Wenzhi's starting salary of six hundred yuan a month was raised to nine hundred yuan, and he now earned a thousand yuan, an unusually rapid wage rise in the factory, the director said. But it was well deserved: before Wenzhi arrived, the factory had needed two full-time cooks, but "now he can do the whole job alone. And he has never been late in serving a meal," Lei said approvingly. "When workers' efficiency improves, we can then afford to raise their salaries." Right now it took a full day for a team of three workers to make one metal plating machine; he would like to reduce that time, he added.

As for Rubo, his first days in the factory had not been as smooth, and he had almost been fired. When he started working a year earlier, the younger Mo had no experience and quickly became a drag on production. "He was an obstacle to others working here and caused troubles," said Lei. When the factory owner decided to fire him, Lei told the owner that Rubo was eager to learn, and successfully convinced the boss to give him another chance. "Rubo cried when I told him the news. I told him to work harder doing the most menial job—helping other workers carry the machines—and he did it," said the manager. "Workers from the most undeveloped regions work hardest. Have you ever seen a guy with money who will work hard for someone else?" he added with a smile.[21]

A day later I had hired a driver and gone south to Shenzhen, heralded today as a hotbed for China's new tech innovation, but then home to seemingly endless migrant worker residency communities. We had been driving for over an hour through what seemed indistinguishable five-story blocks of cement buildings with scuffed gray walls. At street level, by contrast, was an ever-changing tangle of signs, scrawled notices, and neon marquees. They advertised eateries with the spicy cuisines of Sichuan, Hunan, and Guizhou, noodle shops from Henan, and restaurants offering hearty stewed meat from China's Northeast; *dageda or* "big boss" pagers produced by Motorola, the predecessor to mobile phones, were touted, while inside tiny stores cheap tennis shoes, white bras, button-up shirts, and colorful plastic buckets for washing up in dormitories hung from low ceilings. Shelves had bundled-up blankets for cold nights in factory bunks; there were twenty-one different kinds of cigarettes, from almost as many different provinces, and cassettes featuring pop stars like Na Ying, from faraway Liaoning, in China's north.

Steaming pots were filled with snacks, including eggs boiled in tea and corn on the cob; roasted yams, peanuts, and chestnuts let off pungent forest-tree smells. And every few blocks there would be a scuffed old billiard table set out on the sidewalk surrounded by a gaggle of workers, smoking while they shot pool. The huge market clearly catered to the diverse migrant population from across China, with its many different eating and living habits. But shopping required having cash in one's pocket, of course. "Even though we can go there after work, things are too expensive, so we usually can't afford them," Rubo had said to me earlier while walking through a similar neighborhood outside his factory in Dongguan.

After finally pulling up outside yet another indistinguishable scuffed building, I trudged up to the third floor. I was there to see forty-three-year-old Zhou Litai, a native of Chongqing, once China's wartime nationalist capital, who was now gaining fame, at least among the beleaguered factory workers of the Pearl River Delta, as one of China's first occupational-injury lawyers. From a poor farming family on the outskirts of the city, Zhou had dropped out of school after completing only second grade, then joined the army when he was seventeen, and had served in Tibet for five years. After demobilization, he worked in a brick and tile factory in Hunan for some years, followed by a series of other equally arduous manual jobs. Distressed at how he and other laborers were powerless to improve poor working conditions, Zhou had decided to become a lawyer, and after self-study, started practicing in 1986. When a man from his home village died in a car accident in Shenzhen, the father asked Zhou to represent the family. In a surprise victory, Zhou won compensation for the family, not just from the driver of the car that hit their son, but also from the factory where he had worked.

Along with low wages and long hours, factory injuries were commonplace across China. And compensation for injuries was notoriously low, maybe several thousand yuan for a severed hand or a crippled leg; for life-threatening sicknesses like silicosis or lung cancer, which would show up only long after one had left a job in a dust-filled jewelry polishing factory or a chemical-fumes-ridden toy factory, there was usually nothing. With twenty thousand workers experiencing serious injuries every year, Shenzhen was the natural place to work, said Zhou. He decided to stay and set up a small office in the same apartment we were now visiting, and soon was flooded with requests for help.

Inside were more than a dozen workers, some resting on cots or lounging on a couch watching TV while they fanned themselves, while others sat on small stools playing cards. All were staying temporarily in Zhou's stuffy, small apartment, as they waited for their day in court. A scowling Zhou met us at the door and, rather than sitting down for the interview I had come for, instead beckoned for me to follow, and rushed over to the group playing cards. Grabbing one man's arm, he quickly pulled up his sleeve to reveal what had been his hand, now a nub with no fingers. "See!" he said. Without asking permission first, he seized another worker by his pants leg, showing a limb that had been severed just below the knee. The workers—all injured, it turned out—seemed used to this treatment and continued to quietly play cards without speaking. "This is how Chinese workers are treated in the factories," he declared angrily. "Government officials believe keeping a boss happy is like preserving one's money bowl. Their attitude is that finding a boss who will invest is much more difficult than finding workers. That's why the laws are neglected and accidents happen so often." Zhou's work representing migrants was not just unappreciated, but actively resented, he said. "The local government believes these cases seriously affect their reputation and harm the investment environment. From local citizens to the mayor, everyone hates me." Zhou's voice rose in volume. "But if we don't protect workers' rights, it will result in social instability. In the 1920s China was full of worker strikes as a result of the large number of angry workers we had then."[22]

While China at the turn of the century once again had plenty of angry workers, most protests occurred in the state enterprises affected by the Zhu-led restructuring and layoffs. But migrant workers, upset about low wages and dangerous working conditions, were beginning to strike as well. "From about 2002 onwards, the labor movement began to change, and an increasing number of migrant workers started to organize protests. Moreover, the scale, frequency and duration of industrial action increased, and labor unrest evolved from random, sporadic outbreaks to regular occurrences," wrote Hong Kong–based worker-advocacy group China Labour Bulletin in a 2007 report.[23]

Public awareness about their plight was to get a huge boost following the death of one migrant in 2003, twenty-seven-year-old Hubei native Sun Zhigang. (The fact that he was better educated than most migrants, with a college degree, may have contributed to the level of national outrage.) Sun had come to Guangzhou to work as a designer in a textile factory. One day police stopped him on the street for not having a temporary residency card, which he had not yet applied for, and not carrying his identity card, which he had left in his hometown, and locked him in a detention center. His incarceration was legal under a 1982 law called "Measures for Internment and Deportation of Urban Vagrants and Beggars," the same statute used to lock up countless migrants before him, without any public uproar. Sun made a phone call to friends in his hometown, asking them to send his ID. The next call they got was the news of his death; after he had been in custody only three days, the center's guards had savagely beaten him to death on March 20. The murder was reported in the muckraking paper *Southern Metropolis Daily,* and the news quickly spread on Weibo, China's microblogging platform. (Use of Weibo had recently taken off nationally for the first time with the spread of the SARS virus, just then racking China, where it was the primary source of uncensored news about the disease's spread.)

A then-little-known rights lawyer, Xu Zhiyong, who had recently graduated from China's elite Peking University, writing years later described his feeling when he first heard about the incident: "April 25, 2003, as SARS emptied out the streets in Beijing, I sat in front of my computer reading about the Sun Zhigang coverage, tears quietly welling up in my eyes. Over the second half of 2002, I had started to investigate the laws concerning custody and repatriation (of migrant populations), and knew what Sun had gone through." Xu, later to become one of the most outspoken and influential voices for migrants before being imprisoned in 2014 for four years for his advocacy of a more fair and constitutional China, joined with two other law graduates from the same university, and wrote an open letter calling for an official review of China's custody and repatriation system.[24]

Much to many people's surprise, the public uproar over Sun's death seemed to have spooked the leadership, who responded with an unprecedented action. On June 20, then premier Wen Jiabao announced plans to abolish the mandatory detention centers for migrants as of August 1. Then, in late July, the minister of public security, Zhou Yongkang, criticized China's police force, saying it must "resolutely stop malignant violations that offend the heavens and reason, and stir up public indignation."[25] (More than a decade later, Zhou was to get a life sentence, convicted of massive corruption.) While the Sun Zhigang incident is widely seen as the beginning of *weiquan*, China's rights movement—where public pressure and lawyer advocates brought policy change—the victory for migrant workers proved illusory. The *hukou* system was not abolished. And what replaced the black jails— now relabeled social aid centers—did not prove to be that different. "Nominally, these social aid centers existed on a voluntary basis— vagrants were to enter on their own will—however, it was soon evident that, in practice, the government used these stations to detain people against their will," wrote Teng Biao, a cosignatory with Xu of the earlier open letter, to become another of China's best-known rights lawyers before fleeing into exile in the U.S. in 2014.[26]

It was a cold day in Beijing in March in the mid-2000s. I had once more adjusted the wording for the question I hoped to ask at the premier's annual press conference, coming as always at the close of the annual National People's Congress in the early spring. I planned to ask about the *hukou* and its halting reform and what was being done to make it less discriminatory toward China's migrant workers. I had submitted my question in advance to the foreign ministry, playing into their game of creating a scripted press conference with no surprises, which they then could present as an example of China's growing openness. But the spokesperson from the foreign ministry kept coming back to me for revisions or changes to my topic. What was it about my question that he didn't like, I wondered.

Finally, I got an answer: The topic of *hukou* reform was no longer relevant, the official patiently explained, as the policy had been altered to the point where it no longer was a constraint on migrants' work and lives. Why didn't I come up with a new topic for a question? I was confused. I knew that was not the case, or at least, I was almost 100 percent sure the policy still was very much alive. Had I somehow missed this big change in my effort to keep tabs on all the economic and policy reforms Chinese officials were then carrying out? I thought not and told him I would tweak my question just a bit more. I went to the press conference, dutifully raised my hand, still intent on asking about the *hukou,* but was never called on. It was only later that it occurred to me how naive I had been: the last thing this official wanted was for someone to ask the premier to explain how his office was going to fix this decades-old policy, when, for now at least, they had no intention of changing it at all. Rather, the *hukou* policy was becoming the bedrock policy for the reform era's Factory to the World manufacturing economy.

2

The Family

In education there are no class distinctions.

—CONFUCIUS[1]

Not sending children to primary and middle school is an
illegal practice!

—SLOGAN ON VILLAGE WALL

While in most families from the villages, parents and children alike
would follow a similar path, dropping out around the time they
were to enter middle school, then joining the migrant workforce,
there were others that, against the odds, saw a sibling or two make
it through high school and sometimes even continue on to college,
often finding a government job after that. Ruxuan, the ambitious
local official who had taken me to Binghuacun on my first visit, was
from one such family; while both parents had been illiterate, somehow they had impressed upon their five children the importance of
reading. Not only had Ruxuan made it through college and got a position working in a nearby local administration before moving up to
a coveted job in the provincial capital, so, too, had his eldest brother
Mo Ruji attended college and later gotten work as a civil servant; now
Ruji was an amiable cadre in Libo, the nearest city to Binghuacun,
whose hobby was taking photographs of rural Guizhou scenery. Two

sisters had also made it through high school and both worked at a small alcohol-distilling factory in Libo.

Mo Ruchun, the charismatic and clearly intelligent middle brother, however, had been forced to drop out of school when he was only sixteen, when their father's health took a turn for the worse. "My brothers and sisters all got to go to school, but I couldn't continue. Otherwise my parents would not have had enough food to eat," he had said, real regret registering in his voice, as we had sat in his apartment in Libo one evening many years after my first visit to Guizhou in 2000. Like most migrant youth, Ruchun had gone out to work as a migrant, spending time in a startling variety of factories, including lumber, shoes, and electronics. He had worked in a cement company, then raised sheep for a time in the mountains above his village. When I had first visited Binghuacun, he had been back doing that, and we had briefly met. During years spent in cities, he had learned to speak a relatively standard version of Mandarin, China's official dialect, unlike those who had stayed in the village. Ruxuan, his successful brother, therefore, had instructed Ruchun to help me when I departed Binghuacun. (Ruxuan had had to leave earlier for business.) Ruchun had met me in a nearby small town, after I took the same horse cart when leaving Binghuacun that had brought me there. He remembered me giving him a bottle of mineral water and had been struck by what he saw as an act of kindness, he was to tell me years later. Then he had escorted me to the small bus station, where I had boarded a bus to return to the provincial capital.

I was back in Humen for the first time in many years. It was mid-April, coming just before the rainy season and the onset of the sweltering summer, and the air had an expectant tautness to it, as if something were preparing to burst. On the recommendation of Rubo, who I had come to Humen to see, I had booked myself a room in one of the better hotels, not far from where he, his wife, and his five-year-old daughter lived. The Lung Chuen International Hotel, with a sweeping driveway leading up to big glass doors and very little international about it, had a massive Chinese map made of tile built into the wall behind its reception desk; an inset showed the South China Sea, with the so-called nine-dash line demarcating Beijing's sweeping claims to the coastal waters of Malaysia, the Philippines, Indonesia, and Taiwan.

As if highlighting that oceanic piece of territorial hubris, the lobby's centerpiece was an aquarium with two huge sea turtles, maybe six feet long from pointed beak to wedged, triangular tails. The marine reptiles swooped and dived in endless loops around their little circular tank, flippered legs propelling them periodically to the surface for air. No doubt they were miserable in their confinement, I thought, but this example of animal cruelty probably did not rise to the polar bear kept in a nearby city's shopping mall, news of which had recently made international headlines. After parking his little red Honda in Lung Chuen's vast parking lot, Rubo met me outside the hotel's glass doors, seeming nervous to enter the lobby—memories of his past life as a factory worker who would have been angrily run out of such an establishment perhaps reawakening. Now, in 2017, as an entrepreneur running his own small sports clothing business, would he be welcome? He led us quickly to his car, as if anxious not to find out.

In some ways, Humen looked unchanged, a jumble of factories but now mixed with multistory apartment and commercial buildings. The same lack of urban planning, where industry rubbed up against residential neighborhoods that gave way to rice fields, was still evident. Near the hotel ran a strip of new commercial businesses that included a 7-Eleven with its distinctive glowing orange, red, and green sign, above it on the second floor was a children's language cram school called "Spirit Kids English," while nearby a coffee shop blaring Chinese pop music into the street had emblazoned on its window the cryptic English phrase LOVE 85 COFFEE BECAUSE TOP.

Whereas Dongguan, a lawless, rough-and-tumble manufacturing town of the south, had once felt far removed from China's political locus of Beijing, today signs of the newly assertive central leadership under Xi Jinping were visible on its slogan-plastered streets. Streetlamps had affixed long rectangular signs touting Xi's CHINA DREAM the phrase he coined in 2012, shortly after taking power, his plan to bring new prosperity to China while building a more powerful party and country. Next to the bold words, white doves flew in front of a sweeping modern bridge set against a red sunset, while an image of a *huabiao*—a traditional white marble ornamental column engraved with images of dragons and clouds and topped with a *denglong* (a mythical creature that is supposed to send the wishes of the people to the emperor), two of which grace Beijing's Tiananmen Square—floated in the sky nearby. On a wall outside a factory that produced pens was painted a picture of a somber-looking Xi dressed in a gray Mao suit, his hands clasped together as if to signal resolve, with the accompanying words "When the people have faith, the nation has hope, and the country has power."

This was Rubo's home, in a nearby crowded residential block, just a few kilometers away from the electronics factory, with its dismal dorms, where I had first met him, almost two decades earlier. (The factory was still in operation, he told me.) At the base of his building was a stuffed-bun shop, round metal steamer containers stacked up and filled with the hot buns, or *baozi*. A woman sat in front of a small table on which were heaps of fresh bananas and a plastic water dispenser with fresh-cut pineapple soaking inside. There was the typical daily-supplies store catering to migrants, its entrance an overflowing panoply of red, blue, pink, green, yellow, and translucent differently sized plastic buckets and bins for cleaning one's clothes, washing one's face, or mopping a floor. Toilet plungers with glowing blue rubber suction cups were stuffed together with bristly fluorescent green and pink sink and shower scrubbers, all seeming to erupt in multicolored abandon from a white canister. Straw and nylon brooms and floppy white mops sprouted upside down nearby. Shelves inside were stacked with various brands of toothpaste, soap, hand towels, shampoo, and clothes detergent.

Upstairs, Rubo showed me around his small apartment with office. The door from the landing opened into a narrow living room, the balcony at the end overlooking the street and the nearby writing-tools factory, a long warehouse-looking structure with bedraggled palm trees around its perimeter. Along the apartment's wall, with its doors opening into a small kitchen and bedroom, were a dark red Ronshen-brand refrigerator and a stand-up water dispenser made by Midea, the white-goods maker now known for automation devices, following its purchase of Germany's crown jewel of robotics, KUKA AG.

In an alcove near the entrance was where he and his wife, once both factory workers, now ran their own business, clearly a source of pride for both. Rubo's wife, dressed in a long greenish-yellow striped dress with orange, yellow, and red polka dots, and wearing makeup, as always, even though she now worked from home, smiled from where she sat, but then immediately turned back to the computer screen she had been staring at intently when we walked in. During my two-hour-plus visit, as Rubo and I sat talking nearby, this was where she remained almost without break, filling out orders and organizing shipments for the tiny sports-apparel brand that they had bought several years earlier, clearly determined to make their new venture succeed. A few Lenovo-brand laptops and an old laser printer sat on three desks that had been pushed together, the middle one turned sideways and jutting out to create a makeshift cubicle on each side, one of which was where she sat. The only decorations in the room were some leafy green plants and a horizontal scroll in a gaudy gilded frame. Gold characters read "a thriving and prosperous business" against a red background, while shiny gold coins and jewelry inset with blue and red gems were painted along the piece's base. Heavy wooden furniture with an orange sheen, two chairs and a couch all painfully hard to sit on, with a glass-topped coffee table before them, finished off the room's decor.

The other two, smaller rooms actually looked lived-in by comparison. The kitchen, dark despite a small window, had a two-burner gas stove hooked up to an orange canister against the opposite wall; a cooking hood was affixed above it, as in most Chinese kitchens, for sucking out the grease and smell of frying food. A shiny silver Midea rice cooker sat on a counter next to a dish rack holding several rice bowls, each with an image of Mickey and Minnie Mouse, pink hearts floating between them. On a utensil rack mounted on the wall were hanging the usual assortment of spatulas, rice scoopers, dumpling ladles, and a colander. A small bowl of diced watermelon sat on the counter, probably a late-afternoon snack for their daughter.

Meanwhile, their daughter was busy in the narrow bedroom next door. That room was where all three members of the family slept, although at first I found that hard to picture; cots to sleep on were barely visible underneath a tangle of toys—a yellow-and-green-colored car racetrack, a blue Hula Hoop, a small musical drum. A rubber mat featuring Disney's Goofy and Daffy Duck was draped over a clothes rack in the corner. Their daughter stood in front of a Haier-brand monitor watching a cartoon, while at the same time carefully sorting through a bright pink child's makeup box. She looked at me quizzically without answering when I asked her what she was doing. Her expression seemed to say, "Dumb question. Can't you see I'm watching a cartoon and checking out my makeup box, you odd foreign man?"

Even though it was still more than a year away, Rubo and his wife were already struggling with the question of where their daughter would enter first grade in September of 2018. There was a certain irony in this; Rubo had dropped out of school when he was not too many years older than his daughter was now, and had hated every minute of his classes before he finally left. But getting his daughter into a good school now was clearly one of his and his wife's biggest concerns. Under China's rigid *hukou* policy, children of migrants were all but banned from attending public schools in the city. (Those few who got in usually were charged special fees, too, as nonlocal residents.) Instead, they were supposed to enroll in whatever far-off country elementary institution served the village where their parents had been born. But that was not where their parents lived and worked in most cases. Following a series of tragedies involving kids growing up away from their families in the countryside, education officials now said they were tweaking the policy to allow more rural kids to study in urban schools, near their parents. But the reality was that getting one's child a slot in a city school was all but impossible, Rubo said resignedly.

Dongguan, like other cities around China, had begun to experiment with offering *hukou* to a very limited number of outsiders through a points-based system—once a person had earned a certain score, they would be eligible to apply for a local residency permit and all the benefits that came with it. Without question, most coveted was the right for one's child to go to a city school. Points could be accrued based on one's education level; the higher a degree earned, the better. Buying a local apartment gave one more points, as did contributing to the social-welfare program for a number of years. But for most migrants—and Rubo was no exception—earning the requisite points was a pipe dream: They hadn't gone to school for enough years. Most had not contributed the full legally required amount to social welfare; making reduced or even no contributions, so that employers and employees could save money, was commonplace across China. And they almost always didn't have money to buy a city apartment. "If I had a local *hukou,* school for my daughter would be free, then I would just have to pay for books and uniforms," said Rubo. "But even if you buy a house in Humen, you still can't get local *hukou.* The Dongguan *hukou* is only for geniuses, and only special people can get it."[2]

Instead, Rubo and his wife were considering options outside the public schools for their daughter. One possibility was to put her into one of Dongguan's private schools, many of which bragged they were *waiyu xueyuan,* or "foreign-language schools." When I asked Rubo if that meant they taught English classes, he figured it did, but said he wasn't sure; like many of China's less cosmopolitan, Rubo separated the world's tongues into two basic groups, Chinese language—the Tai language he spoke as a Buyi he took for granted—and "foreign language"—a much-coveted ability prized in one's children. (It was not uncommon for Chinese, after listening to someone speaking English, to declare, "Wow! Your foreign language is so good!") But the private schools were costly. Paying a tuition that could run as high as 15,000 yuan ($2,184) a term was a real struggle. An equally large problem was quality. Most were known for having far less skilled teachers and substandard facilities, compared to public academies. (That was true even of those that claimed to teach alternate languages.) A final choice—and this was the most common one for migrants—was to send their children back to the village they came from to study in a boarding school. For Rubo, that was the least acceptable option. "She is too young to live in a dormitory now," he told me. "We want to keep our daughter here with us. We don't want to make her into a *liushouertong.*"

In the second decade of the twenty-first century, the term

"liushouertong"—literally, "left-behind children," referring to the estimated sixty-one million offspring of migrant workers who grow up separated from their parents, or one in five of all Chinese youth—had become well known across China, following a series of tragedies. Perhaps the most infamous incident was when five cousins, aged nine to thirteen, died of asphyxiation in 2012, after starting a fire with charcoal in a large trash bin in a place called Bijie in rural Guizhou, to try to keep warm. The boys' fathers had left them to live alone after they went to work in Shenzhen. Three years later, in the same region of northwestern Guizhou, four children killed themselves by drinking pesticide, after their parents had also left them for work.

Less headline-catching but equally disturbing, researchers began to identify a range of serious health problems afflicting these youngest victims of the *hukou* policy. Malnutrition and physical stunting among migrant children is common, the social scientists' fieldwork showed; the kids eat poorly whether they live in boarding schools or stay with their grandparents in the countryside. The left-behind children on average are three centimeters shorter and weigh significantly less than other Chinese children, showed the joint study carried out by Stanford University, the Chinese Academy of Sciences, and Northwest University in Xi'an.

The psychological toll is equally alarming. According to a 2015 study by Beijing-based research organization Growing Home, 63 percent of rural boarding students are lonely, nearly one-fifth say they are depressed, and many have considered suicide. Drug abuse and petty crime are common. And many are sexually abused by relatives or teachers, showed a 2013 study by researchers from Beijing Normal University and the government-affiliated China Children and Teenagers' Fund. When I first started to report on their travails, in 2014, Sanna Johnson, executive director of the Beijing-based Centre for Child-Rights and Corporate Social Responsibility, a Swedish business consultancy, told me, "The left-behind children often carry some sort of trauma. They usually don't do as well in school, and there is the risk of them getting involved in bad behavior."[3]

Spurred by the hollowing out of the countryside as migrant workers flooded into coastal factory towns in the 2000s, as well as a declining birth rate in part because of the one-child policy, officials ordered a massive consolidation of rural schools. In 1997 China had 630,000 primary schools, many of them small and located in villages; by 2011 there were only 254,000, with average class sizes soaring.[4] As small rural schools were shuttered, much larger boarding schools were established in county townships across rural China, to educate and house the left-behind children. By 2015, there were 100,000 boarding schools serving China; most were known for overcrowding and poor quality.[5]

The Chinese Academy of Sciences is a sprawling bureaucracy with over 60,000 staff, 48,500 of them scientists and researchers. Opened in 1949, exactly one month after the founding of the People's Republic of China, the Chinese Academy was modeled on the then Soviet Union's national science academy, and headed for most of its first three decades by Guo Moruo, a famous Chinese poet, author, and early Communist believer. Now the academy's 104 distinct institutes are scattered across the country, and house everything from rocket scientists and physicists to experts on nanotechnology and climate change. As a business journalist, the academy was not my usual beat.

But one chilly March morning, I found myself heading there, to visit its China Center for Agricultural Policy, and meet economist Scott Rozelle, a sixty-something Stanford professor with sweeping gray hair and the manic energy of a true believer. Fluent in Chinese, Rozelle was often jokingly called "more Chinese than we are" by his fellow mainland scholars. "Scott has probably spent more time in the Chinese countryside than any other foreigner; he knows rural education unlike anyone else," said one professor, who himself had worked in the field for three decades.

"We are better off here because we are under the radar screen. CAS doesn't pay much attention to our research," Rozelle said with a laugh as we sat down in a cold conference room on the third floor of the center.[6]

I had come to establish the rules for a reporting trip in China's West. My purpose: to see the flip side of the country's often-hyped educational success—the overcrowded rural boarding schools of the interior, not an experience usually open to foreign journalists. I would have to provide full anonymity to the principals and teachers I spoke to, Rozelle said. "I don't mind you saying that the dormitory rooms are full of pee because there are no lights, and it's a hundred yards outside to the nearest bathroom, and the six-year-olds are scared to go out at night. So instead they wet their beds and get beat up by the other kids sleeping in the same beds next to them," Rozelle had said on an earlier phone call. "But you can't say Mr. Liu the principal said this or said that, because then he will get fired." (Rozelle was using "Liu", one of the most common Chinese surnames, as a generic example.)

Sitting across the empty conference table from me, he explained, "Our requirement is that you do not name names. You can say Shaanxi"—the Northwestern province known for its rich coal seams and rural poverty—"or Southeastern Shaanxi, but not the name of the county where you are. Only if someone clearly says they don't mind you printing their name, then you can do so. That is the only caveat for this reporting trip."

Leaving Xi'an, it's hard to believe it was once the Tang dynasty capital called Chang'an, meaning "perpetual peace." Laid out on a massive symmetrical grid, with its streets lined with Chinese scholar trees, in the sixth century, it was the largest, most cosmopolitan city in the world, with bustling communities of foreign and local Muslims and Buddhists. The dusty city is home to the Terracotta Warriors, statues of stone soldiers dating back to the much earlier Qin dynasty, now a draw for tourists from around the world. It has experienced the same bubble in real-estate development as all Chinese cities. En route to the countryside, one passes through kilometers of recently constructed high-rise residential towers, most of them empty, before reaching the low-slung factories that clot the city's outskirts.

That familiar picture of urban China in the second decade of the twenty-first century soon ends as the road crawls upward into the Qin mountain range, which runs from east to west, and serves as a boundary between the Yellow River watershed of the north and the Yangtze

River to the south. With peaks over 3,500 meters, this belt of still-wild coniferous and deciduous forest is home to the russet Qinling panda and the 1.8-meter-long Chinese giant salamander, the world's biggest amphibian. From the G5 expressway, opened to traffic in 2007 and with 540 bridges and 136 tunnels along its 255-kilometer length, one sees traditional brick villages wedged into the hillsides; where the road runs through a valley, a BYD electric-vehicle battery factory has been built.

After reaching a prefectural capital, our van leaves the thorough-fare, to climb higher into the mountains. The now-dirt road narrows to a lane and a half wide, with a precipitous drop to a small river on the left and sheer rock face on the right; our driver honks protectively as we round blind corners. We pass an earthquake resettlement village, tidy new brick houses with signs lettered wc identifying the occasional public bathroom. The resettlement community is built just below an aging reservoir, the soaring face of the dam rising just behind the village. I hope this area isn't also prone to seismic activity.

Finally, the van rattles through a gate, and we come to a stop in a school courtyard. Fifteen children, dressed in cheap nylon parkas, with frayed polyester hats and mittens, stand in a circle playing some kind of game of tag with a ball. One side of the brick building is lined with doors that open into classrooms, with dirt-scuffed cement floors and scarred wooden tables and benches. There is also a kitchen, its walls blackened by smoke from a wood-burning oven. Half of one wall outside is obscured by neatly stacked split wood, both fuel for the oven and the heat source for the school.

The principal, a forty-two-year-old man with tousled hair and a worn, smiling face, greets us outside. "Let's go to our administration office, it's more comfortable to talk," he says, and the contrast between the hardscrabble setting and his effort to treat the visitor from afar with solicitude brings a twinge of poignancy. The office sits on the second floor, in a recently added wing situated toward the high end of the narrowing canyon. It was built not many years before, courtesy of a special fund from the education ministry in far-off Beijing, though it has quickly aged to match the rest of the compound.[7]

The principal sits across from us at a long table in the frigid room.

Behind him is a locked glass cabinet filled with the school's prized collection of hardcover books—nothing like the flimsy paper textbooks the children use. Through a small window I can see the tightly cultivated, narrow corn plots snaking up the edges of the mountain, wherever the pitch momentarily eases. "It isn't easy," he says, concern flashing across his face. "Of our sixty students, one-third board here. They are the ones I worry about," he continues. "The others get good meals back in their homes in the evening. My boarders get enough to eat—it isn't that they go hungry; it's just not the right things that they are getting." Later, a serious-faced twelve-year-old boy tells me that he loves the food here. The meat, served just once a week, is particularly welcome, he says.

The principal pulls two shy students, both boarders, into the room to answer my questions. They stare determinedly down at the table, intent on not meeting my gaze. The girl, a thirteen-year-old in a puffy pink parka, with a second pair of knit sleeves layered on top for added warmth, seems slightly less bashful; her eyes flick up to mine, midway through speaking, before quickly taking refuge again in the flat brown sheen of the table.

Do you miss your parents, I ask. No answer. She starts to rapidly knead the cuffs of her sleeves. I suddenly see tears running down her face. I look at her, chagrined that she will always remember me as a pushy stranger that made her cry. The principal gently prods her: "Do you miss them?" She pulls herself together, and says, "Yes, very much." She, like most of the children of migrants, will see her mother and father only once or twice a year, during the rare leave they get from whatever factory, construction site, or restaurant kitchen employs them.[8]

The Chinese Communist Party's claim that it existed "To Serve the People" had always rested in some not small part on its success providing basic education for all. While in the days of the KMT (1927–1949), a period marked by civil wars and Japan's invasion, only a fraction of China's children went to school, that was to change after 1949. Henceforth, the party would provide universal schooling, including for the children of China's hundreds of millions of peasants. The push for nationwide education would go hand in glove with similar efforts for health care; where legions of "barefoot doctors" or paramedics with basic training were sent out to meet the needs of China's hitherto ignored rural masses, collective schools would be established in every agricultural commune and state-owned company, to ensure that all children had a chance to learn. Ironically, the famous line of Confucius "In education there are no class distinctions" would become something like the Communists' rallying cry—despite the fact that the party reviled the Chinese sage. In the rejuvenation of China, education was to be the supreme leveler, the party claimed.

The new leaders did make extraordinary progress. While before 1949, some 80 percent of Chinese were illiterate, by 1964 that number had dropped to just one-third of the population. By 1982 it was 22.81 percent. With the passage of a law on compulsory education in 1986, China's government promised nine years of free education to all its citizens. As China passed the millennium in 2000, five years after my arrival in Beijing, the illiteracy rate was just 6.72 percent.[9]

But despite real achievements, China's education system is deeply unequal. While students in its biggest cities have received the lion's share of resources, those in the hinterlands suffer from overcrowded classrooms and dormitories, and low-quality teaching. That reality is often ignored as observers around the world hold up China's education system as something to be both feared and envied. That tendency was on blatant display in late 2010, after the Organisation for Economic Co-operation and Development's Program for International Student Assessment, or PISA, announced that fifteen-year-old students from Shanghai had tested highest in the world for math, science, and reading. For many in the U.S., it was seen as almost a Sputnik moment— when the then Soviet Union was first in the race to launch a satellite into space in 1957—triggering national soul-searching. In response to the U.S.'s poor showing on the PISA, Congress passed the National Defense Education Act, authorizing the spending of billions of dollars to improve teaching. The shock of seeing U.S. students test thirty-first in mathematics, behind not just Shanghai but Hungary, Poland, and the Czech Republic, helped drive the adoption of the Obama administration's Common Core standards, now in use in forty-two states and the District of Columbia.

"The PISA results, to be brutally honest, show that a host of developed nations are out-educating us. . . . And the jewel of China's education system, Shanghai, debuted this year as the highest scoring participant globally," said Arne Duncan, the U.S. education secretary, in December 2010. "The hard truth is that other high-performing nations have passed us by during the last two decades. Americans need to wake up to this educational reality—instead of napping at the wheel while emerging competitors prepare their students for economic leadership."[10] In an interview with the Associated Press, Duncan called it "an absolute wake-up call for America," adding that "the results are extraordinarily challenging to us and we have to deal with the brutal truth. We have to get much more serious about investing in education."[11]

But using Shanghai, one of the country's wealthiest cities, to laud China's national education system brings to mind another Russian-themed analogy: Potemkin village. China's financial capital, through a combination of high living costs, the household registration system, and a callously efficient public security force, has, like Beijing, become one of China's most segregated, elite municipalities. Not only are the children from Shanghai not representative of the rest of the country, the more than one million migrant children who reside there are barred from attending public schools, and not tested at all. "[PISA doesn't] sample schools with any significant migrant population," said Wu Xiaogang, a professor at the Hong Kong University of Science and Technology and an expert on *hukou* policy, as we sat in a coffee shop near his alma mater, Peking University, on a cold October morning.[12]

Even as the party has long publicly proclaimed equal opportunities for all, the roots of its unfair system were the result of deliberate choices taken during the earliest years of the People's Republic. Taking their cue from Stalin's Soviet Union, Mao and his cohorts decided that scarce educational resources should be concentrated in a limited number of exclusive public schools, starting from first grade and continuing through high school. First set up in the 1950s and still around today, these elite institutions are roughly similar to "feeder" schools in America, whose students eventually graduate into top universities in unusually high numbers. Known as "key schools," they would train the future technocrats and engineers, the "experts," for the newly industrializing China. ("Red and expert"—meaning having proper ideological along with professional training—was what China's education system should aim for, in Mao's formulation.) Only a minority of students, mainly children of well-connected party insiders, would get in, with the majority relegated to lower-quality schools.

That already skewed system was to become even worse following government fiscal reforms in the mid-1990s. The tough then vice-premier Zhu Rongji, later lauded for pulling off China's entry into the WTO, had what seemed an impossible task: reining in the increasingly independent provinces. Amassing significant budget surpluses as they benefited from more than a decade of rapid growth following Deng's reform and opening, the regional governments along China's coast began ignoring policy edicts from the center; outside observers, including Central Intelligence Agency analysts, wrote reports predicting that China was about to break apart like the Soviet Union.

To rein in the wayward provinces, leaders in Beijing realized they must tighten control over the purse strings. Even before Zhu won promotion to premier in 1998, he had succeeded: While provinces had previously returned only some 20 percent of the taxes they collected to the center, they now were ordered to hand over more than one-half. With less money in hand, the provinces stopped acting so independently. But that fiscal clawback coincided with the central leadership's ambitious push to rebuild and expand social welfare, including education and health care, which had collapsed with the end of communes and reform of state enterprises. Now the localities were told they were responsible for funding the new programs. "Beijing was worried about losing control over wealthy provinces like Guangdong. That was the rationale for recentralizing," explains Lynette Ong, a professor of political science at the University of Toronto. "What it did to local government finance is make its share of revenue and expenditure become very unbalanced."[13] (Under China's unitary system of government, local governments are not allowed to levy their own taxes.)

As a result, Zhu's reform unwittingly led to the vast regional gaps in funding for social welfare bedeviling China today. It is why spending on medical care in richer coastal provinces dwarfs that in the poor interior, leading to significant differences in life expectancies; so, for example, the average male in Shanghai lives 80.2 years, while in Tibet only 68.4 years. And it explains why several years ago Shanghai was spending annually on average 14,518 yuan per elementary-school pupil, while in Guizhou the amount is just 3,237 yuan, or less than one-fourth.[14] Not surprisingly, drop-out rates are much higher in Guizhou and other cash-starved regions, than in China's wealthy municipalities like Shanghai and Beijing. When students in a poor county of Hubei were told to bring their own desks to school in 2012, it became a much-discussed topic by shocked families, across the Chinese internet.

Leaving the mountains of southern Shaanxi, where the ground once more levels out in a broad valley, one encounters more substantial fields of corn, and now also rice, which surround the district's largest town. As you enter, agriculture gives way suddenly to busy commerce. A bustle of shops open onto its main street, each with its specialty—mobile phones: *shouji*, cigarettes and alcohol: *yan jiu*—stenciled in Chinese characters across the windows, in lieu of any establishment name. *"Yanjiu"* was a particularly pointed example of the wordplay of homonyms, ubiquitous to China: "Research!," also pronounced *"yanjiu,"* like "cigarettes and alcohol" but with different tones, was reportedly the answer a local official would give when asked for help in issuing the permits needed to open a store or start a factory. The response could mean that more research was needed before a decision on permits could be reached, but also serve as a coded request for a gift of cigarettes and wine, to speed up the process.

Other than communication devices and consumable vices, here in this little town, there are also stores stocking daily necessities: There are little pouches of detergent from Tide, Omo, and the Chinese brand White Cat; scratchy tan nylon stockings; and shelves piled with dusty packages of rice crackers and strawberry-flavored Oreos. There are the ubiquitous red coolers with sliding glass panels that open from the top, filled with cans of Coca-Cola, Snow Beer (in Chinese called "snowflake beer"), milk tea, and mineral water in plastic bottles so flimsy they bend at the middle when you pick them up. On the street outside is a mael-strom of chugging three-wheel tractors, motorcycles that zigzag, and de-livery vans that barrel through, their drivers pressing their hands down on the horn excitedly, like game-show contestants on a winning streak.

Turning off the hectic street and pulling through the white-tiled gate to the local school provided relief from the hubbub. The school compound comprised a large square of new three-story buildings, like a walled city, with a running track and soccer field in the center. Be-side a parking lot, with two Chinese-style pagodas on each side, was a statue of Hua Luogeng, a famous Chinese mathematician. "Only those who are adept at using their time will make great academic achievement," read the inscription at its base. Nearby was a wall for party pronouncements and propaganda.

In a now-familiar routine, the principal, a round-faced, squat man with a serious expression, greeted us as we piled out of our van, and led us to his office. When I complimented him on the neat school grounds, doing my best to speak over droning loudspeakers intoning the rules of proper behavior for students, this quarter-century veteran of China's education system seemed unimpressed; much more impor-tant was grabbing this opportunity to tell a foreign visitor just how difficult it is to run a boarding school, it seemed. While the physical surroundings might be fine—and, indeed, the central government had poured money into constructing new classrooms and athletic fields and renovating cafeterias in schools across the country in re-cent years—the software for learning was woefully lacking. Not only were there not enough teachers for a student body numbering three hundred, most of his staff was older and few had been well trained. Turnover was high, with younger teachers in particular often leaving for jobs in bigger cities; during his three years as principal, he had already lost eight.

His school was forced to deal with the occasional medical needs of students, given that their parents were usually too far away to help them. He had applied to the local education bureau for funding to hire a nurse, but was denied, he said with visible irritation. "We try to deal with the simpler things here. But for anything more serious, we have to send them to the hospital," he said, passing his mobile phone from hand to hand. For the fifty-some-year-old principal, dressed in a brown, scuffed suit and a black belt with a huge buckle reading CHIC, there was no doubt who among his students were most difficult to manage—the left-behind children, numbering about one-half of the pupils, all of whom were boarders.

"Their parents aren't around most of the time. That means the burden of managing them is all on the teachers," he said. "Their emotional development isn't very good, because they have grown up without their mothers and fathers. And if we want to call their homes to deal with some problem, the only person we can reach is their elderly grandparents." He continued to list their faults with resignation: They don't study well; they don't do their homework; they don't come to class; when they do come, they often fall asleep, or play with their mobile phones. We do our best to ensure they have enough to eat and a clean place to sleep, he told me. They had just one so-called *shenghuo laoshi* (literally, "life teacher") to manage the school's seventy male boarders, and a second one for an equal number of female students, he explained. Having someone who could serve as the equivalent of a dorm monitor was now required in each boarding school, according to a new policy set in Beijing; in reality, many schools didn't have one at all. You should meet one to better understand our challenges, the principal said, and led me over to the school's main dormitory.[15]

The girls' "life teacher" had a guarded confidence about her. After being demobilized from the military, three years earlier, she had started this job, and now was about to turn thirty. "I am here to ensure their safety," she said with a tight-lipped smile, clutching a ring of more than a dozen keys. One no doubt accompanied the padlock I had seen hanging loosely from a grated metal door that swung across the stairwell, sealing off the two upper floors of dormitory rooms. *They are locked in the building at night,* I realized with a sinking feeling; news reports of factory workers, karaoke bar staff, and also students dying in fires locked behind bolted doors had been all too frequent in recent years.

"I help the girls learn they should wash their hair twice a week, regularly hang out their bedding to air, and make sure they keep their rooms clean," she explained, as we stood on the open walkway that ran outside the third-floor sleeping quarters. "Helping the children with their psychological problems is also part of my job," she said. "The biggest issue is they miss their parents and are lonely, particularly when they first start." Her male counterpart who managed the boys had a different set of challenges: fistfights and runaways were commonplace among those who lived in the dorms.[16]

Part of the strategy of keeping the boarders out of trouble was to structure their days so they had no idle time, the principal had explained earlier. On the wall of one of the girls' dormitories, a barren room where eight slept in simple blue metal bunk beds, each with a neatly folded blanket at its foot, I saw a daily schedule posted. After rising between 6:50 A.M. and 7:20 A.M., the students would tidy their rooms and get washed up by 7:30, after which they would gather outdoors for ten minutes of calisthenics done to music broadcast over the loudspeakers. Then came breakfast, followed by a day filled with seven classes, each lasting forty minutes. These included the mandatory courses of math, Chinese, English, and politics.

Other than fifteen minutes of exercise in the afternoon, as well as lunch and dinner, the day would be filled with either instruction or "self-study" sessions, with the aim of keeping students occupied until bedtime. Immediately after dinner, at 6:40 P.M., students were herded into classrooms, sometimes with the doors locked behind them, and ordered to read their textbooks and keep quiet until 10:00 P.M. "I miss my parents so much," said one fourteen-year-old boy with a bowl-cut hairstyle and a short stature making him look younger than his age. "When no one speaks to me, I don't feel good."[17]

Hong Kong's Polytechnic University sits near the mouth of the Cross-Harbour Tunnel where it opens into crowded Kowloon. It was a late October day, and the sultry humidity of the summer had recently dropped to just bearable, when I met sociologist Anita Koo in her small office. On a crowded shelf behind her desk were an assortment of books and journals focusing on the mistreatment of migrant workers in China's factory economy, including those working for Foxconn Technology Group, the massive Apple iPhone and iPad contractor. Her research focused on the education of their children and how the household residency system determines where and how they live and study, she explained.

From birth to about five years of age, children usually stay with their grandparents in the villages they were born in, the thirty-some-year-old Hong Kong native explained. Then, when it comes time for them to enter first grade, most join their parents in whatever factory town or urban metropolis they are employed in. (A small number remain in the countryside, not going to school at all, although this practice is less common than before: "Without an end to illiteracy, the roots of poverty won't be broken" and "Not sending children to primary and middle school is an illegal practice!" were two exhortations I had seen painted in faded red characters on brick walls in Binghuacun.)

After arriving in the cities, migrant children attend private schools, often of questionable quality, that have sprung up to serve kids barred from the urban public system. The schools are not cheap, as Rubo was finding out as he struggled with his daughter's education, and run the constant risk of having to suddenly move or outright being shut down, given their often semilegal status, particularly when authorities want to force migrants to leave. But by fifth grade most kids must return to the countryside to prepare for the *zhongkao*—literally, "middle test," the exam they have to take to get into a rural high school. (There is virtually no way for those without urban *hukou* to attend any kind of high school, public or private, in the cities.) That's when most of these eleven-to-twelve-year-olds enter China's vast archipelago of rural boarding schools, home to an estimated thirty-three million students.

That disruptive series of moves, along with being separated from their parents, is the root of their psychological problems. Almost without exception, the students she had interviewed—and Koo had spoken with scores of students in the rural Hebei countryside near Beijing—described the return to the countryside as a huge setback in their lives. While in the cities they had learned etiquette, from "tossing trash in the bin to saying 'hello' in the morning," that was not expected or appreciated in the villages, she explained. Even language proved a problem; many had become more comfortable speaking the official dialect of Mandarin while in the cities, and struggled to communicate in the local vernacular. "Again and again we heard them tell us that after they return, they feel downwardly mobile—they say they feel like they are going back to hell," Koo said. "They ask themselves why they have to be sent back to this backward town."[18]

In a surprising twist, most find themselves also academically ill-prepared, studying at a level one or two grades below their classmates who never left the countryside. That's the unintended result of a well-meaning reform: in order to move Chinese education away from its traditional reliance on rote memorization and encourage creativity, urban schools have begun diversifying their curricula and reducing the stress on exams. Rather than focus overwhelmingly on preparing students for the *zhongkao* and later the *gaokao,* or "high test," that determines where one enters college, city schools have lightened overall homework loads. And they have added new subjects, like physical education and arts, to the traditional core exam subjects.

After being uprooted and dumped back into rural schools that use the original test-focused pedagogy, the returnees are doubly disadvantaged, says Koo.[19] The years spent in schools with broader curricula ironically become a serious liability. "The reform came about because policymakers want China to catch up in the new, innovation-driven economy. They don't want to overemphasize rote memory, and instead want to encourage independent thinking. But this same reform is what makes the migrant students suffer when they return to their villages," she explained.

That shift, along with the stress of living away from their families in impersonal boarding schools, helps explain their poor performance. It's also the reason more and more of these returnees are dropping out. Today only one-quarter of China's labor force has graduated from high school, a rate lower than in Turkey, Brazil, and South Africa, says Stanford's Rozelle. "The Chinese education system is creating extreme inequality," he told me. "The cost of not having Chinese rural children go to school will probably be the collapse of China's economy in 2030. There is no way China can move into becoming a high-wage, skilled economy with four hundred million people who can't read or write."[20]

Meanwhile, while many have credited China's *gaokao*, or college entrance exam, for being an impartial way to ensure that the best students get into the best schools, regardless of social background, in practice it has failed in that role. Instead, children lucky enough to be born in Beijing, Shanghai, and other wealthier metropolises are given a home-court advantage when applying to their local universities, which also happen to be the country's best: they are admitted with lower scores than their rural counterparts, and as a result are far more represented in top schools like Beijing's Peking and Shanghai's Fudan universities. Meanwhile, only a tiny minority of the already small number of rural students who finish high school—most from China's poorer western provinces, which in turn have few good universities—can win acceptance into China's better academies in the country's east. By 2005, the shape of the problem was already painfully apparent amongst male youth. While around 68 percent of twenty-three-year-old men from China's cities had completed high school or gotten higher degrees, only some 13 percent of men of the same age from the countryside had accomplished the same. That gap has not changed much in the intervening years, says World Bank economist John Giles.[21]

Koo, who did her doctoral research on the role of class in Great Britain, sees the education system as key to maintaining a rigid social structure within China. "The remarkable thing in China is that most people view it as a meritocratic system, with public education and the *gaokao* providing equal opportunity to all, which of course it isn't," she said. The government wants students to get at least "a minimum education, because they want good workers, and they want them to be adept for the new economy. But that is it. They see education as a way to train workers, not to educate all of their citizens."

Koo compares education to a vast funnel that pushes hundreds of millions of rural kids into a stark choice. Stay in school despite the unpleasantness of boarding life, with almost no chance of becoming part of the tiny minority that makes it into university. Or drop out and return to the cities to seek employment in factories, construction sites, and restaurants just as their parents did before them. The latter route starts the cycle all over again, with their future offspring also left behind and poorly educated, eventually to become manual laborers, too. And that's a source of deep disappointment for migrant parents who had hoped for a better life for their children.

I saw the real-life impact of that injurious cycle when I visited forty-year-old Chen Jinyan, a migrant worker who had dropped out of school as a youth. Chen had spent most of the last two decades laboring on construction sites in Qingdao, the northern coastal city famous as the home of Tsingtao beer. Now he was back in the Shaanxi town he had grown up in, and with the help of his seventy-year-old father, Chen Dengke, was building a two-story red-brick house; he planned to provide it as a dowry and home for his son when the youngest Chen got married and started a family (Jinyan himself had gotten divorced years earlier).

The fourteen-year-old Chen had disappeared just eight days earlier, one afternoon walking out of the boarding school he had studied at and I had just visited. "It's the first time he's run off; he fell in with some friends who are bad influences, but I'm hoping he will eventually return," the father said to me, pausing from hammering nails into a beam. "I wanted him to study, but how could I make him stay in school when most of the time I wasn't even living here," Chen said. "But we have to go out and find work—we have no choice. We need to make money to live." The grandfather leaned back against the newly built brick wall, cocked his head up in a half tilt as if he were checking for rain: "I took care of eating, clothing, and pocket money. That's all I could do. But the older he got, the more difficult he became," he said.[22]

While I never met Chen's son and don't know if he ever came home, the next day I spoke to another dropout. From the same township in southern Shaanxi, he was now employed as a cook in a Peking Duck restaurant in the provincial capital Xi'an, where he made two thousand yuan a month. He described to me a school far worse than those I had seen, where the sheer discomfort experienced was a major factor in his decision to leave. "The boarding conditions were seriously bad. We had twenty students in a room, with two to three of us sharing a bed—I never imagined it could be so crowded," nineteen-year-old

Chen Xueliang (no relation to the other Chen family) told me, sitting in the empty dining area before his shift began. "Often, there would be no beds, they would simply push the tables together, and have us sleep on them," he said, dressed in a white smock with a tall cook's hat precipitously perched on his head. "My parents—who only made it through third grade—kept pushing me to keep studying. I ran away twice but they came looking for me, and made me return. Finally they gave up," he said ruefully. "My little sister was a good student. My family is poor, so I thought it was better that we spend money on her instead. But sometimes I regret my decision."[23]

Beyond opting out of education entirely, there is another choice: entering one of China's vocational schools, fast-growing in number. For many policymakers, this route is seen as a neat solution. Rural kids who are failing in schools will be pulled out of academic programs, and instead get trained to become part of an upgraded workforce, cogs in the creation of a new economy. "The rise of the Chinese economy is accompanied with quality improvements of Chinese products and services," said China's premier Li Keqiang, speaking at a national vocational education meeting in Beijing in the spring of 2014. "Imagine the scale and level of Chinese products and services if most of the nine-hundred-million-strong labor force can be trained to master medium- and high-level skills."[24]

With an almost seven-decade-old tradition of setting five-year economic and social plans, a practice inherited from Stalinist Russia, authorities have laid out ambitious targets. The number of students in vocational high schools and colleges, which have two- to three-year-long programs, will rise from 30 million in 2014 to 38.3 million by 2020. Meanwhile, some six hundred universities are to be converted into vocational colleges, adding to the thirteen hundred already in existence. China already has the world's largest number of such institutes, including also twelve thousand training high schools, but most are understaffed and underfunded. According to guidelines issued by the State Council, local governments will be responsible for funding the vocational schools, which will also be able to tap low-interest loans and preferential tax policies.[25]

On that same trip to Shaanxi Province, I went to see how this push to expand vocational training was faring. Already there were reports of serious problems. The schools' main focus had become producing low-skilled workers to serve as cheap labor for electronics factories, according to numerous accounts in the local media. Foxconn, which had gained international notoriety after some two dozen of its workers committed suicide over the space of several months in 2010, was now being criticized for its heavy reliance on poorly paid vocational students in its factories.

After visiting the boarding schools, I spent the night in a typical small-town hotel: a glitzy marble-floored lobby with an oversized chandelier and an empty coffee shop, and upstairs, small rooms with hard beds and worn carpet. I found a restaurant that served pork ribs, a local specialty, drank more of the local beer than was perhaps advisable, and felt silently grateful not to have grown up in rural China. The next morning, I climbed back into the van, unrolled the windows to clear my grogginess, and rode to the township's only vocational high school.

The school, which taught more than seven hundred sixteen-to-eighteen-year-olds, offered training for six main trades, the black-suited principal told me as we sat in his cold, cement-walled office. The most popular subjects were preschool education, automobile repair (the first dominated by female students, and second male, he said), and railway service employment. Those wishing to work on the railway, now much expanded with new high-speed routes, would take courses on courtesy, food safety, sanitation, and basic English and standard Mandarin dialect, the fifty-something Shaanxi native explained. Computer science, hotel and hospitality work, and agriculture training made up the rest of the curriculum. Unfortunately, a new policy requiring preschool teachers to have training at the college level would bar his students from that job in the future, he lamented. "So we will be out of luck. Railway will have to take its place as the number-one choice." After two years of classes, each student was required to intern for a year in a company before graduating.

The mandated work year, however, rarely had anything to do with offered trades, the principal admitted. Like most vocational institutions, his school had become a guaranteed source of cheap workers for a particular factory, an auto-components maker in far-off Suzhou, Jiangsu. The relationship was so close that his school had posted three teachers to live in the factory and deal with any problems that arose if, for example, students broke something while working. As in my earlier school visits, a group of students was pulled from their dorms, and roped into talking to the questioning foreigner. While I waited with notebook ready, four of them filed into the office, taking seats in a row in front of me. The internship, the students all agreed, was nothing more than a factory line job, and a not very pleasant or well-compensated one. (The students received a nominal salary, but were inevitably the lowest-paid people in the factory.) None of the four had ever heard of an internship having anything to do with a student's chosen field, at their school or any other institute. "No one in the factory is there to teach us anything—they view us just as more cheap workers," said one nineteen-year-old girl, a southern Shaanxi native. "The older workers should teach us but they don't. If we make a mistake, they attack us for our errors, which will reflect badly on the whole manufacturing line."[26]

Of all the experts I spoke to, none was more certain that the vocational push was a serious mistake than Rozelle. And he had the data to back it up. He and other Chinese colleagues from Shaanxi Normal University had surveyed students at 140 schools in their province, as well as in coastal Zhejiang. What they found was far worse than they had imagined. Not only were the schools unsuccessful in teaching the skills they advertised, such as computers and hospitality, but they were also failing their students in basic subjects like mathematics. "We found they actually know *less* in their third semester than when they entered—that's because they are forgetting what they learned before," Rozelle told me.

With China's leaders like Premier Li hailing the importance of vocational training, large amounts of government money had flooded into schools, leading to a serious corruption problem. Rozelle and his team started to see the scale of the graft when they discovered what they called "ghost schools"; as they chose institutes to survey, fifteen simply didn't exist. Despite being registered as schools, they had no campus, teachers, administrators, or students. What they did have were false rolls of pupils. And for each fake student, the central government provided a fifteen-hundred-yuan annual subsidy. That amounted to a total of $80 billion a year, Rozelle estimated. "There is no assessment of vocational education in China, so they simply don't know what is happening," he said. "The problem is rampant," the principal told me. "These sham schools hire people to pretend to be students" for when inspectors show up, he explained. "Then later they pocket all the subsidy money and disappear."[27]

In February a deep chill hung over the wet mountains of Guizhou—altitude combined with frequent rains making for a climate of particular rawness. Still, I had timed my visit for that season to coincide with Lunar New Year, always a good time to catch migrant workers back in the villages they hailed from, during one of their rare trips home. In the ten months since I had least seen Rubo and his wife and daughter in Humen, the family had expanded: their infant son was only two months old and a quiet child, rarely crying. Despite that, Rubo looked exhausted, his face puffy, as we sat wearing our coats against the cold in the first-floor living area of the huge but largely empty farmhouse he had built for his parents. He explained in a tired voice that he would have to drive alone back to Dongguan, leaving the next day. He would then be able to pick up his family from a nearby airport a day later; they were going to fly back rather than brave the long, bumpy road trip with their infant son.

When I asked him where his daughter would attend school, the start date now just six months away, he did not yet know, only that it would have to be a private school: Earning the required points to get her into a public school in Dongguan had proved impossible; he didn't have enough years of education or sufficient money in the bank either—both important measures. And he hadn't paid his full social-welfare payments, also required if one wanted a shot at getting granted full local status. I tried levity, saying at least he didn't have to worry about his infant son's education for the next several years, before immediately realizing it wasn't a funny topic, and that I was probably reminding him of a future burden he didn't yet want to worry about.[28]

China's leaders are well aware of how the system discriminates against the families of migrant workers, and they say they intend to finally fix it. Along with the massive drive to expand vocational education, authorities have announced a ten-year-long "National Plan for Medium and Long-Term Education Reform and Development," which promises to boost spending on education at all levels and make a fairer system by 2020. The plans calls for efforts to ensure "equal compulsory education for children living with migrant worker parents in cities" and that "regulations shall be studied and formulated to accommodate these children to take entrance examinations for higher schools upon finishing compulsory education without going back to their home villages."[29]

Complicating matters, however, the plan continues to put the burden of meeting these goals mainly on local governments, who with their limited budgets have little incentive to take on the financial costs of admitting students from elsewhere in China. The plan also hedges its bets by stating that the "establishment of *rural boarding schools* shall [also] be accelerated, with priority given to the accommodation needs of the left-behind children" (emphasis added). Says University of Hong Kong Wah Ching Centre of Research on Education in China director Gerard Postiglione, "China has done well getting students enrolled in basic education, but has not done so well in ensuring an equity level of education for students, particularly between urban and rural."[30]

At its most basic, any successful reform must break down the walls that block rural students from studying in the cities, and that separates education into two unequal systems, urban and rural. But offering middle-class and wealthy city dwellers the chance to enroll their children in elite urban schools is a key way the party buys their acquiescence. If municipalities decide to open their schools to tens of millions of students from the countryside, putting huge pressure on scarce educational resources, including classrooms and teachers, China's urbanites will likely revolt. That's one key reason why Chinese public-security forces have cracked down hard when migrant parents and activists work together for more equitable education, a cause that might initially seem noncontroversial.

Rights lawyer Xu Zhiyong, with his trademark short-cropped hair and intense demeanor, was to find out just how sensitive the cause of equal schooling was. After campaigning to end the arbitrary detention system following the death of worker Sun Zhigang, in 2003, Xu increasingly focused his work on fighting the educational discrimination facing migrant-worker children. This work, combined with his creation of a rights-focused NGO, while organizing intellectuals across China to meet and discuss civic rights, drew the ire of China's police. After helping organize a protest by migrant workers demanding that Beijing's schools accept their kids, he was arrested on the charge of "gathering crowds to disturb public order" and sentenced to four years in jail, at a trial held in Beijing in January of 2014. The surprisingly harsh punishment seemed a warning to others considering doing grassroots organizing. Xu's long closing statement to the court, cut short by the judge, who called it "irrelevant," was an impassioned call for migrant workers and their children:

"When I think of the hundreds of millions of children whose fates were permanently decided by the *hukou* segregation, of generation after generation of Chinese people who have been hurt by this evil system, of the countless Chinese who died in the custody and repatriation system, today I stand here as a defendant, filled with no grudges but pride for having worked to eliminate the segregation system with Chinese characteristics and for having fought for millions of children to be able to live with their parents and go to school," Xu declared. "Here in absurd post-totalitarian China I stand trial, charged with three crimes: promoting equal education rights for children of migrant workers, calling on officials to publicly disclose their assets, and advocating that all people behave as citizens with pride and conscience. If the country's rulers have any intention to take citizens' constitutional rights seriously, then of course we are innocent."[31]

3

The Land

No three days are clear, no three feet of land are level, and
no one has three ounces of silver.

—OLD GUIZHOU SAYING

City dwellers scorn country people for their closeness to
the land; they treat them as if they were truly "soiled."
But to country people, the soil is the root of their lives.

—FEI XIAOTONG, FROM THE SOIL: THE FOUNDATIONS OF
CHINESE SOCIETY[1]

Spend time in its green fastness, and you will eventually hear Guizhou
described in this way: "No three days are clear, no three feet of land
are level, and no one has three ounces of silver." This proverb of uncertain provenance is usually offered apologetically, a local's explanation for Guizhou's poverty and backwardness. It is popular because it
is truthful. Although not the rainiest province—Hunan, Guangdong,
and Fujian are all wetter—Guizhou is one of the very cloudiest; its
capital, Guiyang, is overcast for nine months of the year. Its many
rugged mountains leave little land to cultivate, and it is one of China's
poorest places.

Location and landscape define Guizhou, to an extent even more
obvious than elsewhere in China. Situated in the country's south-

west with a subtropical climate, the province suffers no extremes of heat or cold: average temperatures range from just 10 to 20 degrees Celsius. Excessive humidity, however, creates Guizhou's notorious enveloping fogs, long a source of torment for visitors. When spring becomes summer, "hills are shrouded in a miasma of suffocating vapors. People suffer from headaches, pressure in the chest, diarrhea, and other illnesses. Epidemics of malaria are not infrequent," wrote one unhappy Chinese explorer in 1638. Situated on the eastern edge of the Yungui Plateau—the upland sloping wedge that rises from the hills of Hunan and Guangxi to the Tibetan Plateau—Guizhou's elevation ranges from a low of 2,300 feet (700 meters) in its east to some 6,600 feet (2,000 meters) in the west.

Guizhou's topography is distinguished by its many mountains, strange, humped clumps, disrupting flat ground, that cover 87 percent of its area. Without the province's abundance of easily erodible limestone, the source, too, of its deep watery caves, Guizhou's mountains would not have their odd forms; its geology is only infrequently laid bare, a slash of gray Devonian rock emerging from deep green, as if a giant cat had wandered through, lazily scratching its claws down a mountain's virid, steep brushy sides. With no more than 5 percent of its land arable—an exhausting and inefficient form of terraced agriculture on its hills is common—Guizhou has always been poor. Among its inhabitants are more than forty different ethnic minority groups making up some two-fifths of the population; the remainder are Han Chinese (Han is the official name for ethnic Chinese), most of whom emigrated there over the three centuries of the Qing dynasty. Among the ethnic groups are the Buyi, some 2.9 million Tai speakers, the vast majority of whom live in the southern half of Guizhou, and include the Mos of Binghuacun.

These characteristics—overcast, little productive land, and poverty—have distinguished Guizhou for at least as long as there have been records. For Guizhou, its topography has been its fate: "The countryside is gloomy and impenetrable. Heavy rains are frequent. The fields must be terraced [because] the soil is stony. Slash and burn agriculture prevails. The paddies and marshes yield no abundance, and the mulberry trees and hemp do not yield much profit. The annual tax revenue does not equal that of a large county in China Proper (*neidi*)," wrote Guizhou's governor Aibida in 1750. "Miao, Zhong [Buyi], Ge, Luo, Yao, and Zhuang tribes swarm like bees and ants. Many of them still believe in ghosts and spirits. They are addicted to violence, whether it be major retaliatory attacks or smaller acts of banditry and plunder. They are easy to incite and difficult to pacify. As a result, it is not easy for the imperial court to find steadfast and competent local officials. Those who are appointed place little importance on their positions. . . . They are dissolute and let matters drift; nothing is of consequence to them. In this way, poison brews and becomes thick. Once released, it cannot be stopped. . . . Thus it is that no benefit can be derived from Guizhou."[2]

Despite the governor's harsh appraisal, the Qing court, ensconced in the Imperial Palace in faraway Beijing, viewed Guizhou as essential to their territorial ambitions. Gloomy and impenetrable it might be, but controlling the province was key to ensuring access to neighbor Yunnan, with its rich resources including copper, which in turn served as the southern gateway to strategically important Tibet, on its vast high plateau between the Qing Empire and India.[3] One way to strengthen its hand over Guizhou was by encouraging Han to emigrate there, in part by using cash and tax incentives. (The Qing, although Manchu, an ethnic minority themselves, had long used the emigration of Han to solidify their control over regions where other minorities lived.) With the influx of people, the population doubled from 1.5 million in the mid-sixteenth century to 3 million by 1733, then doubled again to 6 million by 1775, according to one estimate. The province experienced "a demographic explosion," writes Jodi L. Weinstein in her book *Empire and Identity in Guizhou: Local Resistance to Qing Expansion.*[4]

The influx of new people put huge pressure on Guizhou's already scarce resources, creating tensions with its indigenous population, many of which were pushed off the province's best rice-growing land by the immigrants, and ended up cultivating corn, barley, and other hardier crops in the harsh mountains. Similarly, the switch by the Qing to a new policy of replacing local chiefs with those appointed from Beijing sparked anger and ultimately outright rebellion.

"Heaven will exterminate the Han Chinese, native headmen, and imperial troops" was the rallying cry used by the Buyi leaders of the Nanlong Uprising of 1797. Combining guerrilla-warfare tactics with supernatural beliefs and charismatic leadership, the rebels quickly took control of every town in the province's west. Only after sending in large numbers of troops from outside did the Qing finally quell the revolt, in the fall of that year.

Tensions remained, spawning a series of other uprisings throughout the Qing dynasty. Much larger was the "Miao Rebellion," 1854–1873, in reality a series of revolts that involved perhaps as many Buyi as Miao, as well as other ethnic groups; in the brutal suppression by Qing forces, most of Guizhou's cities were destroyed and possibly as many as 4.9 million people died, or more than half the province's population, according to some historians. "At the present time, traces are everywhere to be seen in the shape of ruined towns and villages and lands lying waste and desolate," wrote one Western visitor in 1882, almost a decade after the fighting ended.[5] Given its tendency for insurrection, "a riot every thirty years and a major rebellion every sixty years" was coined to describe the region.[6]

Guizhou is still plagued with poverty, in particular afflicting its minorities, and tensions over limited resources have continued until today. In recent years those strains erupted most dramatically in June of 2008 when some thirty thousand Buyi and Miao in central Weng'an County rioted, overturning and burning police cars and torching government offices. The immediate cause was the death of a sixteen-year-old girl; while authorities claimed she had committed suicide, most local residents believed she had been raped and murdered by two young men with family connections to powerful local officials.[7] The incident came less than a month before the opening of the Beijing Olympics, a particularly sensitive time for China, eager to project an image of stability to the world. Reducing the tensions in Weng'an became a major priority for top officials, including then party general secretary Hu Jintao. After thousands of paramilitary police had been sent in to quell the riots, a senior Guizhou official was dispatched to the remote and poor county for an investigation. The explosion of anger in Weng'an was about much more than the girl's untimely death, the authorities' report concluded. Equally important was a history of mistreatment of residents; corrupt officials in cahoots with local mafia gangs had seized land from villagers to develop coal and phosphorous mines; thousands more were forced to leave their homes to make way for a huge dam and reservoir, and received little money in compensation.[8]

In recent years an alternative to the cycle of poverty and protest has opened up. Just as Rubo abandoned country life in Binghuacun in exchange for factory work, in part to avoid falling into bad habits, rural youth in Guizhou and across the countryside can find employment in the more developed provinces along the eastern and southern coasts. "Instead of resorting to banditry and rebellion, young people in search of better prospects can leave Guizhou for the booming coastal province of Guangdong," writes Weinstein. That exodus of young people, so common for all those from Western China, has left villages with far fewer inhabitants, and most of them elderly. Those younger migrants who have left for export factories often return only for festivals, or sometimes funerals.

The rain had been coming down for days already now, adding new menace to Guizhou's already perilous roads. Our driver was a friend of Ruchun's, Qin Jijie, a local real-estate developer. The building boom in Libo, so common to small-town China, had apparently been kind to him: He dressed a step above most locals, wore a bulky gold watch on his wrist, and bragged about the features of what he called his American vehicle, a black BMW SUV. He was recently divorced and seemed more intent on using this rare meeting with a foreigner to gauge his chances of finding a wife from overseas than on driving. "I can't find any good women in China. Next time, you should bring an American girl to introduce to me," he suggested. "Do you think she would like me? Is Guizhou too poor and backward for Americans?" I responded with what had become my stock answer when locals apologized for the region's backwardness—that yes, it might be poor, but the beautiful scenery made up for any shortcomings—and avoided directly answering his marital query. He seemed unsure about the trade-off but still eager. "Once you find her, you can send me her picture, before you visit next time," he said.

As we drove out of Libo, the downpour grew in intensity. Ruchun, oddly, had assured me I would not need a raincoat when we had left his apartment in the county seat earlier that morning—only later would I realize it was one more example of the lopsided hospitality that I often had to struggle to understand. What he had meant was that, as befitting an honored guest, he would ensure I spent no time outside in the inclement weather. But getting cold and wet in any case was not my concern at that point; instead it was surviving the ride to Binghuacun. As our car sashayed around the tight mountain curves, I kept a watchful eye on the frothing, water-sheeted asphalt unwinding before us. While the road was now very slippery, that was not the real peril. Instead it was the rocks and mud that had washed into our path. But despite my concern, Qin seemed perfectly capable of keeping a watchful eye on the road while discussing his future marriage prospects.

A death had happened in Binghuacun, the eighty-plus-year-old matriarch of one prominent family passing away from old age. That meant it was time for a trip home for Ruchun, and for many other villagers who had left long ago. While the mass exodus from the countryside of the last few decades had meant the end of many village traditions, honoring an elder's death was still viewed as an essential rite important enough to draw many temporarily back. In the afternoon, the body was to be buried, and later a banquet was to be held. "We are all one family, all surnamed Mo in Binghuacun," explained Ruchun. "So we all have to take care of things together." Ruchun's successful younger brother, Ruxuan, now working as a Guiyang party official, also had made a cameo a day earlier, to pay his respects. I had hoped this would be my chance to finally catch up with Ruxuan, whom I had seen only one time, briefly, in the years since 2000, but he was once more to slip away: "Sorry. I suddenly have a meeting in another city. I am leaving this afternoon for the airport," he had told me over mobile phone while still in Binghuacun. I had been in Guiyang, just one day before setting out for the village.

By the time we arrived in Binghuacun, thankfully having safely navigated the obstacle-spotted, slick road, the rain had lessened slightly, but still was steadily coming down. As I stood just inside the front door of Ruchun's parents' house, shielded from the downpour outside, I watched the funeral procession pass by, a long line of villagers in ponchos and broad-brimmed round bamboo hats, many in flip-flop sandals to pad through muddy puddles. The group moved quickly, people banging on drums and clanging cymbals, others throwing out strings of red firecrackers, the bang and crackle of small explosions ricocheting in the muffled misty air. Some carried long bamboo sprigs they swung rhythmically as they walked, while others clutched handfuls of burning incense. Six men hoisted the black wooden coffin on ropes, carrying the old woman's body out of the village and up the mountain to a high spot near a small Buddhist shrine, where it was to be buried.

Later came the eating and drinking. A water buffalo had just been slaughtered. Earlier I had wandered over to the communal outdoor butcher-table-cum-wood-oven and tried to make conversation with some elderly men overseeing the operation, only to find they spoke only the Buyi dialect. The deceased's oldest son was hosting all the funeralgoers at a banquet in his family's wooden farmhouse, in the heart of the old village that clung to the hillside overlooking the river. The dark second-floor living room, above the stable where buffalo, ducks, and chickens were kept, as was common in the Guizhou countryside, was filled with round low-lying tables, each surrounded by relatives and friends sitting on small stools. In the middle of each was a brazier with a wok where slices of pink buffalo meat, chunks of tofu, and chopped-up vegetables were being sautéed over a wood fire. More plastic bags filmy with blood and flesh of the buffalo were carried in and dropped by each table, for refilling the wok. The ubiquitous little teapots, both aluminum and ceramic, were filled with heated home-made rice wine and placed on each table. The fifty-some-year-old son, dressed completely in traditional white funeral garb, with a white cloth turban wound around his head, moved around the room, greeting guests and handing out packs of Guiyan-brand cigarettes—the best in Guizhou, Ruchun was careful to point out to me.

The rain had finally stopped, and outside young kids with snotty noses were pretending to play mahjong, at tables set up under government-provided emergency-response tents, large characters on their tarp roofs reading CIVIL ADMINISTRATION DISASTER RELIEF. I had just said goodbye to Mo Wenke, the long-ago-retired village party secretary. He had had ambitious plans to develop Binghuacun, when we last met, in 2000, and I was still hoping to find a time to talk to him about how those had fared. "After an afternoon of drinking, I may go to Libo," he had told me, as one possibility for meeting later, but sounding unsure that he would actually leave the village that day. The order of priorities for everyone here seemed clear: the afternoon was for drinking, as Wenke had put it, not eating, or talking, although that certainly would happen, too. Calls of *hejiu! hejiu!* (drink! drink!) had rung out as I left the house, as people had raised their porcelain rice bowls filled with wine, in a last attempt to toast with the foreigner. "At funerals, cattle are butchered and dressed, and relatives and friends are invited. Drinking from the 'oxhorn of happiness,' the guests often get drunk and sometimes even wind up killing each other" was how a Buyi funeral was described by one observer in the eighteenth century. Drinking was unavoidable, but fatalities were not going to be part of this afternoon.[9]

Ruchun had arranged one more stop before we returned to Libo, dropping by another house where there was someone to share drinks with. Each visit to Binghuacun required meeting and doing toasts with a select group of local notables, with Ruchun escorting me from house to house, to fulfill our social responsibility. The purpose seemed twofold. Respect was shown to whomever we visited, as we were making time to come drink with them. At the same time, Ruchun seemed eager to show off his foreign friend, a rare thing to have in a Guizhou village, which seemingly conferred on him a reputation for worldliness. I was happy to play my role. The only catch was that I had to avoid drinking too much.

As we approached the final house, up a hill behind the newer section of the village, I told Ruchun that he must tell the waiting people that I had to work later in the afternoon, so couldn't drink much. Inside the dimly lit room, a group of men sat around a table, younger and visibly drunker than those attending the funeral banquet. They were all local cadres. Ruchun introduced me to the most senior of them, the head of the Libo economic development agency, a florid-faced man who exuded the expansive confidence of a ranking local official. He had been temporarily seconded to this remote area of Guizhou with the purpose of introducing silkworm cultivation, as a new economic means, part of a raft of poverty-alleviation policies being pushed from Beijing. "American friend! You must drink with us!" the cadre roared at me. When Ruchun dutifully explained that I could not stay long because of work, the official pshawed: "I have a meeting later this afternoon and I'm drinking!" he said, thrusting a bowl filled with the rice liquor into my hands. After we had downed the contents, tipping the bowls to each other to show they were empty, he launched into impassioned speech: "America is very good! America is amazing! China under Xi Jinping is amazing! Our economy keeps getting stronger, farmers are becoming better off, and Xi plans to eradicate all poverty by 2020—amazing!"

For Xi to have a shot at making all Chinese better off, not just those from the cities but those from the countryside, too, he and his policymakers will first have to solve the land problem. Disputes over who owns and benefits from the soil have defined, again and again, key moments in China's history. With almost ten million square kilometers of territory, it is the world's third-largest country, after Russia and Canada. But with mountains and vast deserts occupying much of its west, agricultural land amounts to only 1.35 million square kilometers, making up less than 15 percent. Most striking is how little land there is when compared to the vast population: divide it into equal allotments, and each person would get about one-quarter of an acre, less than half the global average. And as its leaders like to point out, while it has a fifth of the world's people, it has less than a tenth of its arable land.

Scarcity of land has forced China to innovate. Farmers terraced high mountains to plant rice, and the world's earliest irrigation system, the Dujiangyan, built in 256 BC during its Warring States period, is still used to water otherwise barren fields near Chengdu, Sichuan, today a laid-back city of teahouses clacking with mahjong players and Louis Vuitton and Chanel shops with locals newly rich from flipping real estate. But it also has been the cause of great strife. Peasants have launched mass rebellions and emperors have fallen, all struggling over land. That was the case for Wang Mang, who ruled over 6.9 million square kilometers for part of the first century AD. Wang was born into a royal family and a life of privilege, but at some point in his fourteen years as the only emperor of the Xin dynasty, his thinking veered rapidly toward the radical. By developing China's first national social security system and seizing all landholdings over one hundred acres and distributing five-acre parcels to each farming family, he won support from the peasants. "The strong," wrote Wang, "possess lands by the thousands of *mu* [about one-sixth of an acre], while the weak have nowhere to place a needle."[10]

But then things went badly wrong. In the company of his imperial harem, including twenty-seven Beauties, three Harmonious Ladies, nine official wives, as well as eighty-one attendants, Wang ordered his forces to prepare for the arrival of rebel soldiers, eager to topple him and put a halt to his dangerous egalitarian policies. Neither he nor his ideas would survive. After a thousand of his loyalists made a last effort to defend his rule, on a late afternoon in AD 23 Wang was killed and chopped into pieces by an angry mob, his tongue eaten by a soldier. Wang's successors quickly gave back the estates to their previous owners, and once again China's peasants were returned to their serflike existence. But over the centuries the land question continued to grip leaders and revolutionaries alike, at times igniting the kind of millenarian movements that the party today still fears.

"All lands in the country are also to be mutually supporting with respect to abundance and scarcity. If this place has a drought, then draw upon the abundant harvest elsewhere in order to relieve the distress here," stated "The Land System of the Heavenly Kingdom," the treatise penned by Taiping Rebellion leader Hong Xiuquan, the utopian who claimed to be the younger brother of Jesus Christ. Hong, part of the Hakka, a group of Chinese known for their historical penchant for migration across the country and abroad, led an uprising of tens of thousands of peasants and miners known as the God

Worshipers, seizing control of much of southern China from 1850 to 1864. He advocated that all land be collectively owned, with families organized into groups of twenty-five. The crops would be allotted according to need, with the surplus going to the state: "The land is for all to till, the food for all to eat, the clothes for all to wear, and money for all to spend. Inequality shall exist nowhere; none shall suffer from hunger or cold."[11]

Watching the unfolding rebellion from his exile in London, a thirty-four-year-old Karl Marx was sure he was witnessing the trigger for global transformation. "It may safely be augured that the Chinese revolution will throw the spark into the overloaded mine of the present industrial system and cause the explosion of the long-prepared general crisis, which, spreading abroad, will be closely followed by political revolutions on the Continent," Marx predicted, writing in the *New-York Daily Tribune* in 1853, fourteen years before he penned *Das Kapital*.[12] While that didn't happen, the rebellion indeed emboldened others. "The Taiping not only caused the government to raise taxes and pull troops out of provinces like Guizhou, but they showed the Qing regime to be vulnerable," writes historian Robert Darrah Jenks, calling it a "powerful stimulus" for the Miao Rebellion.[13] When the Heavenly Kingdom of Great Peace, as Hong called his reign, finally collapsed under attack by imperial forces in 1864, Hong poisoned himself in his palace in Nanjing. Like Emperor Wang's, Hong's radical prescriptions were abandoned, but his ideas were to inspire the future leader of modern China.

"Mao Zedong's revolution was aimed at solving the peasant problem. In 1978, Deng Xiaoping's reforms were also trying to solve the peasant problem," says Ma Wenfeng, an affable agricultural analyst, who grew up in a farming family in Henan, central China's rural heartland, also where Rubo's wife came from. "China's present leaders, too, know they must solve the problem of the land—without fixing this, making the land more productive, without finding work for the *nongmin* [farmers], China's economy won't keep developing."

I was working on a story looking at efforts to modernize its still-backward agricultural industry and wondering why it always involved companies going overseas to make acquisitions. The most prominent example was COFCO, or China National Cereals, Oils and Foodstuffs Corporation, the state-owned behemoth with vineyards in Chile and a sugar processor in Australia, which was then buying stakes in Dutch and Singaporean commodities traders. "For an agriculture company to make money they need scale, so they must buy up farms. But we still have more than six hundred million farmers who need to make a living off of the land—we can't allow too much consolidation at home, or what will these people do?" explained Ma.[14]

It was the rare sunny morning without smog, and I had scheduled several face-to-face interviews, perhaps too many for the sprawling, car-clogged capital Beijing. Ma's office was in the city's northeast. My next appointment was far to the south in the China World Trade Center, home to multinationals Apple and ExxonMobil. I arrived just before noon after a long taxi ride crawling down the capital's Third Ring Road and met the head of a U.S. agricultural trade association in Aria Restaurant, a popular haunt for foreign executives and the Chinese businessmen who do deals with them. Over steamed scallops, salmon fillet, and chardonnay, the association's chief explained how the growth of the new urban middle class was driving agricultural policy. With more money to spend, China's well-off were eating more pigs, cows, and chickens, and so upping demand for feed grains such as wheat, barley, and corn.

Surging food needs also are behind the leadership's decision to quietly abandon a centuries-old policy of food self-sufficiency, and instead encourage agricultural firms to *zouchuqu*, or "go out." COFCO, with financial backing from Beijing, was about to finish its second big overseas acquisition in as many months, aiming to become the country's version of a Cargill or an Archer Daniels Midland, the giant American agribusinesses. "China's agriculture has limited supplies and rising demand, so they have to go abroad," said the foreign exec. "But as I always like to point out, it is ironic that a country that was founded on the principle of taking land away from its own landlords now wants to go out and buy it up around the world."[15]

Following the victory of the Chinese Communist Party in 1949, the early years of the new People's Republic of China were defined in large part by the stripping of property from the landlords and rich farmers and its redistribution to peasants, often with great violence. Where others had failed in remaking the land structure, Mao Zedong, through force of will and propitious timing, was the one to finally succeed. Under the slogan "Land to the tiller," first used by founding father Sun Yat-sen in 1924, land was doled out to farmers. While farmers' newfound property rights would be short-lived, the country has not returned to the old land system that had persisted for centuries.

Some four decades after his death, in 1976, quite suddenly Mao was once again in the news. As the new leader Xi Jinping decisively abandoned the post-Deng era's consensus style of leadership and the policy of "keep your head low and bide your time," instead amassing power and boldly asserting China's interests abroad, the comparisons started pouring in. Was Xi even more powerful than Jiang Zemin? Than Deng Xiaoping? In reality, scholars and journalists concluded, he was the most powerful leader since Mao. Xi's striking reemphasis on ideology, in politics but also in the education system, the media, law, and business, was also credited to the enduring legacy of the man Chinese have long called the Great Helmsman.

Born in 1893 to a moderately well-off farming family, Mao was to look to the countryside to find the impetus for the future revolution. That rebellion would come from land-deprived peasants, while the urban proletariat would play a secondary role, in contrast to the Russian revolution and traditional Marxism-Leninism, was perhaps the young rebel's most important realization. "In a very short time, in China's central, southern, and northern provinces, several hundred million peasants will rise like a mighty storm, like a hurricane, a force so swift and violent that no power, however great, will be able to hold it back," wrote Mao in 1927. "They will smash all the trammels that bind them and rush forward along the road to liberation. They will sweep all the imperialists, warlords, corrupt officials, local tyrants, and evil gentry into their graves."[16]

After coming to power in 1949, Mao exhorted the peasants to violently rise up; they seized the land of tens of millions of landlords and rich farmers and beat some 4.5 million of them to death, in just the first few years after the founding of the People's Republic. The goal, as stated by the new leader in a 1950 decree, was "to eliminate feudal, exploitative land ownership by landlords and implement peasant land ownership, so as to free the rural labor force, develop agricultural production, and open the way for the industrialization of New China."[17]

The peasants would not enjoy their new rights for long, however. Mao's vision of a New China was inseparable from his desire to industrialize. Taking his cues from Stalin but always wanting to outdo him, he chose steel as the centerpiece of his goal to industrialize and declared that the country would rival Britain and the West in production within fifteen years. Never mind that it was a pipe dream, all of society must mobilize. And the country would need legions of low-paid and compliant farmers to grow the grain and produce, and raise the meat, for newly minted industrial workers.

That meant farms had to be collectivized. After that happened, just a few years later, in 1953—resisted by many and also with its share of bloodshed—Communist cadres were in charge of the land, rather than peasants. And the farmers, who toiled long hours under the new bosses in huge communes, would face restrictions on their movement with the imposition of the *hukou* policy later in the 1950s. In an irony little discussed then or even now, the biggest beneficiaries of Mao's peasant revolution would be the cities and the people who live there—not the countryside. The rural masses post-1949 would become second-class citizens, their primary purpose in the new system to support the cities.

Sweeping changes were to come to the countryside, including the creation of ten-thousand-strong farmer megacommunes in 1958, and then their rapid dismantling after Mao's death. Mao's volatile nature and the necessity to halt horrendous tragedies like the famines of the Great Leap (1958–1961) ensured that. But over the decades, the basic outline remained the same: farmers locked to the land with little power over their livelihood. It took Mao's death before real change was to come.

The road to Xiaogang runs through run-down village after village of scruffy cement and white-tiled farmhouses; broken glass, discarded plastic bags, and empty tins litter the ground, rangy yellow-furred dogs nosing in the debris. Scuffed passenger cars, flatbed lorries, delivery minivans, and zippy motorcycles careen along the thruway's bumpy, unmarked length, horns blaring, while tired-looking, elderly farmers dressed in Mao-traditionalist blue ignore the cacophony, walking on the narrow shoulder, backs to the traffic, seemingly unafraid of being struck down. PEOPLE CHERISH SAFETY, STAY TO THE RIGHT. CARS CHERISH SAFETY, DRIVE SLOWLY, admonishes a sign, making the dubious suggestion that pedestrians that don't step into the road will be out of reach of vehicle bedlam. Little blue farm trucks are parked wherever there is space as temporary shop kiosks; from their open backs apples, peaches, and pears are sold, with attached loudspeakers blaring out the various deals on offer. Blankets are draped over tables and chairs outside, in order to air them out in the morning sunshine. Billboards for *baijiu,* the popular clear hard liquor made from rice, sorghum, or barley, stick up above the squalor, suggesting that drinking is the main leisure activity for those who live here.

Fengyang, long known as one of the most impoverished counties in Anhui, an already poor province, shows the less savory side of reform and opening. Hundreds of small, slapdash factories populate the region, including smoke-belching glass manufacturers and effluent-spewing papermakers; workers in the factories make barely enough to get by and live in close proximity to the pollution. This part of Anhui became infamous for its "cancer villages" in the mid-2000s, when thousands of people living along the banks of the Huai River were struck down with gastrointestinal cancers after being exposed to its severely polluted waters. But Fengyang is also home to the village of Xiaogang, the place heralded as the birthplace of one of the most important economic reforms to emerge from China's opening: the "household responsibility system," allowing farmers finally some control over their land.

What was to become national policy celebrated by the leadership came from the grassroots, and indeed went against the express commands of the center. In 1978, eighteen farmers from Xiaogang, facing a severe drought and not enough food for their families, decided to secretly divide the local commune's land into individual plots. A quota of crops would go to the local authorities, as before. But once that was met, farmers would decide what to grow and where to sell any additional produce. They agreed to stand up for one another no matter how the authorities responded, and signaled their commitment by signing a document in their own blood. With Mao gone, Deng and his reformist allies Zhao Ziyang, then running Sichuan, and Wan Li, party secretary of Anhui, decided to allow the bottom-up experiment to continue. By not crushing the grassroots movement, the party ensured its rapid spread; later it was to be officially sanctioned. *"Yao chifan, zhao Ziyang, yao chimi, zhao Wan Li"* ("If you want to eat grain, ask for Ziyang. If you want to eat rice, look for Wan Li") became a popular rhyme at the time, crediting the leaders' decision to allow the reform.

"Before launching the household contract system, food was not adequate to feed everyone," explained one of the farmers who then served as a commune production team leader, in a popular account. "Families boiled tree leaves, bark, and any edible wild plants; we ate whatever we could find. After consulting with some other villagers, I made up my mind to contract land to individual households no matter what penalty would be imposed on me. We didn't want to starve anymore."[18]

The first sign one is approaching Xiaogang comes suddenly when the road widens and becomes even asphalt, with fresh white and yellow traffic markings, rather than the potholed, cracking pavement of before. Decrepit farmhouses disappear from its sides, and neatly planted saplings, red-leafed shrubbery, and craning blue and white tall light posts replace them. There is a four-columned, white stone *paifang*, or ceremonial gate, as one enters, with green glazed tiles on its roof. FENGYANG COUNTY, XIAOGANG VILLAGE is written on it in huge stylized characters by Fei Xiaotong, now deceased, but once China's most famous anthropologist and sociologist, and a noted expert on village life. Beyond the gate almost all the architecture is uniform, two-story whitewashed buildings; on the first floor, tall pillars separate the little tourist shops and overpriced restaurants. The only exceptions are two huge mausoleum-like museums, one that features dioramas and dozens of photos and charts, outlining the history of the household responsibility system, and the second one to remember the life of Shen Hao, a model official who is said to have died from overwork in Xiaogang, with the tan shirt he frugally wore day after day, and a replica of the run-down office he worked from. "Xiaogang Village, as the national red tourism scenic spot, the base for patriotism education, and demonstration site of agritainment, has very high value resources," a notice informs the curious visitor.

Today Xiaogang seems to be a village without farmers; instead most residents are employed in local businesses catering to red tourism—when Chinese travel to sites known for revolutionary Communist Party history. A few locals idly play mahjong in one quiet shop, while tourists mill about on Reform Road, the main street through town. Later I meet thirty-something Xiao Guangfei, a friendly engineer from Huainan, Anhui. When I ask him why he has decided to visit Xiaogang, he has a ready answer: "I am interested in any place that has helped my country become developed and strong. And I am interested in the reform history because it has made China strong. I am patriotic," he says proudly.[19]

The road continues through Xiaogang before it ends at a large parking lot overlooking lush green rice fields. Here tourists and officials get their pictures taken in front of a bucolic representation of what the party calls its successful agricultural reforms. Demonstrating how important a pilgrimage spot it has become for even the top echelons of the party, Xi was to visit Xiaogang just three weeks after me at the end of April 2016.[20] Photos show him beaming as he meets farmers, and later gravely examining a tassel of rice surrounded by local officials.[21] "I come here today to review the reform. That is to unswervingly adhere to the Party's basic line for 100 years, to continue the reform and opening up, and to write a new chapter," Xi said. Farmers and agriculture "are integral to the country's modernization and to the goal of building a moderately prosperous society," he added, using the term *"xiaokang,"* translated as "moderately prosperous" in party jargon.[22]

Just beyond Xiaogang—named a model village for "Happy Rural Families" by the province some years earlier—is the neighboring hamlet of Damiaoyu.[23] Dusty lanes run between beat-up farmhouses, with water buffalo sprawled in splashes of hay in front courtyards. One sixty-some-year-old with squinting, skeptical eyes peers at me from under his battered blue Mao cap, then gestures at me to come over, offering me a cigarette. Our conversation will be a staccato of smokes, one following the other, and no pause for a breather. As well as keeping a cigarette in his right hand available when needed, he has another tucked behind his ear; he is smoking one in a brown holder, held determinedly between clamped teeth. When I ask what it means to live next to Xiaogang, I set off a tirade.

"We here are right next to Xiaogangcun but we are poor. We have eight mouths to feed and we can't do that from just five *mu* [about four-fifths an acre] of land," he says bitterly as he leads me into his house. He has guessed my age, on his own volition, as between thirty and forty. I tell him I am older than that, almost feeling guilty when I do, once again realizing that he has badly misread my years, only because the Chinese countryside can age people like him so quickly. Inside are his wife, his daughter-in-law, and her four daughters. His son works in a factory in Hangzhou, some four hundred kilometers away. Yellow-furred village dogs snuffle for scraps under the wooden kitchen table, leaping out of the way as he pulls out a bench for me to sit on. He hurls a cigarette to the ground in front of a neighbor who has just wandered in; the man bends over, picks it up, and lights it. "What you see there is all just appearances. They have spent money to make the houses look beautiful. But that doesn't really help farmers or improve their lives. That is just for show. It's for people like you who come to visit here and for leaders who come to see their propaganda. They don't care about us farmers. What happened there has nothing to do with our lives. We are poor. Life is difficult."

The mother, dressed in a long black parka with a ruff of fake fur, her hair tied up in a bun, is holding her youngest daughter in her arms while occasionally helping translate her father-in-law's country accent into more standard Mandarin. Suddenly she chimes in: *"Xiaokang!* The leaders say they want to make the whole country prosperous! Who are they fooling! We don't even have enough to eat now." Not sure how to respond to their anger, I ask to look at the rest of their house, and step into the attached bedroom. It is a chaotic mess of rumpled bedclothes, rolled-up straw mats, a box containing bottles of bean-curd milk, and plastic bags stuffed with clothes, all piled on the hard cement floor. Two washtubs are filled with cheeping day-old chicks—a hundred of them, the mother-in-law informs me with a smile. On the wall is a calendar with a picture of Jesus Christ on the cross. "I am a Christian—is that good?" she asks me. "Good! Very good!" I frantically answer.[24]

Despite huge progress in wiping out poverty, the countryside still has large numbers of poor people and incomes continue to fall behind the rest of the country. This unfortunate fact is in part because of the *hukou* system, which restricts rural people's ability to fully integrate into the cities. Equally responsible, however, are the continuing limits on farmers' rights to the land. While they were given freedom to decide how to use the land they lived on, they were not given ownership. This partial reform was equivalent to "half-baked privatization," according to dissident intellectual Liu Xiaobo, the 2010 Nobel Peace Prize winner who was jailed for his writing and died under prison guard in 2017. Before 1978, "the Communist regime . . . was, in effect, the sole landlord in China. Rural people in the Mao era, while farming 'state land,' were something like serfs. In the post-Mao period people became, at best, more like tenants," Liu had written, describing the changes to the land regime.[25]

The core of reform in the countryside is "sticking to collective ownership of rural land," Xi reiterated on his visit to Xiaogang—party-speak for continuing the ban on land sales. Given the central role that nationalizing land and eliminating private ownership in the countryside played in its revolution and ideology, the party is loath to reverse course. The leaders maintain that through "the collective," land in the countryside in effect belongs to all the people, an argument made much earlier by Mao. (In the cities, the land officially belongs to the "state," but the development of what in effect are real-property markets has by contrast been allowed.) And in the eyes of the government, land plots doled out to farmers, no matter how small or unproductive, are also seen as a fallback for rural Chinese, a source of food and income even if at a subsistence level; the government fears, too, that if farmers were able to freely sell their land they could be taken advantage of by unscrupulous businessmen, losing their means of subsistence and saddling China with a large landless population prone to rebellion. As people in the countryside have watched their counterparts in the cities become increasingly wealthy through the right granted them to buy and sell property, while they have remained relatively poor, the party's logic has been hard to stomach.

With a real land market taboo, policymakers in Beijing have instead gradually strengthened farmers' "usage rights," starting with pilot programs in places like Hainan Island. On a hot day in March 2001 I took a bus southwest from the provincial capital, Haikou, down the western coast to Dongfang County, one of the island's poorest regions and home to an ethnic minority called the Li. With its sleepy farming villages, it felt worlds away from the golf courses and yacht club then being built in the new resort town of Sanya, a little over 150 kilometers away on Hainan's southern tip.

There were two main planks to the Hainan reform program. One was issuing user certificates to the island's many individual banana and mango growers; that was supposed to make it harder for authorities to seize land for development, a problem in Hainan as nearly everywhere in China. The second was lengthening the thirty years farmers were usually granted rights to use the land to seventy years. The aim was that newly confident agriculturalists would invest in irrigation projects, new seed crops, and new cultivation techniques, thus boosting productivity and local incomes.

But that hoped-for outcome was slow in coming, I realized as I listened to the party secretary of Baoban District, which included ten farming villages with a total population of twelve thousand people. While land certificates and longer-term use rights were of course welcomed, explained the forty-seven-year-old Fu Shihuan, with a face tanned dark from the tropical sun, a powerful state-owned banana plantation, the Red Spring State Farm, with 10,000 *mu* (1,647 acres) of land that abutted the villages, wasn't honoring the new rights; with its connections to local party officials giving it cover, the state agriculturist had been seizing fields in recent months, to expand its cultivation acreage and likely to develop real-estate projects.

It was a muggy morning, and the windows were opened for a cross breeze through the three-story white-tiled government building we were sitting in. A poster of a glowing orange-colored Mao presiding over Tiananmen Square hung on the wall, as did an award praising local cadres for enforcing the family-planning policy. A dusty courtyard had several tired-looking jackfruit trees and some scrubby palms; a rooster occasionally crowed, breaking the torpor. "Villagers feel that for generations they have farmed this land, now how can it be transferred to the state farm with no good explanation?" said Fu plaintively.[26]

The problems of the collective land system go beyond the travails experienced by farmers, who together with migrants, still make up more than half of the country's 1.4 billion people. With the average size of a farming plot just 1.5 acres, China's agricultural sector is deeply inefficient, and makes up less than one-tenth of the economy. But the value reaped from land is far larger, even if farming has nothing to do with it. Today land sales, still not allowed for farmers, account for at least one-half of revenues for the country's tens of thousands of city, county, township, and village governments. If it is in the "public interest," as the 1998 Land Management Law vaguely puts it, acreage officially classified as agricultural can be converted to industrial and commercial use. Then officials can legally sell it at far higher prices to developers hungry for more land for construction on the outskirts of cities. "There is no economy in the world that remains in this anomalous situation of having confiscated and nationalized land, and then somewhat hypocritically started selling it off," points out author and journalist Orville Schell. "This is a long-term, one-time booster to the state economy. But it can't go on forever."[27]

City officials, acquiring land and loans at far-below-market rates, have gone on an orgy of urban expansion, building massive malls and outlandish municipal buildings. Cheap land and credit have made common the phenomenon of the Chinese ghost town—places like Yangzhou, Jiangsu, an ancient city now home to vast new luxury residential developments that are largely vacant. That reality is what led investor Jim Chanos to refer to China as "Dubai times a thousand—or worse" in 2010, predicting an imminent crash that has yet to come.[28]

Land, too, is used for collateral as cities borrow to finance even more construction. Local governments already had debt amounting to 29.95 trillion yuan ($4.3 trillion) at the end of 2017. When off-budget or hidden borrowing worth as much as 40 trillion yuan ($5.8 trillion) is combined, it amounts to an "alarming" 60 percent of GDP, according to S&P Global Ratings. As loans have grown, revenues from land are being used to cover interest payments. A fall in prices and collapse in property values could cause a series of debt defaults by regional governments across China. "The potential amount of debt is an iceberg with titanic credit risks," said a report by S&P.[29]

Cities and factory zones have encroached deep into fertile growing regions. Already damaged by excessive use of pesticides, the soil has been further poisoned by industrial effluent including the heavy metals cadmium, nickel, and arsenic. One-fifth of all of China's arable land is now polluted, showed a survey released in spring 2014 by the environmental protection and land resources ministry. Over a tenth of the country suffers from acid rain, which is particularly severe in the Yangtze River Delta. Officials say the country is now nearing its so-called red line, the minimum amount of agriculture land they claim is necessary for national food security, or 120 million hectares (297 million acres). As early as 2007, the former premier, soft-spoken Wen Jiabao, whose wife and other relatives together amassed at least $2.7 billion during his years in power,[30] warned that the country was facing "unbalanced, uncoordinated, and unsustainable development."

With city residents up from less than a fifth of the population in 1978 to just over half now, China's urbanization rate is still low compared to the 60 percent common in countries at a similar stage of development. And some three hundred million of those in the cities are migrants, some of whom have lost their rights to the land they once farmed. Without a city residency permit, they cannot access affordable health care and urban pension programs, or send their children to public schools in the cities; they are also uncertain about how long their employment will last. That forces them to save more for the future—what economists call "precautionary saving"—leaving them much less money to spend. Meanwhile, those who stay in the countryside struggle to earn a living farming on small plots of land, reluctant to invest their meager earnings in improvements like irrigation and better seeds, keeping crop productivity low. All this helps explain why household consumption still is a relatively small part of the economy.

China's leaders know that a system that disenfranchises half its people is unsustainable. Li Keqiang, the latest premier and the first to have dual degrees in economics and law, has touted what he calls "people-centered" urbanization—meaning not just more city construction but also allowing migrants fuller rights. The policy of expanding rural land usage markets is supposed to boost farmers' incomes while providing migrants a way to earn some money as they leave for the cities. Land consolidation creating more efficient larger farms is expected to produce more grains, fruit, and vegetables to feed the growing appetites of the middle class. In parallel, the rigid *hukou* policy is to gradually be relaxed in certain cities.

The authorities, however, have no intention of allowing real free migration, as frequent campaigns to evict workers from cities show plainly. By offering residency permits only selectively, the government aims to steer migrants into smaller urban areas, such as Baoding, Hebei near Beijing, or Zhenjiang, Jiangsu, not far from Shanghai. But the larger cities are likely to be the main draw for migrants. As is true everywhere, "the population flows will follow the jobs and quality of services that a region can offer," wrote Shen Minggao, formerly a professor at Peking University and an economist at Citigroup Hong Kong, in a March 2014 report on China's urbanization, questioning the government's micromanagement.[31]

The costs are expected to be high. In 2014, a finance minister estimated it would cost 80,000 yuan for the housing, welfare, and other costs associated with integrating each new city dweller, amounting to a total of $6.8 trillion. The payoff is supposed to come as each new urbanite spends an additional $1,600 more a year, boosting overall consumption.[32] To wean localities off their reliance on land revenues, they plan to develop new sources of funding. Cities will issue more municipal bonds. Tariffs on water, electricity, and heating fuel will be raised, and a nationwide property tax may eventually be launched. (Resistance from officials who own multiple apartments has been a formidable obstacle to date.)

Chongqing, with a population of twenty-nine million, and which has added several million new urban residents over the space of just a few years, suggests where China may be heading. Despite the downfall of its former chief, Bo Xilai, the charismatic princeling son of a party revolutionary, who was thrown in jail for life for corruption and abuse of power in 2013, it has continued to grow rapidly—but much of its growth has been driven by massive land grabs.

In 2013, I went to Chongqing to see how farmers' lives were changing under rapid urbanization. I started the day by visiting newly citified folks, who had traded their small farming plots for official urban residency. Proud in their apartments, little one-bedroom alcoves lodged many floors up the sides of towering new high-rises, they at the same time seemed stuck halfway between their roots in the fields and their still-undefined futures as city folk.

Sitting in their cramped apartments, I asked what most pleased them about their new lodgings. Hot water, having one's own toilet, they eagerly answered. The thought occurred to me that in this building these earnest, suntanned former farmers were probably higher than they had ever been previously. As I walked through the barely finished residence grounds, loudspeakers droned repeated didactic messages: "Keep your balconies orderly"; "All trash must be put in receptacles"; "Walk on the designated paths and cherish the greenery"; "Motorcycles must be parked in the proper place." Getting to the elevator on the ground floor of the buildings had proved challenging, with muddy motorbikes pushed inside for shelter and occupying most of the small entryways.

The place was impressive in its own way: an entire new community of apartments but also a grocery store, a laundry, a library, and a gleaming job-training center with a neon signboard advertising positions for cleaners and handymen. It had been built to meet the needs of some ten thousand farmers who had recently tended rice and corn-fields in a village called Daling, not far from here. The community seemed almost self-contained: all jobs available were for positions to serve the new residents, who, no longer farmers, needed those same jobs. Adding to that sense was the isolated feeling the community had. The ten or so high-rises seemed almost arbitrarily dropped into an endless succession of lush green rolling hills dotted with countless small patches of land cultivated with rice and corn. With the present pace of urbanization, however, none of the open land would be here in ten years, I thought.

"My bathroom here is better than my old bedroom," said one for-mer farmer as he eagerly showed me around his twelfth-floor, seventy-square-meter (753.5-square-foot) apartment, with its Konka TV and Galanz microwave. (His shy forty-eight-year-old wife concurred when he, answering for her, said that switching from a coal-burning stove to the new gas-fired one was the best part of their move.)[33] Their daughter had started a small clothing shop, and business was good, too, he said. He had won a coveted position as a building super and had made a quick call on his mobile phone to report a broken elevator before taking me to his apartment.

While no doubt the new setting had made a lot of farmers happy, that was not its main purpose. Instead, the land-for-*hukou* swap pro-gram had two other purposes. Firstly and crucially, it opened up new agricultural land for development, enriching many local officials and real-estate companies. At the same time, the creation of a new version of Daling was part of a national strategy to convert farmers to urban-ites, expected to consume far more as they moved into the middle class. In 2012, for the first time in history, more Chinese resided in cities than in the countryside; policymakers were eager to encourage this trend to continue.

In the new Daling, that goal seemed in sight, although, as I kept reminding myself, the satisfied local farmers had been selected to talk to a foreign reporter by the officials who had arranged my visit. The officials, in turn, all worked in a vast economic-development zone whose continued success depended on gobbling up more agricultural villages to make space for companies who would build new factories, pay corporate taxes, and create wage jobs. My purpose later that day was to talk to those who had less happily left their land.

By 1:00 P.M., I was far from the model village of high-rises, wandering about in another newly built urban zone. I was starting to think I was lost or, worse yet, playing a perverse game of treasure hunt. As instructed, I had climbed out of a taxi at the intersection of two broad avenues, now almost empty, built in hopeful anticipation of future vehicles and wealthier residents. The woman I was trying to meet was giving me odd directions via a series of abbreviated calls over mobile phone: "Go across the avenue to the auto shop," she told me. "Turn and walk left for several hundred meters." "Now cross back over the road." "Turn left at the first intersection and walk another two hundred meters. . . ."

It was very hot. Chongqing is known as one of China's "three big furnaces" (the other two are Wuhan and Nanjing, both downstream and also Yangtze River towns), and summer temperatures hover in the nineties Fahrenheit, while humidity can reach 80 percent. Sweat was quickly mapping dark patterns across my white shirt. What was the woman thinking? Was she just really bad at giving directions? Or was she trying to shake off anyone who might be following a reporter?

The road I was on had lost the shoulder on its right side, and now a steep bank rose up some thirty feet. Another vast residential development of twenty-story high-rises was under construction on top of the bluff. A plump-faced forty-five-year-old, with a look of perpetual wariness, met me in front of the Shimalu, or "Stone Horse Road," wet market, enclosed under a hangar-size roof. "That's where our land was," she said, indicating the new buildings rising up across the road. "We used to have our own house and farm," she said slowly, now looking fixedly at me as if expecting an answer to why everything had gone so wrong.

Mindful of the instructions I had been given earlier about meeting people who had experienced *chaiqian*, or "relocation" (the two characters meaning "tear down" and "move")—don't stay long in one place, get your questions in fast and get out, they are all watched closely by the authorities—I suggested we continue our conversation in the flat she and her husband had recently begun to rent. We cut between a convenience store and a shop selling Xiaomi mobile phones, and entered a residential compound, the housing grimy and squat.

As we trudged up three poorly lit flights of stairs, I wondered whether we were being followed. One of the gloomy landings would be an ideal place to accost a disoriented foreign journalist, I thought anxiously. I was carrying my laptop, something I had been warned not to do, given the risk that it could be seized by local police. Was I making a serious mistake coming here? We entered a cramped apartment filled with the stale smell of cigarettes, where her husband was waiting for us. It took no urging to get him to begin chronicling his and his wife's misfortune. The day they knew local officials were serious about taking their land, he said, was when hired thugs broke his arm and leg; it was in January, deep in the gloomy rainy season.

"The local government that orders evictions is always working in cahoots with a real-estate company. When the thugs came to throw us off our land, local cops and land-office officials were there, too, but did nothing to stop the violence," the bullet-headed farmer said in a flat tone. "Now I can't work because of my injuries. My wife was earning money selling ducks and chickens, but then avian flu came and ended that. But that doesn't concern them. They only care about getting rich. Although the central government of course doesn't want urbanization to set back our living standards, that is what has happened."[34]

The biggest obstacle to successful land reform is local governments that continue to rely on land sales for their operation, and officials who often benefit through kickbacks and sweetheart property deals. Along with its ideological bias against privatizing the land, the central government has not yet figured out other adequate sources of income for localities to tap, with land-related revenues amounting to as high as $1 trillion a year.[35] (Most of that goes to township governments and above; very little goes to the villages.) Farmers in more than 40 percent of China's villages have had their land expropriated, receiving only a nominal fee in compensation, showed a study in 2011 by Seattle-based nonprofit Landesa.[36] The World Bank estimated that the rural population has been shortchanged 2 trillion yuan ($321.34

billion) in lost land earnings over the past twenty years, amounting to 4 percent of China's 2013 GDP.[37] (That figure could be much higher, say others.)

Farmers who resist suffer beatings and worse; at least forty-one set themselves on fire from 2009 until the end of 2011 to protest property grabs, according to London-based Amnesty International. "Forced evictions [represent] the single most significant source of popular discontent in China," says Amnesty's 2012 report, *Standing Their Ground: Thousands Face Violent Eviction in China*.[38] In one of the more brutal incidents, eight people died fighting over requisitioned land in a village outside of the southwestern provincial capital Kunming in the fall of 2014. Four of them were construction workers burned to death by an angry mob of villagers, official media reported.

I had another encounter with a couple of dozen aggrieved farmers from Chongqing on a cold winter morning in Beijing some six months after my trip to the southwest. Their story was typical: Local officials eager to build high-rises had evicted them from their land. Now they had come to the capital to demonstrate in front of the U.S. embassy, in a last-ditch move of desperation. As one explained to me, outgoing U.S. ambassador Gary Locke was returning to Washington, as his term as diplomatic chief in China was nearing its end; surely he could appeal for help from then U.S. president Barack Obama, the head of a country they still viewed as the world's advocate for democracy and human rights.

The farmers, most well into their late fifties and sixties, were dressed in ill-fitting clothes out of place in China's capital city. But they took advantage of the long line of visa applicants snaking down the sidewalk in front of the gray, bunkerlike U.S. outpost, built just before the 2008 Beijing Olympics, to disguise their intentions, as they moved closer to the entrance. Then all of a sudden they began their protest, donning white tunics cut from sheets on which they had written the character for "*yuan*," or "injustice." "Our land was taken—give it back!" they chanted, thrusting their fists in the air, while bystanders looked on in surprise.

Tough-looking young plainclothes security agents dressed in olive-green winter jackets and black knit caps, along with uniformed police, quickly surrounded the demonstrators, roughly grabbing the placards from their hands, and started herding them away from the embassy gate. Most striking was the farmers' lack of any fear; "Have you no shame?" they yelled. The motley group was far from the "mighty storm" of peasants that Mao had spoken of so stirringly eighty-seven years earlier. But as I watched the farmers angrily confront the authorities, I could see the scale of the challenge the party still faces in the countryside.

The high-speed train approaches its platform in Shijiazhuang like a blunt-nosed gray and white snake, a long blue line running down its body; with these markings, is it poisonous? Two headlight-eyes pierce inquisitively through the tan morning smog. People huddle in dark clumps in the darkness of the vast cement structure that is a Chinese railway station, the snake engorging and disgorging. This is where it comes to feed and excrete, in thirty-minute intervals, in locations across the country. It is how the country folk go to and from their villages, to the gray factories and dusty construction sites.

The Taihang Mountains that rise west of the provincial capital are cloaked in an acrid cloud of sulfur dioxide, nitrogen oxide, and ozone, from the glass, cement, and steel factories of Hebei Province.[39] In the winter it is at its worst and today the air we breathe has an abundance of the tiny, most lethal particles, or those 2.5 microns or less in width; air quality has broken the ceiling of five hundred particles per cubic meter, or is "crazy bad," as the U.S. embassy in Beijing once referred to it on its Twitter stream. As you leave the city behind, move through these villages of dirt-scratch farms, the smog or *wumai* stays with you, hanging over the ridges, creeping around the dust-coated trees, and it seems out of place, somehow wrong. Accept the poverty, remoteness, lack of employment, but then shouldn't one at least get clean fresh air?

The village of Shangxule seems deserted. Glance down its long, muddy streets and at most you may see an old man bundled up in a faded blue winter overcoat, cane in hand, quickly rounding a corner. There is no other sign of life but ears of bright yellow drying corn held in circular mini-granaries of chicken wire, some three feet in diameter and five feet tall, perched on flat farmhouse roofs. Shangxule, like Binghuacun, like tens of thousands of other villages across China, is what has come to be known as a *kongchaocun*, or "empty nest village." That is when outmigration leaves the countryside populated only by the very elderly and toddlers that have been left in their care. While in theory Shangxule has a population of some twelve hundred people split among three hundred families, the reality is that most have left and only a few hundred people still live here; the vast majority of them are the aged and very young.

Sixty-nine-year-old Dong Xiangzhu sits outside her front door on a tiny wooden bench, looking over the farmhouse courtyard. On her long, ruddy face, common to natives of China's northern plains, she has a worldly look of having seen it all, despite the fact that she has rarely left this remote village. The sudden presence of a foreign reporter, the first ever here, doesn't faze her: "Who lives here now? Other than the kids, it is just us elderly folk trying to not get sick so we can keep on farming," she says. "But I can't work in the fields anymore." She slaps her knee for emphasis, then later keeps smacking it as we keep talking, presumably to punish the arthritis that is acting up. Her daughter, who now works in an online finance company in the provincial capital, explains to me that the elderly here all have joint problems from years of laboring in the fields; as is true in most villages, they work into their seventies or until they are no longer able. "I can still plant wheat and corn," chimes in her seventy-year-old husband, Gao Chouni.[40]

Lovely, lush-plumaged dark red and ocher roosters peck at the hard-packed dirt in front of us, then drink from a bowl, tipping their heads back to the heavens with each sip, as if savoring a fine wine. A pig breaks loose from a pen at the side, then goes on a squealing rampage through the small courtyard before being beaten back into his alcove at the side of the house with a big stick wielded by Gao. The animals provide food and, if they breed well, occasionally extra money for the couple. Peanuts, sweet potatoes, and *fentiao*, vermicelli made from mung beans, hanging in translucent white streamers from racks in front of houses, supplement the staples of wheat and corn in their diet and pocketbook.

By 2050, one-third of all Chinese will be elderly, up from a little over 17 percent now, bringing soaring health costs and new social burdens. Less acknowledged is that hardest hit will be villages like Shangxule, with aging in the countryside happening 2.3 times faster than in the cities, as young people desert the villages. Already outside the cities there are some eighty million people over sixty-five, making up about three-fifths of the country's aged.[41] Compared to their city counterparts, rural elderly are far more likely to have physical disabilities,[42] and they have far higher rates of untreated hypertension and respiratory diseases.

Depression among the elderly living in the countryside is a growing problem, and suicide rates are more than three times that of those in cities.[43] And the fact that their children usually live far away in the cities, unable to regularly check on them, only makes them more vulnerable. One-fifth have incomes falling below the official poverty line, a far higher proportion than in cities, while 40 percent become poor because of illness in the family, according to Su Guoxia, a director in the State Council Leading Group Office of Poverty Alleviation and Development. As a result, families are often unwilling to seek medical care unless absolutely necessary. "Even though older people are getting less healthy in rural China, they are getting less health care," says Albert Park, an economist at Hong Kong University of Science and Technology. "If we can stand the pain we don't go to the hospital—it's too expensive," says Shangxule's Dong.

Dressed in tan shorts and an orange shirt to beat the heat, Mo Rubo leans forward to keep his back off the hard wood of his living-room couch. He shifts uncomfortably on the seat edge as we discuss his parents back in Binghuacun. "We brought them here a bunch of times, but they couldn't get used to living in Changan—no one spoke to them, and when they did, they couldn't understand them. The longest time that my mother came was for six months to take care of my daughter when she was an infant.

"I built them the new house in Binghuacun because they are getting older. They are too old to climb the mountain to the old place, so I built the house next to the river to make their lives a little easier," Rubo says, frowning. "If we could live in Libo, I wouldn't have to worry about my parents getting old, I could see them whenever necessary. Isn't my village nicer than here? I want to go home but there is nothing to do there. I am forty-one years old. Too young to retire!" he says, a smile finally breaking over his face.

Later that evening, while eating in a Hunan-style restaurant near their apartment, we continue discussing the choice to remain in Changan, far from his parents—a taboo in traditional Chinese culture, where the eldest son is expected to take care of and even live with his mother and father. His wife listens with a tight-lipped smile; this clearly is a discussion they have had before. When I ask if she would like to move to the village, she answers with an emphatic nod no. "They eat hot pot all the time, which I can't get used to. We eat noodles in Henan," she quickly answers, referring to her home province. It is clear she has issues with Binghuacun beyond culinary choices. I recall Rubo's mother complaining that her daughter-in-law, who stands out from the villagers in her colorful stylish dresses and makeup, doesn't take well to the rustic life and cuts short her son's visits home. "I love the village life, it is so comfortable, but it is difficult, too," says Rubo. "Because when you want to buy things, it isn't easy. Kids need school, people need medical care, and neither is good there."

4

The Party

Our dictatorship is the people's democratic dictatorship
led by the working class and based on the worker-peasant
alliance.

> —MAO ZEDONG, "ON THE CORRECT HANDLING OF
> CONTRADICTIONS AMONG THE PEOPLE," FEBRUARY 27, 1957

Before, we all played the cat-and-mouse game.

> —PETER WANG, GENERAL MANAGER OF ZHI QIAO
> GARMENTS CO., NIKE SUPPLIER

The Panyu Migrant Workers Center is one floor up a grimy stair-
case in a prematurely stained cement building that sits amid tattered
palm trees and a jumble of toy, electronics, and textile factories. One
spring morning in 2005 the center has a couple of dozen migrants
hanging out in a stuffy room, some playing Ping-Pong or Chinese go,
while others quietly pore through much-read Chinese comic books
and magazines with names like *Chinese Lawyer* and *Youth of the City*.
On a packed bookshelf nearby, pamphlets explaining rules for Chinese Communist Party membership sit next to a U.S. Department of
State–issued booklet, *Issues of Democracy*. Maps of Guangdong Province, China, and the world hang on the walls, next to photos of work-

ers taking classes, and banners that read BOOKS BRING BOUNTY TO ONE'S LIFE and KNOWLEDGE CAN CHANGE FATE.

Luo Guangfu, a grave-faced twenty-seven-year-old who grew up on a farm in Chongqing, has just finished a twelve-hour night shift working weaving machines in a nearby textile factory in Panyu, which sits just southeast of the provincial capital Guangzhou. He is here for a seminar on China's new labor regulations, even though it cuts into his sleeping hours. The seminar is taught by one of the center's small volunteer staff, all of whom are migrants, and Luo is eager to learn. "If a worker doesn't know China's labor law, then he's in big trouble. When a factory doesn't pay us enough, we can use it to confront them," Luo says.[1]

The center's director is Zeng Feiyang, a former civil servant and lawyer, who comes from a town in the mountainous and poorer northern part of Guangdong. "Workers' understanding of their rights has grown rapidly. That's a very happy thing," he says. Thirty years old, he sports a simple buzz cut for a hairstyle, and has bushy black eyebrows behind broad glasses. "We were the earliest organization when we opened in 1998; now workers' NGOs are proliferating." His center also earns money doing worker training for companies such as Reebok.[2]

Halfway through the first decade of the twenty-first century, workers in China, beginning in factory-dense Guangdong Province, began to wake up to their rights. Entry into the World Trade Organization in 2001 had brought a flood of foreign investors, and more and more people now were employed in factories or on construction sites that had little or no connection to the Chinese state. With new bosses from Taiwan, Hong Kong, the U.S., and Europe, workers discovered that the basic workplace conditions of salaries, hours, and safety varied far more widely than before and could suddenly change. An elaborate human-management system where in the cities, state-owned enterprises, and in the countryside, communes, had once determined not only every aspect of employment but basic life choices like when one could have a baby—even birth-control pills were doled out through one's employer—was rapidly coming to an end. As the party purged itself of its decades-old caretaker role—a system that had been called the "iron rice bowl" for the benefits it offered urban Chinese workers, including housing, medical care, and education— in its place had emerged a raw capitalism that had little interest in laborers beyond their blood and sweat. That left them with a stark choice: passively accept what was offered them, no matter how bleak, or grasp any means available to get employers to treat them better.

Migrants, living far from their hometowns and the officials who— at least on paper—represented them, not surprisingly were most vulnerable. A local party cadre might give money to a village fund supporting healthy childbirth or for an annual holiday, but usually had no role whatsoever in migrants' lives in the cities. Back in Binghuacun, a red sign plastered on a wall showed that Mo Ruxuan, the younger brother of Ruchun, had donated three thousand yuan, the largest sum among seventy-six people, for village events including a banquet celebrating the 2016 Mid-Autumn Festival. Pictures of Ruxuan, who had rapidly risen through the ranks and now worked in Guiyang, were posted on a nearby stand used to promulgate party news, under the title CARING LEADERS NOTICE. He was pictured gesturing to a visiting provincial finance office director. But having a successful relative meant nothing for the Mos who had left Guizhou. Outside the village, China's laborers were usually ignored by the state.

Indifference toward the laboring class of course was a huge shift from the attitudes that prevailed during China's revolutionary years. Like any good Communist, Mao from the beginning knew that the proletariat was supposed to play the key role in his country's transformation. Workers—then usually not migrants—were heralded as "masters of the country," or *guojiade zhuren,* in official propaganda. "The industrial proletariat represents China's new productive forces, is the most progressive class in modern China and has become the leading force in the revolutionary movement," wrote Mao in "Analysis of the Classes in Chinese Society," in March 1926, more than two decades before the founding of the People's Republic.[3] The Chinese state "is a people's democratic dictatorship led by the working class and based on the worker-peasant alliance," Mao wrote years later, in February 1957.[4] Deng Xiaoping, one of some sixteen hundred young

Chinese sent to France from 1919 to 1921, had firsthand experience of the life of a worker, where he labored in a steel mill and factories making paper flowers and rubber boots.[5] Borrowing a leaf from their Soviet Communist brethren, China's new leaders instituted the tradition of regularly naming and publicizing the deeds of exemplary Model Workers, who were intended to show the citizens of the People's Republic how to be good servants to the party. For countless children growing up across China, the most memorable Model Worker of the 1970s was a candy seller in a Beijing downtown department store. He was renowned for never needing a scale when doling out treats, so good was he said to be at estimating weights.

Mobilizing workers and organizing strikes in cities like Shanghai was a key part of the underground Chinese Communist Party's strategy in urban China in the years before 1949. And it was at least a partially successful one, as party members leveraged worker protests to "liberate" China's cities from under the control of their Nationalist rivals. But after the founding of the People's Republic of China, that began to change. As Mao adopted the "Big Push" strategy of Stalin, which emphasized the development of industrialization, especially heavy industry, the importance of having a docile labor force became key. Strikes were no longer allowed and each worker was closely managed by his or her employer, or *danwei*, literally translated as "unit." And outside the cities, rural workers always had far fewer benefits than those provided to those in urban state enterprises. After Mao's death and the launch of economic reforms, most workers became important mainly as just a source of cheap labor for Chinese and foreign investors alike.

Today Chinese society largely looks down on the farmer-turned-migrants that make up the majority of China's working class. Occasional halfhearted pity for them is dwarfed by a strong strain of scorn and resentment among most urbanites. As "outsiders," or *waidiren*, they are a convenient scapegoat, blamed for everything from city road congestion and high food prices to petty crime. "Farmer!," or *nongmin*, today is a dismissive epithet used to curse or make fun of the migrants. And despite the party still heralding the importance of workers, featuring them in its annual entertainment and propaganda lollapalooza, the Lunar New Year CCTV Gala Show, and publicly declaring the importance of the state-controlled union in ensuring their well-being, the reality is very different; they are expected to be obedient and accept their second-class status.

Even as the party ended its tutelage over workers, however, it did more than just keep them as ideological props; as it backed out of day-to-day management of their lives, it created a legal infrastructure to regulate those who became the new bosses, and ensure they did not mistreat workers too badly, in part to prevent social unrest. China's first labor law was enforced haphazardly after its adoption, in 1994, and was largely limited to dealing with work hours and salary issues. But in the early years of the twenty-first century, shortly after China entered the World Trade Organization, officials began more seriously to police the human-resource practices of the growing numbers of foreign factory owners. In quick succession authorities first promulgated a law on occupational disease in October of 2001 and then, just eight months later, brought out a second law, on worker safety. At the same time, encouraged by the state press that was publicizing the importance of the new regulations and growing international attention on sweatshop issues, labor and legal scholars at universities and self-taught workers turned lawyers in the new labor NGOs began to teach migrants about their rights.

As many a worker was to find out, a strong law was not sufficient; what was needed was its implementation. And, not surprisingly, the new factory bosses were eager to avoid taking any actions that would raise costs. Faced with the tough new regulations, they searched for work-arounds and found clever ways to hide continuing abuses, all aimed at keeping the same profit margins as before. As a new global anti-sweatshop movement began targeting companies like Nike and Walmart for problems in their supply chains, the multinationals began to demand that their suppliers comply with the new laws, afraid of how a labor scandal could hit their stock prices. A multimillion-dollar industry of monitoring factories for overtime and wage violations in China sprang up, with international brands and retailers hiring auditing companies like Cal Safety Compliance, Bureau Veritas of France, and SGS of Switzerland; they marshaled teams of local hires to march through factories, inspecting whether they were following the new laws and meeting newly created corporate codes of conduct.

The new auditing industry, however, suffered from lack of co-ordination, with each brand or retailer seemingly more concerned with protecting their reputation than creating a workable system of improvement that all suppliers could aspire toward. That meant big Chinese factories that produced for multiple brands or retailers often struggled to meet conflicting codes of conduct, and received some-times almost daily visits from inspection teams, who inevitably de-manded facility tours, access to payroll records, and interviews with managers and workers. "McDonald's, Walt Disney, and Wal-Mart are doing thousands of audits a year that are not harmonized," said Auret van Heerden of the Fair Labor Association, a former antiapartheid activist from South Africa with a long mane of white hair and a coffee "addiction." Among factory managers, he said, "audit fatigue sets in."[6]

Not surprisingly, factories quickly became adept at gaming the new system, keeping multiple faked books—one for tax inspectors, one for auditors, and a real one for the company's business purposes. They also developed elaborate routines to hide abuses when being inspected and often paid off inspectors with bribes. "First notify un-derage trainees, underage full-time workers, and workers without identification to leave the manufacturing workshop through the back door. Order them not to loiter near the dormitory area. Secondly, im-mediately order the receptionist to gather all relevant documents and papers," read the instructions for managers facing an audit at one Chi-nese fabric export factory in Guangzhou. The directive also ordered workers to quickly put on earplugs and face masks in the event of a visit.[7]

From the outside, it is hard to spot the small toy factory that sits off a busy street in Shenzhen. One enters through a small, dingy meet-ing room, used to host visiting buyers, before reaching the first factory floor. Paint fumes choke the air in the poorly ventilated space, where young women hunch over die-injection molds, carefully spray-painting tiny figurines of Snow White, Cinderella, and other Disney princesses. I have come here with the compliance manager of a top U.S. retailer, who has been in the monitoring business for many years. Disturbed by how commonplace audit dodging has become, and how some big brands have opted to turn a blind eye to the funny business, he has brought me here to show me how it works. The Chinese factory manager who accompanies us is clearly nervous, as we have arrived with only half an hour's advance notice, and tries to rush us through an impromptu factory tour. Asked what is behind a locked door, he at first insists there is nothing of note. When pressed, he finally pulls out a key and opens it. Inside is a second workshop, filled with a smaller number of women, some of whom appear to be under the legal working age of sixteen. One jumps up and tries to hide behind her coworkers as we enter. The factory manager, looking distraught, admits that this second room is used to hide the most egregious rule breaking that goes on in his factory.

"Before, we all played the cat-and-mouse game," says Peter Wang, general manager of Zhi Qiao Garments Co., whose run-down factory sits among mango groves and rice paddies in Panyu, two hours northwest of the Shenzhen toy factory, and produces athletic apparel for Nike. Its six hundred employees work stitching machines and wield large steam irons, making sports jerseys and shorts. After getting caught by Nike for breaking regulations, the factory has cleaned up its act, the beleaguered Wang says. "Any improvement you make costs more money." Paying overtime wages—time-and-a-half pay after eight hours on weekdays and between double and triple pay for Saturdays, Sundays, and holidays—is most difficult, he says. "The price [Nike pays] never increases one penny," Wang complains, "but compliance with labor codes definitely raises costs."[8]

Even as officials publicly demanded that factories comply with the new rules, it often seemed halfhearted. At the local level, governments were uninterested in making life tougher for investors that brought both tax revenues and jobs. And ultimately, even senior policymakers in Beijing knew that a dirt-cheap labor force was key to China's continued economic growth. Brands, for their part, seemed more interested in ensuring that they had plausible deniability by carrying out audits rather than actually expecting their suppliers to change practices. Workers were supposed to mutely accept their transformation from being, at least in in principle, a vanguard revolutionary force to being mere cogs in the industrial economy. The law was supposed to prevent the most egregious mistreatment, but factory hands must not speak out.

Their passivity would help maintain the deal the party had struck with China's city folks—rising incomes in exchange for stringent limits on civil rights and a ban on openly criticizing China's leadership. Where pliable workers helped Mao industrialize, now their marginal status was necessary to buttress fast economic growth and lift living standards for those new middle-class urbanites. When I had first met Mo Wenzhi, he had told me how his father had died when he was very young, while working on a dam project. Wenzhi did not blame anyone and accepted the loss of his father as part of the lot of poor, rural Chinese like himself, saying simply, "He worked too hard, so he died." That was the unassertive attitude the party wanted.[9]

The problem was that workers were proving to be less and less acquiescent, and demographic changes were playing a part in the shift. In 2005, in an astonishing about-face for a country once envied by global businesses for its seemingly innumerable workers, serious labor shortages began to emerge in the factories of the Pearl and Yangtze River deltas. In part the legacy of the one-child policy, which had dramatically lowered birth rates, the shift also came from a sharp rise in demand, with an ever-growing concentration of manufacturers coming to China, including setting up shop outside the delta regions, and vying for migrants to fill their factories. That meant workers could begin to be choosy, leaving jobs where they earned less, able to quickly find employment elsewhere. The era of having to hand over identity cards and become a virtual prisoner of one's employer was coming to an end, and factories slowly began to improve working and living conditions, in order to attract and keep their staff.

Beyond an economic environment shifting from one always favoring capital toward one more balanced to labor, the new generation of migrants, born in the 1980s or later, were different from their parents. With their own smartphones and access to the internet, they were more aware of their rights. They were better educated and more in-terested in finding work they liked rather than just earning enough to send remittances home to the village. Above all, they were becoming savvy about the ins and outs of China's expanding raft of labor laws and how to use them. "If you want to come out and be a worker it is important to have a strong understanding of the law," said Qing Yong-zhi, sitting one spring afternoon in a Shenzhen apartment rented by a friend. Qing, born in 1984 in Bijie, Guizhou, the town to later become infamous for the tragic deaths of left-behind children, now worked in a Shenzhen-based Japanese-owned factory that made handicraft cloth fans. "My father's generation saw the law as a tool of capitalists, not something for workers."[10]

Labor organizers were becoming a real force, too. Now not just teaching about the new regulations, they were encouraging migrants to take action, training them in collective-bargaining tactics, as well as trying to influence policies. At the turn of the century, China had only a handful of legal advocates for workers. Chongqing-born Zhou Litai, the unlicensed "barefoot lawyer" who had represented factory hands seeking compensation from job injuries, was one, as was Panyu's Zeng Feiyang. But a little over a decade later, China had some eighty labor-rights groups, in Beijing, Shanghai, and Chongqing, and in Guangdong, home to about half of them, and they were playing an increasingly key role in an ever-stronger workers' movement.[11]

Zhang Zhiru was one such activist, now running his own small office called Chunfeng Labor Dispute Service Center in Shenzhen ("*chunfeng*" meaning "spring wind," a hopeful name suggesting new openness in China). Zhang, who was born in a rural part of Hunan Province, in central China, and who had dropped out of middle school when he was fifteen, got his first job working in a shoe fac-tory in Dongguan, then later taught himself labor law. In the fall of 2011, he decided to run for the local People's Congress in Shenzhen, saying he would serve the city's millions of migrants. The authori-ties were not pleased with his effort to participate in what had long been a largely rubber-stamp exercise for connected officials. First, he had been warned by local police that he was risking arrest for "undermining" the election. Next, cadres had announced a new rule that blocked those without local *hukou* from participating in the electoral process. Zhang pulled out.[12]

I met him for the first time half a year later in a crowded restaurant in one of Shenzhen's vast industrial suburbs, to talk about the newest factory dodge: the use of temporary workers. Zhang, as I was to discover as I got to know him better, seemed unflappable and always ready to leap into a conversation about workers' rights, no matter what might be going on around him. "I have a little question—should our center work to improve the conditions for temporary workers? Or should we campaign for a complete ban on using temporary workers?" he asked me, as the room packed with diners buzzed with sound around us. It was not clear if he expected an answer.[13]

The question seemed irrelevant given how prevalent the use of temps had become. At the beginning of 2008, the Labor Contract Law had come into effect, toughening regulations on overtime and mandating new social-welfare payments for all employees, which could add more than a third to factory wage costs. There was a loophole, however. Temporary workers—in China called "dispatch workers"—were not protected. As local governments began to enforce the law, companies responded by replacing full-time workers with temporary ones. According to one estimate, the number of temp workers had reached sixty million by 2012, up threefold since the enactment of the law. And reliance on temps was common not just in small export factories, but also in the country's largest state-owned enterprises, like PetroChina and Bank of China, as well as in many multinationals. "Factory owners are smart businessmen. If they figure out that the labor contract looks too expensive, they are going to find a way to find a detour—that is what's happening now," says Martin Ma, China director of Solidaridad Network, a Dutch nonprofit that works to improve factory conditions in China. "I have run into a number of factories that used to have a thousand full employees. But today they have only fifty working in the trading department."[14]

"Nokia Life District" is the name unofficially bestowed upon a several-acre neighborhood in Dongguan's Nancheng District. Streets here are lined with inexpensive restaurants, mobile-phone service shops, and pharmacies. The first clue one has arrived is the sight of throngs of young men and women in their late teens or early twenties, all dressed in the same blue-and-white shirts, similar to those that the Finnish company's employees wear worldwide. They are part of a ten-thousand-strong migrant force that labors in the huge mobile-phone factory that sits nearby. But despite the smocks, very few of these people are actual employees of Nokia. Instead they are temps who have been brought to the factory by labor-dispatch companies. That means they are paid about three-quarters the wage earned by Nokia hires doing similar work, can't get bonuses, can't live in company dormitories, can't join the official union, and often are bullied by the factory managers, says Liang Bing, a twenty-year-old who grew up in Hunan Province and has joined four other workers in a coffee shop minutes from the factory gate, on a warm evening in early 2012. Less than one-third of his colleagues actually work for Nokia, he estimates. "Nokia just wants to save money and avoid responsibility. We are just a force they abuse."[15] Nokia said its most recent audit of the Dongguan factory found it "clean, properly managed with the respect of employees, and free from any discrimination," declining to specify what percentage of the workers were contract labor.[16]

The first large worker protests of the reform era came in China's Northeast, following the massive downsizing of the state sector launched in the late nineties and early 2000s. In the spring of 2002, tens of thousands of industrial workers demonstrated in two factory cities: Daqing, Heilongjiang, important for its vast oil reserves, and Liaoyang, Liaoning, an iron and ferroalloy production base, both originally developed by Japanese in the 1930s. With police monitoring the road that ran from the provincial capital Shenyang to Liaoyang, I had slipped into the smokestack city one night in late March, with the help of a taxi driver sympathetic to the striking factory hands. They had lost their jobs, with salaries unpaid, after the factory went bankrupt. "Here, put this on," the driver had said, throwing a baseball cap into the backseat where I sat. "You are going to have to slump down ahead, as we are coming to a road check." With my light hair covered, I scrunched down, pretending to sleep, with my face shadowed under the hat's bill; we were waved through by the sleepy officer and continued into Liaoyang.

The scale of the protests in China's rust belt had spooked the government in Beijing, which had responded with force, while polishing tactics that would be used with countless protests to come: identify and arrest protest organizers, punishing them with long sentences meant to frighten future activists; reprimand local officials for not properly managing the dispute; and throw some money toward the masses of aggrieved workers as a temporary salve. In Liaoyang, the two main protest organizers were sentenced to seven- and four-year sentences, respectively, on charges of subversion.[17] The local paper reported that thirteen officials were guilty of corruption and announced they were to be punished. And according to local press reports, workers had received half of their back wages and were promised later unemployment benefits or pensions. All of this was seen as a way to nip in the bud the possibility of angry workers linking up across factories or regions, as had happened earlier in Eastern Europe and elsewhere.[18] "The Chinese regime is very much worried about the Solidarity experience in Poland coming to China," Lee Cheuk Yan, head of the Hong Kong Confederation of Trade Unions, told me in an interview one evening in the grand old British-built white granite building that then housed the Legislative Council on Hong Kong Island.[19] Lee, born in 1957 in Shanghai, was banned from entering China, after he traveled to Beijing during the Tiananmen protests to support striking students and workers.

But while the first wave of demonstrations came from the state-owned industrial economy in China's cold Northeast, no Chinese Lech Wałęsa was to emerge to lead a workers' movement. And the party proved remarkably successful in dealing with the mass layoffs that came with the restructuring of its old economy, pushing many of the already middle-aged workers into early retirement. Others found work in private companies, often low-paid, called in China *xiahai,* or literally "enter the sea." What would emerge later as a far more serious

source of instability was protests by the migrant workforce in the export factories of far-off Guangdong, some twenty-three hundred kilometers to the southwest.

Wang Kan, a labor expert and professor at the China Institute of Industrial Relations in Beijing, has a bookish, gentle manner that be-
lies his research area: the often fractious relationship between Chinese
workers and factory managers. As we sat in a Korean-owned coffee
shop in Beijing, our usual meeting place, it soon became clear to me that
Wang's latest survey had uncovered a trove of information on what was
fast becoming a sensitive subject in Xi's China: labor protests. Workers
who had joined wildcat strikes had surged from under 10 percent in
2006 to 47.5 percent in 2015. Meanwhile, those using official channels to resolve problems had fallen from around 60 percent to under
one-half. And while protests by migrants earlier had typically been
of a smaller scale, that was changing, he explained. While in 2006
less than one-third had participated in strikes with more than ten
people, a decade later that number had grown to include almost all, or
96 percent. Over the same time period, the percentage saying that fellow laborers provided the most effective support in strikes grew from
44 percent to 63, while those who relied on the official union never
reached higher than 8 percent and had fallen to zero by 2013. "There
is more of a group consciousness," said Wang. "We asked workers
why they joined strikes. Most said they joined strikes to help their fellow workers. And the reason for that is experience—more and more
workers have either witnessed or participated in strikes."[20]

In recent years Guangdong's labor shortages had become a serious
problem for companies, and my visits there had revolved around
meeting factory managers and hearing them gripe about rising wages
and high turnover. This trip was to be different, however. I was going
to get a look at the largest strike China had seen in years. Over forty
thousand migrants had joined demonstrations in April of 2014 over
unpaid social-welfare payments at eight factories in Dongguan, all

owned by Yue Yuen Industrial, the world's largest shoemaker and a top supplier to Nike and Adidas. Four years earlier, workers had struck in the nearby city of Foshan at supplier factories to Honda Motors operations, heralded at the time as a sign of the beginnings of a new labor-rights movement, but involving far fewer workers. This trip south I also wanted to see what role the region's labor NGOs were playing; staff at Zeng Feiyang's Panyu center and Zhang Zhiru's Shenzhen Chunfeng had both been coaching the striking factory hands in negotiating tactics, I had heard. Another tiny NGO, not involved in the Yue Yuen strikes but busy helping other workers, was single-handedly run by fearless activist Wu Guijun. Years earlier, Wu had been injured in a furniture factory, then fined by the boss for missing work while he was in the hospital. Shocked by how little respect was accorded workers, he started to volunteer in labor NGOs. Later he had led a strike in another furniture factory that was shutting down without paying its workers, was jailed for one year, and in a rare victory, was later released when it was determined there was not adequate evidence of any crime by Wu, and even was given a small sum in compensation; he used that to start his own labor support group.[21] But even as I made the last preparations for my visit, reports began circulating among the close-knit activist community of a crackdown; Lin Dong, a colleague of Zhang's, was arrested on the charge of spreading online rumors, a crime in China, after posting information about another strike on the WeChat messaging service. The word was that Chunfeng's director himself had been forcibly taken away by the feared *guobao,* or internal security force, and that his whereabouts were now unknown.

Finding the newest location of the Chunfeng office was a challenge. In the two years since I had last visited, Zhang had had to move his home and attached office multiple times; police ordering landlords to stop renting to people and groups they perceived as troublemakers was a common form of harassment in cities across China. (Later in the year, Zhang and his wife and son would carry out their own mini-demonstration, standing with signs outside city offices protesting their latest eviction.)[22] It seemed that Zhang was being pushed even farther into the outskirts of Shenzhen, already a sprawling city. I considered the disturbing fact that the person I had arranged to meet—Zhang Zhiru—apparently had been kidnapped, in the short few days between when the appointment had been confirmed and my arrival here, as my taxi navigated the narrow lanes of a migrant worker urban village.

Zhang's disappearance, disturbing as it was, gave me the opportunity to meet his new deputy, an idealistic and bright son of migrants, who had recently started working at Chunfeng. The twenty-some-year-old had grown up in a small farming village in Jiangxi, a land-locked and mountainous province that had once served as a base for Mao and other revolutionaries, and even today was still poor. He had studied hard and, by scoring high on the national college exam, had become the relatively rare example of a poor rural youth who makes it into college. Later he was to get a master's degree at the Central Party School in Beijing. As the Jiangxi native explained, his success had made him something of a celebrity in his village; in the minds of his relatives, who were all farmers, he was on track to get a job in China's vast civil service. And while salaries might be low, everyone knew that working for the government meant plenty of lucrative, if often illicit, opportunities to make money on the side. When he opted to come to Shenzhen and get a job at Chunfeng, the villagers were dismayed. "With a university degree, I got a job making even less than many workers make, so many of them were really disappointed," he said with a rueful smile on his face, as we sat in the meeting room combined classroom at Chunfeng, which opened onto the first-floor entranceway and elevator. "But I know what it's like for migrant families. I was a left-behind child. I decided I want to find a powerful way to change this unequal environment for migrants in China. Here we think the best way to accomplish this is through the collective-bargaining system for workers. That's what we were doing at Yue Yuen. So many workers trust Chunfeng. But now the government is holding our director Zhang and Lin Dong," he said, starting to sound distressed.

In his new job, he got a quick education in dealing with the authorities and their thuggish tactics. He was given the responsibility of opening a second office in Dongguan, to be closer to where many of the factory disputes were occurring. But in the office's just four months of existence, he had been forced to move four times. Without a family to worry about, he said he had been able to bear the constant upheavals. But it was far more difficult for a Chunfeng colleague who was married with two children, and had his elderly mother living with them. "We were followed everywhere. Not by the police, but by bad men who they hired to watch us. Then the *guobao* came to speak to us. They told my coworker that if you keep working in Chunfeng, you won't be able to have a home here in Dongguan anymore. And it won't just be you—your mother, your children, even your sister's family, they will all have to move, too. That night, we all cried. I think what they were doing was immoral," he said, his voice breaking. "They said to me have a bright future, you don't have to do this kind of work. They warned me that I should be cautious in choosing my work and lifestyle. You don't want to do something you will regret. And they told me Mr. Zhang is doing illegal things but hiding it by wearing a legal cloak. I asked for evidence. I told them if you have evidence, I will oppose him. I will fight against Zhang myself. But they had nothing to show me." In December, Zhang told him that it was time to give up on plans for a Dongguan office, and he moved back to Shenzhen.

It was now almost midnight. As we continued to discuss the travails of Chunfeng, suddenly Zhang strode into the office, dressed as usual in a neatly pressed white shirt, with a purposeful look on his face. "The *guobao* just gave me a ride back," he said, and set down some bags of soft bean curd he had brought back for his family. The young man, sounding exultant, said, "Zhiru! You've returned!," and called Zhang's wife on his mobile phone, telling her she must come down immediately from the apartment where they lived upstairs. Zhang had been on "vacation"—what it's called when Chinese security agents forcibly take people they want to silence to a guesthouse or tourist spot for some mandatory relaxation time. He had been picked up by two officers he knew all too well from their previous visits to the Chunfeng office, and they had driven him to a hotel on the outskirts of Guangzhou. Zhang had spent two days and nights there in what he said were very pleasant surroundings. "There was water and there were mountains," he explained, using the common

Chinese expression denoting a scenic spot. When, after the first night, he demanded they let him leave, the agents had quite civilly said that was impossible, and urged him to send out a message on his WeChat account saying he was taking some time off. "Going on vacation during the biggest labor action in China in years? How could I do that? I refused to write it," Zhang said indignantly. Then late on the second day they had abruptly said he could go home. They set off in the same car on the three-hour drive south back to Shenzhen, where I was to see him late that evening. "They spent lots of time trying to discourage me from helping the Yue Yuen workers," Zhang said. "But I told them I was doing nothing wrong—only trying to help resolve the strike."[23]

Two days later, on a rainy afternoon, I am on my way to Gaobu, Dongguan. The massive, aging Yue Yuen complex, with eight separate shoe factories, sits along the Dong River, the eastern tributary of the Pearl River. As our van passes through a gate entering the factory zone, I slump down in my seat, afraid of being seen. Dozens of black-and-white police cars and the green vans of the armed police line the roads, while parked buses are filled with napping officers. Police, some with automatic rifles slung at their waist, walk in small knots by the glistening trees. I feel sick to my stomach as I peer through the rivulets running down the vehicle's window and decide to not roll it down for a better look and pictures. I reassure myself that it is simple common sense—that opening the window would likely result in our car being waved to a stop, an encounter that at best would end with me ordered to leave and not come back. "It is a little sensitive for foreigners to see all of this," my driver says, starting to look nervous. We pass a factory wall festooned with a red banner that states, "All YY workers can take free computer classes," which I read out loud. The driver scoffs and says the strikers are banned from hanging any protest banners and only positive messages are allowed.

Through a Chinese labor-rights organization based in Queens, New York, I had gotten the name and contacts for a twenty-seven-year-old from Sichuan who had been employed at Yue Yuen for four years. While he had agreed over the phone to meet me, that had changed in the twenty-four hours since we had last spoken. "It's not convenient to come out and talk," he had said, sounding jumpy, when I had called him on his mobile, as we had driven into Gaobu. "The authorities—the police and armed police—are watching us carefully and won't let us leave the factory. And they will grab anyone talking to outsiders." Why had most of the workers, at least for now, ended their strike, I had asked, grabbing what I knew would be the only opportunity to question him. "Because the factory managers and the local government and police are working together. Whether we are working in the factory or eating outside, they monitor us. They are in front of us, behind us, constantly watching us, and they are at every factory entrance. They told us if you aren't willing to work, we will take you away. But the central government [in Beijing] has promised us workers we will be treated properly. We won't stop demanding our rights," he had added quickly before ending the call.[24]

His was an argument heard across China. While local governments were seen as corrupt and in cahoots with factories, both aligned in their mutual desire to abuse laborers in their pursuit of money, the officials in far-off Beijing were certainly on the side of the workers and would stop any mistreatment, if only they knew about it; didn't the laws they wrote make that clear? It always made me feel sad, no matter how often this mantra of faith was repeated. The reality, of course, was that Beijing was much more concerned about preserving stability, and would never accept workers taking matters into their own hands. They had instead the party's own creation, the All-China Federation of Trade Unions—the world's largest union, currently with 302 million members—in charge of managing workers. And given the Chinese leadership's dual obsession with, on the one hand, avoiding the bogeyman of *luan,* or chaos, and on the other also ensuring rapid economic growth, the ACFTU usually frowned on any worker activism and sided with management.

This was not a new thing. When the ACFTU was created, on May 1, 1925, its structure and purpose had both been consciously modeled on the Soviet Union's worker union. And while it did have a role alerting the party to worker concerns, its primary purpose was never about resolving grievances. Instead, it aimed to channel the party's directives down to the working masses and help mobilize them for political campaigns. "The dictatorship of the proletariat . . . cannot work without a number of 'transmission belts' running from the vanguard [the party elite] to the mass of the advanced class, and from the latter to the mass of the working people," wrote Vladimir Lenin, in an essay entitled "The Trade Unions, the Present Situation and Trotsky's Mistakes."[25]

Indeed, the party has had a history of curbing the power of the unions, whenever they started to actually represent workers. During a wave of strikes in machinery, textile, and fertilizer factories in Shanghai in 1957, the national head of the ACFTU, Lai Ruoyu, a former soldier from the arid northern province of Shanxi, broke with the party's official line on the cause of the unrest. While some cadres said it resulted from new workers "who were immature, impure and imbued with a low-class consciousness," Lai instead criticized the unions for not aiding the factory hands. "After the socialization of industry, the unions [have] become useless in the eyes of many workers," Lai said in a speech to union cadres in Beijing in May 1957, describing the union officials as "breathing out of the same nostril as enterprise management." Shortly afterward he was purged by the party and was not officially rehabilitated until years after his death, from liver cancer in 1958.[26]

Attempts to create an independent union were dealt with harshly in the years that followed, including during the Tiananmen Square movement some three decades later. Former railway worker Han Dongfang, who was a leader in the creation of an independent union, the Beijing Workers' Autonomous Federation, during those student and worker protests, was imprisoned for twenty-two months following the crackdown on June 4, 1989, and was released only after he contracted tuberculosis in jail.[27] He later fled to Hong Kong and founded China Labour Bulletin. CLB, which he still heads, has played a more important role than probably any other organization outside the Chinese mainland in supporting the labor movement through funds and training, including the Panyu center and Chunfeng during the Yue Yuen shoe-factory strikes. "We are not pushing for Solidarnosc in China. We are not trying to overturn the party or the union. We just want the union to serve the workers," said the charismatic Han while drinking wulong tea in the JW Marriott in the upscale Pacific Place mall, on a fall afternoon in Hong Kong.[28]

That was not how it was viewed by the leadership in Beijing, who have long feared that domestic labor activism will be manipulated by groups outside China who oppose their rule, and morph into an anti-party movement. Less than a year after the Yue Yuen strikes, a sweeping crackdown had been launched on the movement and its organizers, under the orders of the country's most senior officials. Dozens of activists were interrogated by police and told to stop helping workers, with many arrested. The Panyu center was singled out for attack, accused of accepting funds from overseas. (It had received funds from CLB in Hong Kong, as well as the Ford and Asia Foundations in the U.S.) Zeng Feiyang was arrested for "disturbing public order," a crime in China, for his center's work supporting another major strike involving shoe-factory workers, this time in Panyu, at a factory producing for Ralph Lauren, Calvin Klein, and Coach. Zeng also faced a smear campaign by the state-controlled media, which reported that the married director had frequented prostitutes, had at least eight girlfriends, and had shared sex videos of them. "Hostile foreign forces are intensifying their infiltration. They are attempting to wreck the solidarity of the working class," China's top trade-union official, Li Yufu, warned in an interview with *Outlook*, a state-run publication, in March of 2015. Wang Kan explained "The Communist Party is trying to get rid of the veterans, the existing activists that have already established social networks, and destroy their legitimacy. They want to get rid of the troublemakers."[29]

As the independent labor movement was being systematically crippled, Xi Jinping harshly criticized the official union for not doing its job of maintaining a stable work environment and called for its overhaul in a meeting that summer. Mass organizations including the union must avoid "being alienated from the people," Xi said. Later that fall, ACFTU directors began a sweeping plan to remake their organization. Its goal was to reduce the bloated union staff by 40 percent by the end of 2016, down from 680,000 full-time officials, while getting millions of new workers to join, including migrants. At the same time, the union reform plan called for setting up hundreds of thousands of new service centers across China, that would provide both entertainment and training: workers would be able to watch movies and take classes in everything from computers to labor law. Probably more important, the centers would also hold discussions on party propaganda and closely monitor workers for signs of discord and possible unrest. The union must lead the masses of workers to follow the party, the state news agency reported in a summary of the plan.

"Xi's idea is to influence the hearts and minds of workers so the transmission belt has been reinvented," Wang Kan said. "But if the union spots some trouble or a strike is going to happen, then they will tell the local government and public security, so they can take action to control it."[30]

It is a warm and sunny day in early November of 2016 and I am back in Panyu. It's been eleven years since Zeng Feiyang proudly showed me around his center and I met textile worker Luo Guangfu, the eager student of China's then new labor laws. After languishing for nine months in jail, Zeng recently pleaded guilty to "disturbing public order" and was given a three-year jail sentence with a four-year reprieve; three other colleagues from the center also were sentenced on the same charge. The one standout is Meng Han, a fifty-two-year former hospital guard turned activist who worked for Zeng and is now facing trial for the same charge. Across the street from the imposing, dark red, eight-story Panyu District People's Court where he is to be tried are run-down car-repair shops. In front of a half-finished high-rise apartment project, with weeds growing up haphazardly in a vast yard, is a red party propaganda banner that reads JUSTICE AND FAIRNESS.

Meng has faced sleep deprivation and harsh interrogation in the almost one year since he was detained by police, his trial delayed as he refused to confess or denounce his colleagues. Last month, Meng's elderly parents were forced to move from their apartment after their water was cut and unidentified thugs defaced their door with axes. The *guobao* visited, urging them to persuade their son to cooperate.[31]

After months of sustained pressure, Meng finally pleads guilty and is sentenced to twenty-one months in jail on this November day. "The police accused us of trying to change the ACFTU. Well, has this so-called trade union fulfilled its responsibilities? Of course not! Instead of solving problems, they just turn up for the show. By coaching the workers and helping them to defend their rights we were doing a job that the government could not do. The trade union should be of the workers and for the workers, not an organ to protect the interests of the bosses," Meng had said to his lawyers some three months before his trial and sentencing.[32]

Earlier this same year, the authorities in Shenzhen have forced Chunfeng to cease operating, and its staff, while not in jail, have had to abandon labor organizing. Zhang Zhiru spends his time finding fake products in markets, then reporting them to the local commerce bureau, for which he receives a small reward. His former deputy has started a day care for a handful of young children; their parents are among the more than one hundred thousand employed at the nearby Longhua Foxconn iPhone factory, infamous for the rash of suicides by its employees, six years earlier. The kids will have to be sent back to the villages when they get a bit older, as they do not have the proper *hukou* that would allow them to attend Shenzhen's primary schools. When I arrive at 10:00 A.M at the modest center—a one room apartment now converted into a tiny children's play and study area, it is already hot outside, and Zhang's former deputy cuts up a chilled watermelon, its juice pooling in little puddles on the table. We have to speak loudly to hear each other over the noise of a whirring fan and the excited yells of the young students milling about. "I tried to find a job with a labor organization here. But I found out I got put on a list that the *guobao* distributed. They told everyone they shouldn't hire me," he explains. "All the NGO leaders have been forced out; the organizations remain but now they can't do anything important like collective bargaining, and today only teach classes on lifestyle habits like hygiene and diet."[33]

We are all wondering what comes next here in China, he tells me in a plaintive voice; it sometimes seems as if we are going backward. He asks whether I think the Chinese political system has become too brittle to last long-term. No, I say, most people will continue to accept the present leaders; they are becoming better off, and there are few in China anymore that are really poor. (I have been seized by a sudden bout of paranoia: Have the police instructed him to ask me this? Will he report on our conversation? Why did I tell him I am writing a book? How would they respond to that?) He, however, isn't buying my cop-out of an answer. He counters using his scholarship: "According to [Alexis] de Tocqueville, it isn't being poor that causes people to rise up; it is the realization that others are unfairly doing much better. You know our workers are a big problem. They feel like they are being left out of the new China."

5

The Robots

Emptying the cage and changing the bird.

—POLICY SLOGAN ENCOURAGING FACTORIES TO ADD
ROBOTS AND UPGRADE PRODUCTION, POPULARIZED BY
WANG YANG, GUANGDONG PROVINCIAL PARTY
SECRETARY FROM 2007 TO 2012

A screw fell to the ground
In this dark night of overtime
Plunging vertically, lightly clinking
It won't attract anyone's attention
Just like last time
On a night like this
When someone plunged to the ground

—XU LIZHI, TWENTY-FOUR-YEAR-OLD FOXCONN WORKER
WHO COMMITTED SUICIDE IN SEPTEMBER 2014

The overnight train to Shiyan leaves the capital Wuhan just after dinner, snakes most of the night across eastern Hubei's alluvial Jianghan
Plain, formed by the Yangtze and the Han rivers, before rattling into
the rugged Wudang Mountains around dawn. This is the far northwestern corner of the province, and in a measure of how remote this region is, Taoist monks and nuns, looking for solitude and distance from

China's populous east, already had settled here more than a thousand years, or five dynasties, ago; with seventy-two temples, thirty-six nunneries, twelve pavilions, and thirty-nine bridges spread across peaks, ravines, and valleys, it is sometimes called the cradle of Taoism.[1] Not far away is the Shennongjia Nature Reserve, home to queer crags and thick forests, said to be home to a Chinese version of Bigfoot, and where *Avatar* was filmed.[2]

Shiyan, where the train arrives midmorning, is not much of a tourist or pilgrimage destination. Oddly, given its isolated location, it is one of the country's largest truck-manufacturing bases, winning it the nickname China's "Auto City" in the press. Dozens of assembly and parts factories are scattered throughout the hilly municipality that runs along the upper lengths of the Han. It is the Chinese version of a factory town—the majority of its close to one million urban residents work at, or have family members employed by, Dongfeng Motors, long China's biggest truck maker, and earlier known by the utilitarian socialist name of Second Auto Works, when it was established here in 1969.

Originally just a tiny mountain village with only ten households, Auto City is the creation of a policy brewed up in one of the country's most autarchic moments. After a bitter split with the Soviet Union that led to Khrushchev ending aid and withdrawing thousands of Russian engineers in 1960, and nervous about the escalation of the U.S. war in Vietnam, China's leaders feared attack by both countries. In response they launched the "Third Front" in 1964, a massive investment and infrastructure program in the mountainous west of which Second Auto was a key element, with the aim of shielding the industrial economy from a war fought along the coast. With well over one-third of all investment in the country going into Third Front projects over the seven years it ran, its proportional scale even dwarfed that of the Develop the West plan, of decades later. "We must pay close attention to Third Front construction: it's a way of buying time against the imperialists, against the revisionists. . . . In Third Front construction, we have begun to build steel, armaments, machinery, chemicals, petroleum and railroad base areas, so that if war breaks out we have nothing to fear," Mao Zedong told his economic planning officials in January 1965.[3]

"Many plants related to No. 2 Auto were constructed around western Hubei, including rubber and tire, paint and bearing factories," wrote political economist Barry Naughton, in 1988. "Further up the Han River, around Ankang and Hanzhong, clusters of machinery plants were built. This period marked the peak of concern over war with the Soviet Union, and many plants were actually dispersed into narrow mountain valleys, and even dug into caves. Around Hanzhong, for example, five large machinery plants were built, but each was built in a separate small mountain valley, so that transport and communications between them was nearly impossible. The No. 2 Auto plant was broken up into more than 20 major workshops that were placed in the mouths of a series of valleys extending 32 kilometers from east to west. The dispersal of productive capacity reflected the military orientation of the program, and was designed to minimize the damage from air attack."[4] Across China, industry was moved into remote and hard-to-reach locations.

But two decades into reform and opening, officials in Beijing decided that its long-protected auto industry, including remote industrial outposts like Shiyan, must shake off its insular past. As China's leaders carried out sweeping reform of the state sector, companies fell into two categories, with separate strategies for each. Under *zhuada fangxiao,* or the "grasp the large, let go of the small" policy, big companies in strategic industries were to be kept and strengthened; smaller ones could be merged or even go bankrupt. Second Auto Works, smaller only than First Auto Works, which had been set up with Soviet financing and expertise in the 1950s in China's Northeast, should be reformed into a globally competitive auto company. To pull that off, China's planners turned to Miao Wei, an ambitious young official whose ancestors came from the coastal county of Changli, Hebei, near Beijing. Changli, population just under half a million, is a hardscrabble farming region that borders on the Bohai Sea. Today a state-owned alcohol company and wealthy entrepreneurs from elsewhere in China are developing Changli as one of the country's top wine-growing regions, and a few faux French châteaus dot the landscape of dry grass and red sandstone hills.[5]

Miao who had been born in nearby Beijing was to leave the arid climes of northern China before he turned twenty. Coming of age during the Cultural Revolution, he had been sent south to work in the Anhui countryside as a sent-down or rusticated youth. But following the end of that tumultuous era, when universities had finally been re-opened across China, he had won admittance to one of the province's prestigious science academies, the Hefei University of Technology. After getting a degree in the internal combustion engine department, he began working in the state-owned automobile industry, where he was known for his open mind and readiness to try out new business ideas. In 1999 he had been appointed general manager of Second Auto in Shiyan with the writ to transform it from an uncompetitive has-been into a national champion for the new reform era. He pledged to resign if he failed in remaking the auto giant, recently renamed Dongfeng—or "East Wind."[6]

"Twenty years ago, this was a very secret place. No foreigners were allowed here," said the forty-eight-year-old Miao, who has a long smile he often uses and is partial to rimless silver spectacles. It's a cloudless afternoon in July of 2003 and we are sitting in his sprawling office, models of three Dongfeng trucks and a Sunny sedan, Dongfeng's bestselling passenger car, on his neatly ordered desk. Behind him is a shelf full of books, including a compilation of the major companies of China and papers authored by Miao on enterprise management. "[In 1969] the Soviet Union and China had a very tense relationship. It was the Cold War and the U.S. wanted to cause troubles. So the government decided to put this facility deep in the mountains. Transportation and infrastructure were not very competitive and the local economy was not so developed, as you can still see today. It may seem ridiculous. But at the time it seemed reasonable: in preparing for war, first, you hide your plants; and second, the plants should be separated physically. This does not make it easy to do business today."[7]

Miao's ambitious plans included shifting Dongfeng away from its longtime emphasis on truck manufacturing, making up about three-quarters of business, to producing more for China's fast-growing passenger-car market. And while new sedans would be manufactured in more accessible locations, like Wuhan and Guangzhou, truckmaking was to stay in Shiyan. Ranging in load size from three tons to thirty tons and usually painted a standard red or blue, Dongfeng's lorries, which had at first been produced for the People's Liberation Army, were now sold to state construction companies across the country. Tucked between green mountains in the city's downtown is one factory, constructed in 1969, the year the company was founded, with a huge banner on its wall proclaiming CARE FOR EVERY WORKER. CARE FOR EVERY TRUCK. A small leafy park with a temple inside the facility grounds is for retired employees' recreation, explains a manager, who wears a big red badge featuring a gold hammer and sickle. Some eighteen hundred blue-smocked factory hands, average age thirty-six, man production lines with equipment dating back to the factory's opening, some thirty-five years earlier. "Up until now, we haven't needed to change the technology. These lines still satisfy all the needs of the market," the friendly manager says. "But going forward we will move along the road to international standards."

To start making better trucks and cars, Dongfeng needed an infusion of capital, technology, and management expertise, and the best way to get that was partnering with foreign automakers. Miao had signed joint ventures between Dongfeng and France's PSA Peugeot Citroën, South Korea's Kia, and, very recently, with the Japanese auto giant Nissan, headed by the then still renowned turnaround manager Carlos Ghosn. This last deal was a particularly bold move. Resentment toward the Japanese for their earlier invasion of China in the run-up to World War II still ran strong, and Miao faced criticism for allowing a company from a former enemy nation to buy into one of the country's top automakers. With an investment of $1.03 billion, Ghosn had secured Nissan a 50 percent share—a first, as all previous foreign partners had been restricted to having at most a 49 percent stake in Chinese auto companies.[8] "Under the leadership of Miao Wei, there is a clear strategy to leverage not only foreign companies' technology, but also their management expertise, to turn around Dongfeng," Zhu Hansong, an investment banker at Goldman Sachs who had worked on the Nissan deal, had told me in his office in Beijing shortly before I left for Hubei.⁹

Miao, under the orders of officials in Beijing, had ensured that many of the joint venture's new vehicles would be under the Dong-feng brand, not just Nissan. He had also gotten the Japanese partners to agree to allowing a strong party organization within the manage-ment of the new company, as well as bringing in the official union to oversee the workers; while a fixture of state enterprises, typically the party and official union were not included in joint ventures at the time. Under Miao's supervision, the staff of Dongfeng, which had 120,000 employees at its peak, had already been whittled almost in half, mainly through offering early retirements. Miao had pushed for most of the remaining employees to be moved to the new joint-venture company, a demand the Japanese had accepted. Like all big state companies of the day, Dongfeng had functioned as far more than just an employer. The company had its own hospital and schools for staff and their children. It had its own newspaper and even a televi-sion station. There was a Dongfeng police force and a company fire department. And all of those divisions did not earn any money and had many staff, most of which had never manned a factory line. "Dongfeng was originally its own small society," Miao explained. But Miao was well aware that one way to lower costs at Dongfeng was by further reducing its workforce. So as part of an agreement with the city, Dongfeng was to hand over all of these social units to the local government, as well as slowly start to bring automation to its labor-intensive factories, plans that had spooked employees.

All staff that remained, many of whom were the second genera-tion to work at Dongfeng, were going to have to sign a new work contract as they were transferred into the Nissan joint-venture enter-prise, which had been formally established only some three weeks earlier. That new agreement would end Dongfeng's role in provid-ing cradle-to-grave benefits, and link salaries and promotion to work performance. "We think this company will have a brighter future. We will introduce advanced technology from Japan, improve man-agement, and improve product qualities," said Guan Suiqing, a thirty-three-year-old quality-control inspector, parroting the official line, when I had met him in the factory. Guan, who had a six-year-old son and a wife who also worked at the company, had started at Dongfeng as a twenty-year-old on the assembly line, and his parents had worked there before him. "On the other hand, we have a lot of pressure on our shoulders. As workers we have to learn lots of new things," Guan said, adding that the "very detailed" contract he had signed just a few weeks earlier gave him a small raise to 1,500 yuan, or $180 a month, but also reduced his welfare protections.[10]

These changes had already sparked a protest of sorts. The day before my interview, some three hundred recently retired former employees had gathered outside the management building and had demanded to see Miao. They were worried their pensions would be cut, now that they were the responsibility of the city, no longer Dong-feng. The general manager had invited a group of ten of the former employees to meet him in his office. He had assured them that the municipality would not suddenly slash their retirement funds. "Their pensions have already been merged into the city pension system and they are worried what this means. They were nervous about their future lives I tried to make them feel better," he explained. When I asked whether their concerns were warranted, Miao did not have a direct answer. "I am not hiding this from you. The people part is the most complicated. We still have more than seventy thousand employees. From the point of view of labor productivity, this is not good. From a joint venture's business perspective, this number is not good. But from a social stability perspective, this may be necessary. If the people are separated from the assets, this could cause social instability," he said. "In a changing society, everyone's interests are affected, are adjusted. That will bring contentment to some and discontent to others."[11]

Contentment or discontent. Equanimity or disaffection. After the reforms of its state enterprises and the layoffs of tens of millions of industrial-factory hands, China was dealing with an entirely new labor issue a decade later. With turnover surging, keeping workers happy or at least not upset was what the factories of Guangdong were struggling with. And if Dongfeng's restructuring had represented the shedding of China's past, the world's largest electronics contract manufacturer Foxconn's attempt to manage its restive workforce of more than one million was symptomatic of the new age. Apple's number-one supplier, which earned half its revenues from the Cupertino company, was reeling from a succession of some two dozen staff suicides in five months at its two sprawling Shenzhen factories, which had blown up into a global scandal. Even as it had rushed to deal with the aftermath in 2011, it would continue to struggle with a larger problem: its labor force, older and now more male than female, was dissatisfied with factory work, got into disputes and sometimes fights on the job, and didn't stay around as long.

Foxconn, like other export-oriented manufacturers, had grown its business on the hard economics of scale, speed, and the ability to drive costs down: its factory complexes in Shenzhen are surrounded by hundreds of suppliers and are less than an hour from the city's port and airport, providing rapid access to key components including batteries, chipsets, Wi-Fi modules, and radio-frequency transceivers. Equally critical to its success had been reliance on huge pools of migrants willing to labor at very low wages. The numbers—seven million migrants in Shenzhen, making up 66 percent of the city's population, most earning a scanty income—were the base on which its manufacturing success was built, and had been ever since it first opened here, in 1988.[12] But now there were signs of fraying.

That strain was apparent on a visit in the spring of 2014 to Foxconn's huge Longhua factory that produced iPads and Hewlett-Packard servers. My tour had been arranged by Louis Woo, a likable former Apple manager partial to turtlenecks, now a top executive and special assistant to the chairman of Foxconn. Woo had earned a bachelor's, master's, and Ph.D., all at Stanford University, and had once taught there as well as at the State University of New York at Albany and the University of Chicago. Woo had been increasingly the company's go-to guy to meet inquisitive reporters and spooked investors, following the string of employee suicides several years earlier. As worker after worker jumped to their death, Foxconn had initially tried to downplay it (the actual number of suicides in a staff numbering close to a million was not high; in fact, the rate appeared to be below the national average in China), but accelerated into full corporate emergency mode sometime after the ninth migrant jumped to his death.

Foxconn had hired Burson-Marsteller, an agency with a founder, Mark Penn, who had deep experience in dealing with corporate crisis communications. While declining to discuss what specific relationship Burson had with Foxconn, Penn used classic public-relations-ese, when interviewed by *AdAge* magazine at the time, saying that "there are certain outreaches we have assisted them with."[13] As part of its charm offensive, Foxconn had allowed reporters, including from *Bloomberg Businessweek,* to tour the factories, speaking to managers and workers. Meanwhile, the brusque company founder and chairman, Terry Gou, prone to infelicitous malaprops, had stopped making as many public appearances, while Woo stepped into the breach. Even so, Gou seemed incapable of avoiding the kinds of comments that could offend. "As human beings are also animals, to manage one million animals gives me a headache," he had said in 2012 at a company party.[14]

The silver-haired Woo had emphasized that he would allow me to see and talk to whomever I wished, and give me as much time as needed to do my interviews. And indeed, he had let me freely wander what the company liked to call a campus, stopping people at will to ask them questions, with no Foxconn staff in tow to monitor or cut short any conversations, unlike the obtrusive, managed visits one got at most factories. Longhua in some ways did seem college-like, with three Olympic-size pools, numerous basketball courts, little shops on its banyan-tree-lined streets selling Haier minifridges and Xiaomi mobile phones for its 135,000 residents. There was even a coffee shop, the Foxconn Café, which served cappuccinos and lemon citron tea. But the benign impression faded quickly when one came to its high-rise dormitories. Several floors above the ground were strung the "suicide nets," flimsy-looking webbing running several feet out from the sides of each building, hung from narrow, rusted bars that jutted out periodically, there in theory to catch any resident who might decide to follow the tragic example of past factory hands and jump from the windows far above.

Foxconn, however belatedly, had responded to the rash of earlier suicides by creating a whole infrastructure of staff and mechanisms to deal with employee angst. They had instituted a twenty-four-hour grievances and emergencies hotline run by counselors, including twenty with certified psychology training, split between here at Longhua and the equally large Guanglan manufacturing facility, in another district of Shenzhen. There were special apps the company provided on everything from how to find the right person in the official union when a work dispute erupted to local entertainment and restaurant offerings. I was ushered into one of the so-called Care Center counseling rooms, the walls painted pink, a little picket fence, with flowers and butterflies painted along their base. (At first glance the design just above the floor appeared to be mold spreading up the wall, in the clammy room.) Well-worn sofas were set around a small round table with a plant with frayed dark green leaves on it. "We can provide face-to-face answers to worker problems here. We want them to feel good when they come. So we have picked warm colors for the decoration," a counselor explained to me earnestly. The staff in the Care Center seemed to have little to do, however, and each worker I spoke to was uncertain as to what its services were for and if they would ever use them.[15]

On a giant soccer field, with crumbling cement bleachers along its length, I found twenty-one-year-old Bai Yaojie, a native of Tianshui, Gansu, where his parents were wheat farmers, napping in the shade. After dropping out of school when he was sixteen, Bai had come to Guangdong for factory work, following in the footsteps of his older brother. He had recently met his girlfriend, who came from Guizhou and worked in a nearby market selling clothes to other migrants. When I asked him what it was like to work at Foxconn, pointing out that his wage of 2,000 yuan ($220) a month must be close to twice what he could earn back in his home province, he laughed. "We can't save money here. We spend it all. My salary isn't that high and living costs in Shenzhen are too high," he said. "Work here on the line is extremely boring and life feels meaningless. And I think all of us workers feel the same." His plan was to return to his hometown with his girlfriend by year-end, get a driver's license, and start driving his own truck, delivering small goods to shops, to earn enough money to live on.[16]

When I later told Woo that many of the employees I spoke to had plans to leave soon, he had confirmed that this was the norm for the factory. Foxconn was struggling to deal with turnover rates that ran as high as 10 percent per month, and it was getting worse, Woo said. "As is true for everyone else, we do have a problem of retaining people. During the first weeks you have the phenomenon of new employees saying, 'Wow, I didn't realize that working in manufacturing required me to wake up at six thirty in the morning to come in at 7:00 A.M.,'" Woo had told me in his measured and convincing professorial tone. "And it's not how much you pay them. It's not the working environment. Instead it has to do with nature of the work. But unfortunately today, no matter how hard we try, can't make a manufacturing job glamorous, or effort-free, as the new generation of workers would like it to be."[17]

That reality was behind the company's recent announcement of plans to add as many as a million robots over the next few years to its mainland factories. "Terry has been focusing on automation, robotics. The employees—and this is even more so true of the younger generation of today—don't want to continue to do work that is very mundane, that requires a lot of repetition and is boring. So our plan is to take those jobs away from them and give those to automation," he said. (Woo always referred to his boss by just his first name, which I couldn't help thinking was a deliberate strategy to humanize Gou, known for being an imperious manager.) "It is already happening in all our facilities. One of these days I want to show you the automation we already have. You go into a pitch-black factory—machines don't need lights!—and our products are being pumped out. It is very environmentally friendly," he said, beaming at me. Later as I scanned the news for reports of progress on Foxconn's automation, some disturbing news about the company popped up. Less than six months after my visit, another worker, a twenty-four-year old named Xu Lizhi, had jumped to his death, and, unusually, had left behind him a body of poems he had written about his time at Foxconn. One he had published earlier in the year had poignantly described a suicide:

A screw fell to the ground
In this dark night of overtime
Plunging vertically, lightly clinking
It won't attract anyone's attention
Just like last time
On a night like this
When someone plunged to the ground[18]

While factory managers started adding robots and subtracting workers, policymakers in Beijing were watching what was happening in the country's manufacturing heartland, with growing concern. Even as shortages became more prevalent, so did demonstrations, with the massive protests in the Yue Yuen's Gaobu shoe factories happening at the same time I had visited Foxconn in Shenzhen. China's cadres knew that the economic success of the last few decades had been built on producing cheap goods that global consumers were eager to buy. China's then huge and growing labor force had provided what economists call a "demographic dividend," contributing about 0.9 percent to annual economic growth, according to World Bank estimates. Now that dividend was gone and China faced the formidable challenge of rising wages squeezing company profits and damaging economic productivity. The country had reached the Lewis turning point—named for Sir Arthur Lewis, the late Nobel laureate—which comes after a labor force begins to shrink as fewer and fewer migrants come from the countryside. Failure to overcome this latest challenge could snare China in the middle-income trap, no longer competitive in low-end industries but also unable to move to a higher-value-added economy. Liu He, a long-faced, gray-haired economist and fluent English speaker, who had earned a master's degree in public administration at Harvard University's Kennedy School, and whose father's family—like Miao Wei's—also came from Changli, was tasked with dealing with this problem. He had studied how industrial economies face challenges over time and had even written a book on the topic. And he was in a position to do something about it: Liu had recently become Xi Jinping's perhaps most trusted economics adviser.

Liu's favored position was no surprise for those who knew the cloistered world of Beijing party politics. Liu and Xi's relationship extended back to their youth, when the two went to neighboring elite schools in Beijing for China's red royalty. Now the timing was propitious. Liu was eager to play a larger role in policy making, while Xi wanted to burnish his image beyond just wielding raw political power. Xi had somewhat surprisingly seized upon what he called "supply-side structural reform" as the centerpiece of his economic contribution—but of a different variety from Republican America's version, instead focusing on closing "zombie" companies and sending subsidies to favored industries. But with little knowledge of even basic economics, Xi needed an expert to flesh out and support his chosen theory, and Liu was more than ready to do that. Over the course of 2016, several anonymous commentaries touting Xi's theory appeared in the party flagship *People's Daily,* all apparently penned by Liu, helping the theory become a common topic of seminars and getting it positive attention in the rest of the state media.[19]

Looking at the experience of other countries, Liu and his fellow economists seized upon Japan as an example for the economic challenge China was now starting to confront. This was a change from earlier years, when Chinese had looked to Japan as an unqualified technological success. Now they saw China's island neighbor as once having dominated the world's manufacturing, before rising labor costs and an aging workforce had lost it that mantle. Productivity had stalled and then stagnated, hitting economic growth. They feared that China now ran the risk of losing its industrial preeminence, as factories departed for countries with cheaper, younger workers. Indeed, China itself had played a central role in the so-called hollowing out of Japanese industry; they did not want to see that now happen to them, too. To avoid that fate, China must push the development of robotics and do so faster than even Japan had. "Xi and his advisers think that that sooner or later, we could become another Japan. And the failure of Japan is it failed to act quickly enough. Cheaper labor will not exist anymore [in China], so we will have to replace workers with robots," Wang Kan, the labor expert at the China Institute of Industrial Relations, explained to me. Earlier in the summer, Wang had joined a small group of economists and labor experts at a meeting with Liu. "In the short-term, China will face lots of shocks. But after twenty years, there will be fewer and fewer young people. Industrial upgrading with robots [aims to] overcome that. When we met with him, Dr. Liu He expressed his view that automation will make it possible for China to conquer the future," Wang said.[20]

The leadership's fears of losing manufacturing preeminence had combined with long-held ambitions to become a global technological power in a new industrial policy announced in 2015, called Made in China 2025. With a heavy focus on robotics and automation, and inspired by Germany's "industry 4.0" strategy, the new policy would allow China to transform from "a manufacturing giant into a world manufacturing power" over its ten-year life span.[21] And in an interesting turn of fate, Miao Wei, in his new role as head of the Ministry of Industry and Information Technology, was charged with carrying it out. The youth who had once labored in the Anhui countryside, then later earned his stripes dealing with excess industrial workers, at the height of state enterprise reforms at the turn of the century, would now be charged with overseeing the country's next big labor downsizing and the biggest change ever to come to its manufacturing sector: the end of its reliance on a migrant workforce and its replacement with robots.

At its unveiling in Beijing by Premier Li Keqiang in May, attended by Miao, the ambitious dimensions of the plan were revealed. China's leaders aimed to transition their country away from its previous four-decade-old "factory to the world" role of producing low-value-added products, like toys, shoes, and simple electronics, that had been built on low wages and lax environmental standards. The manufacturing economy would move to a much more capital-intensive model, where companies would be able to make their own high-end technology and sell it competitively around the world. "Nine tasks have been identified as priorities: improving manufacturing innovation, integrating information technology and industry, strengthening the industrial base, fostering Chinese brands, enforcing green manufacturing, promoting breakthroughs in 10 key sectors, advancing restructuring of the manufacturing sector, promoting service-oriented manufacturing and manufacturing-related service industries, and internationalizing manufacturing," the official Xinhua News Agency intoned. Over the ten years ending in 2025, ten sectors, namely information technology, aerospace, high-tech ships, railway equipment, new-energy vehicles, power equipment, new materials, biomedicine and medical devices, agricultural machinery, and, critically, numerical-control tools and robotics, were to be become world-class industries. The government would use preferential policies to encourage their development, including tax breaks, subsidies, loans and bonds, and government procurement. Several billion dollars would be earmarked from the national and provincial budgets to set up "manufacturing innovation centers" across China. As Miao said at the time, by 2025 "China will basically realize industrialization nearly equal to the manufacturing abilities of Germany and Japan at their early stages of industrialization."[22]

As was true with many of China's new economic policies, the origins of Made in China hearkened back to Guangdong some years earlier. The province's export economy had been suffering under rising labor costs for almost five years when the global financial crisis hit in late 2008, devastating its already shaky economy. As consumers in the U.S. and Europe slowed their buying of its cheap toys and textiles, thousands of already-struggling factories shut down, and some twenty million migrants lost their jobs. That was a wake-up call for its rising-star party secretary, fifty-three-year-old Wang Yang, then known as a proponent of economic reform. Under a policy colorfully called "emptying the cage and changing the bird," Wang and his deputies had already been encouraging factories to move away from labor- and energy-intensive, polluting export industries to newer and cleaner ones, including software, new energy, and biotech. Tax breaks were used to encourage the new industries while lower-margin industries were squeezed with tighter labor and environmental regulations. While the efforts slowed temporarily at the height of the downturn, its officials emerged from the crisis even more certain of the need to upgrade the economy. "What Guangdong is facing, all of China is facing," Wang Yiyang, vice-director of Guangdong's development research center, said in an interview with *Bloomberg Businessweek* in 2009. "We have to find new sources of competitiveness."[23]

Later that year, Beijing celebrated the sixtieth anniversary of the founding of the People's Republic of China on October 1 with a massive military parade through Tiananmen Square. Along with the fighter jets and goose-stepping soldiers, China showed a less bellicose but equally important side of its ambitions. Among thirty-four floats that rolled through the square was one with men dressed in blue-and-yellow overalls and yellow safety helmets, and women in the gray cloth pants and white cloth hats worn in textile factories, "showing the industrial workers' vibrant and majestic appearance," as a government website described it at the time.[24] While that was squarely a nod to the past, other floats showed China's future technological ambitions. One had a replica of a bullet train and a passenger jet to depict China's aspirations in transportation. Another float featured oil rigs, but also highlighted green energy, and was studded with windmills and flanked by hundreds of red-helmeted workers, each carrying a solar panel. And a third had twenty of China's top scientists and engineers standing above a giant slanted keyboard that made up the float's side. Above them were a ten-foot-high microscope, giant test tubes filled with blue liquid, and a white telescope. In huge, red, three-dimensional characters on the float's front was written INDIGENOUS INNOVATION, the then-popular slogan promoting domestically developed technology. Encouraging homegrown technology would also become a key feature of the Made in China 2025 policy some six years later, with explicit market-share targets for the new products, including Chinese-made robots.[25]

To see Made in China 2025 firsthand, Guangdong is also the place to go. Not only is it home to thousands of manufacturers turning to automation as a means for survival, but it also is a showcase for the government's sweeping policy of upgrading, and home to what is now one of the country's biggest robot producers. As the province where labor shortages among its 9.3 million manufacturing workers first emerged, its cities have adopted their own mini-versions of Made in China, providing subsidies to factories that buy robots. Meanwhile, Guangzhou, as the provincial capital, has been anointed as a model

Roadside restaurant for migrant workers outside Shiqing Hardware Machinery
Equipment Factory, Dongguan. *Greg Girard, 2000*

Mo Wenzhi, cook at the Shiqing Machinery Factory. *Greg Girard, 2000*

Mo Rubo, welder at the Shiqing Machinery Factory. *Greg Girard, 2000*

Mo Rubo and girlfriend in factory dormitory. *Greg Girard, 2000*

Nike supplier factory in Guangdong. *Greg Girard, 2000*

Mo Meiquan and Mo Yukai in rice fields in Binghuacun. *Greg Girard, 2000*

Elderly women and children outside traditional Buyi houses in Binghuacun. *Greg Girard, 2000*

Guangzhou auto factory workers going off shift. *Dexter Roberts, 2017*

Labor activist Wu Guijun (right) in Shenzhen restaurant. *Dexter Roberts, 2017*

Labor activist Zhang Zhiru in alley outside office in Shenzhen. *Dexter Roberts, 2014*

Elderly farmer Dong Xiangzhu (left) in courtyard of home in "empty nest" village of Shangxule, Hebei. *Dexter Roberts, 2016*

Grandfather and granddaughter, Binghuacun. *Dexter Roberts, 2017*

Mo Ruchun (right) buying fish from river, Binghuacun. *Dexter Roberts, 2017*

Slaughtering a pig for lunar new year, Binghuacun. *Dexter Roberts, 2017*

Retired party chief Mo Wenke (right) and Mo Ruchun (stirring pot, far right) at funeral banquet, Binghuacun. *Dexter Roberts, 2018*

Mo Bochun, village party secretary (left), discussing plans to transform Binghuacun into tourism destination. *Gráinne Quinlan, 2016*

Mo Wangqing, migrant returnee who has started a fish farm in Binghuacun. *Gráinne Quinlan, 2016*

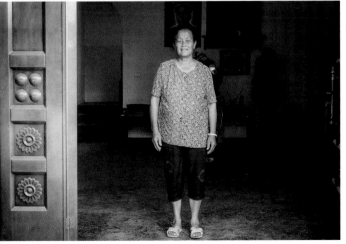

Mo Rubo's mother standing at the door of the house Rubo has built for her, Binghuacun. *Gráinne Quinlan, 2016*

Elderly lady passes high rise under construction in Libo. *Dexter Roberts, 2018*

Mo Ruchun and Mo Rubo with author, Binghuacun. *Dexter Roberts, 2018*

for the ambitious new policy, and its most successful companies have been showered with low-interest loans and subsidies, as they branch into favored sectors, including new-energy vehicles and drones.

China still lags far behind many other countries in robot "adoption," as manufacturing consultants like to call it. Factories long accustomed to relying on cheap labor have been slow to invest in expensive automation machinery. That has been true in spite of the ambitions of Chinese leaders going back decades. When Deng Xiaoping visited Japan in late 1978, at the beginning of China's economic reforms, he had been astonished at the sophistication of its industry. "We must admit our deficiencies," Deng told his Japanese hosts. "We are a backward country and we need to learn from Japan." When he visited a Nissan plant near Tokyo that had just started using robots, he was shocked to hear how many cars it could produce per worker, contrasting it with China's labor-intensive auto industry. "Now I understand what modernization is," he said.[26] By 2017, China's factories still only had 97 robots per 10,000 workers, tiny compared to the 308 per 10,000 in Japan, 322 per 10,000 in Germany, and 710 per 10,000 in South Korea, the country with the highest rate of automation in the world. But China is moving quickly to catch up. Chinese factories bought almost 138,000 robots that year, up 59 percent over 2016, accounting for more than a third of all sold globally.[27]

And the country's factories have little choice. After a decade in which manufacturing wages doubled, China's workers are no longer cheap. By 2015, average wages of 4,126 yuan a month had matched those in Brazil and were already much higher than in Mexico, Thailand, Malaysia, Vietnam, and India. In Guangdong, three out of ten migrants quit their jobs every year, and for employees under twenty-eight years old, the rate is 37 percent.[28] While some manufacturers have moved their operations to lower-wage countries in Southeast Asia, for example, others simply shut down. Binghuacun's Mo Rubo had chosen the latter option for a tiny factory with four workers he had opened in Guangzhou to make his company's sport clothing. "It became too difficult to manage. So I got rid of the factory after a few years," he explained. But for many larger-scale operations, upgrading has been the natural choice. A robot costing 200,000 yuan ($29,000) that replaces three people could pay for itself in twenty-two months in inland China, and in just over a year on the higher-wage coast.[29] A year after Rubo closed his factory, about one in every ten manufacturers in Guangdong was using robots, and 44 percent had installed automation equipment. That, of course, meant job cuts; Guangdong manufacturing employment fell by 6.6 percent that year, with more than one-half of factories reducing their staff.

Government-offered preferential policies have accelerated the rush to add robots, including many that do simple tasks like painting, welding, and sanding. Guangdong Province announced in 2015 that it would provide 943 billion yuan ($137 billion) in subsidies to about two thousand local companies, including both robot makers and those making autos, home appliances, and construction materials, that wanted to automate their plants. As its migrant population shrank, Dongguan had announced its own program, called "Robots Replacing Humans," with 200 million yuan earmarked for companies that planned to upgrade, covering about 10 to 15 percent of the cost of new robots. Tax exemptions and refunds and low-interest loans were also on offer for companies. And what was happening in Guangdong was being repeated in manufacturing regions across the country. Coastal provinces including Zhejiang now offer incentives to encourage automation, as does inland Hubei, a thousand kilometers due north of the Pearl River Delta, home to Dongfeng, and where Miao Wei spent most of his career before moving to Beijing in 2008.

Some 450 kilometers down the Han River from Shiyan, back in the flatness of the Jianghan Plain of Hubei, is Hanchuan, an industrial town named for the waterway that runs through it. Thirty kilometers farther south is Wuhan, where Miao Wei served as party secretary after leaving Dongfeng. A haze hangs over the region when I visit in June of 2017, issuing from the many factories that pock Hanchuan and produce everything from glass and aluminum frames for buildings and car windows to textiles and packaging materials. Like Guangdong, Hubei is facing the double whammy of rising wages and high turnover among its 3.4 million industrial workers, pushing firms toward upgrading; while 6 percent of factories have already added robots, 46 percent are using automation equipment like numerically controlled machine tools for drilling, milling, and shaping metal—even more than in Guangdong—and close to half of manufacturing firms have recently cut staff, with their workforce dropping 3.3 percent a year.[30]

When sixty-six-year-old Hu Sr. opened a small factory to produce baby strollers and wheels, back in 1984, finding enough workers and paying them was something he never worried about. His thirty-four-year-old son, Hu Chengpeng, who recalls playing in the facility as a child and who took over as CEO five years ago, says ensuring that the factory's lines are fully staffed is the biggest challenge. Turnover among the 420 migrants employed in the factory's dark and gritty workshops is running at 20 percent, while wages have been growing by double digits every year. "Labor costs are getting just too high," Chengpeng says. That's behind his recent decision to buy forty new robots, each costing 40,000 yuan ($5,850), the cost of which was covered in part by an interest-free loan from the city's finance department. The new machines replaced dozens of staff who worked cutting plastic molding. "We are implementing our automation strategy right now," his father says proudly, adding that eventually the factory will use a quarter fewer people, and won't have to reduce production—now at eighty thousand strollers a year.[31]

While smaller private companies like that owned by the Hu family have been able to tap into local government funds to modernize production, far more money is available for large-scale state-owned firms, those that Xi Jinping has said must become "stronger and bigger." Back south in Guangzhou, municipal authorities have created four 10-billion-yuan ($1.5 billion) funds and are offering tax exemptions, one-time subsidies, and even low-cost or free land to support firms diversifying into the new industries that fall under the Made in China 2025 plan. Guangzhou Automobile Group Co. (GAC), China's sixth-largest passenger-vehicle and SUV maker—it was founded in 1955, and now partners with Fiat, Honda, Isuzu, and Toyota in making cars—has long benefited from the city's preferential policies. Now that the use of more robots in factories and the production of new-energy vehicles are national priorities, GAC is focusing on both as key strategies and getting lots of support, says forty-eight-year-old president Feng Xingya in an interview in the company's showroom in the city's business district of Zhujiang New Town.

The land for a vast new-energy-vehicle factory facility that will be largely automated and is set to start production in 2019 south of the city was provided for free by the Guangzhou municipality, the president says. Feng's company, which gained international attention for its uniquely named brand the Trumpchi, is also making use of low-interest loans and tax-reduction policies. "This is the most supportive environment we have ever experienced," he says. If production continues to rise with the launch of new-energy vehicles—plans call for producing two hundred thousand electric vehicles a year by 2020[32]—then GAC's seventy-six thousand employees may not need to be reduced, he explains. But Feng plans to add even more of the spiderlike orange German-made KUKA robots to his assembly lines, the brand that dominates auto factories worldwide. "There are three key reasons. The number-one reason is quality. Robots don't make mistakes. Number two is rising [wage] costs. Third is delivery periods. When you use machines you can save time. No worker can work for twenty-four hours," he explains.[33]

But policymakers don't just want more productive factories; they want them using far more China-made robots. One year before Made in China 2025 was launched, Xi Jinping had already called for a "robot revolution," saying that robots will be the "crown jewels of manufacturing." In 2017, officials set a target of growing the share of domestically produced industrial robots from only around a quarter now to 70 percent by 2025. The biggest challenge: companies that can design and make the three core components of servomotors, drivers, and control panels; today many of China's estimated eight hundred producers of robots buy those from overseas makers like Fanuc and Siemens, then slap metal around them, says Chai Yueting, director of the National Engineering Laboratory for Electronic Commerce Technologies at Tsinghua University. "China has lots of robot companies. But their technology often is from the Japan or U.S.," says Chai. "China's own specific robot technology is still very limited."[34]

Guangdong Province, and in particular the Shunde district of Foshan, which sits on the western bank of the Pearl River just south of the provincial capital, has emerged as the center for China's efforts. The district, long known for its scrappy electronics firms, is now home to fast-growing robot makers, big and small. E-Deodar is a manufacturer of fifteen-thousand-dollar robots, a third cheaper than the foreign brands, which are used in everything from furniture to electronics factories in the Pearl River Delta. On the same floor as its small forty-robot-a-month manufacturing line is the laid-back management office, with a coffee shop where a human-looking robot serves coffee to its youthful employees. "People ask me, how long can you make robots? I say, it's simple, we will make robots until there's no more people in factories," explained Max Chu, the general manager, who sports short-cropped hair and a casual sweater vest when we meet in late 2017.[35]

Just a twenty-minute drive away is Midea Group, the world's largest appliance maker, which has become China's best hope for a globally competitive robotic champion. Once recognized mainly for its cheap air-conditioning units and water-dispenser machines, the company dramatically changed its business when, in 2016, it bought 95 percent of KUKA AG, a 120-plus-year-old automotive robotics maker based in Augsburg, Germany, for $4 billion. The acquisition fit nicely with Midea's own plans to continue to automate its own couple of dozen factories and slash its workforce, already reduced by half from two hundred thousand in 2011 to about a hundred thousand. But, equally important, the KUKA purchase is helping Midea dominate the fast-growing China automation market, selling to other companies. "We believe there will be huge and explosive growth in the robotics and automation sector in China in the next few years, but yet we are only at the beginning," chairman Fang Hongbo told Bloomberg in an interview in the gleaming skyscraper that houses company headquarters.[36] Midea aimed to almost double the revenues earned from its automation business to 20 percent by 2020, according to the fifty-year-old chairman, who has worked at Midea for twenty-five years.[37] In the spring, his company started building an 800,000-square-meter smart-manufacturing industrial park nearby

that would focus on building robots with KUKA, for "smart manufacturing," logistics, health care, and homes, with an investment of 10
billion yuan ($1.46 billion).[38]

The deal to buy the European company had been a controversial
one, with German politicians worried about losing technology to
Chinese competition and, in a perhaps ironic twist, fearful that the
Augsburg-based robot-making factory workers might be laid off. As
part of the agreement, Midea agreed to maintain KUKA's head count,
and not close its plants in Germany or delist its shares or move its
headquarters, until the end of 2023. Andy Gu, Midea's deputy CEO,
who had gotten a Ph.D. in demography from Cornell University, had
flown repeatedly to Germany to deal with concerned politicians and
corporate leaders. Now, shortly after the sale closed in early 2017, Gu
and KUKA's German CEO, Till Reuter, a bespectacled former investment banker who had worked for Morgan Stanley, Deutsche Bank,
and Lehman Brothers, were both in Shanghai for an electronic-
appliances fair. Sitting in a plush meeting room at the Pudong
Shangri-La Hotel, which looks over the Huangpu River at the historic Bund, the executives played up the synergies of the agreement.
KUKA, which dominates automation for the automotive industry
and was already one of the three top robot brands globally, would be
able to leverage Midea's huge sales and distribution network to grab
new business in China, including building service robots to meet the
health-care needs of the rapidly aging population, according to Gu.
"We are going to expand into more industries to be more diversified.
Midea will help us to open the doors," said Reuter. But the Chinese
manager had finished on a less synergetic note. "KUKA has a reputation for reliability, but as you know, as a German company, they are
not really well known for low-cost products," Gu had told me. "We
need to really work very hard to figure out how we can really reduce
these costs."[39]

Less than two years later, in November of 2018, Midea had ordered
the German CEO to resign. "A person familiar with his exit said Mr. Reuter had a different strategy in China than Andy Gu, chairman of the
group and vice-president at Midea," and also said that "Mr. Reuter had

no desire to leave early," the *Financial Times* reported at the time.[40] The surprise departure sparked a new eruption of concern in Germany about China Inc.'s plans for its technology crown jewels. Other recent deals that had also raised disquiet included Chinese automaker Geely's purchase of DaimlerChrysler in February of 2018. Germany's domestic intelligence agency had recently released a report warning of the Chinese government using its state companies to undermine the European country's economy and security. "We certainly do have to be concerned with this if we have the impression that behind the potential buyer lies a foreign state with interests that go far beyond the acquisitions," Hans-Georg Maassen, then Germany's top spy, told reporters in Berlin.[41]

Meanwhile, as a trade war between the U.S. and China heated up, the Trump administration singled out Made in China 2025 as a blatant example of Chinese protectionism and industrial policy that undermined U.S. industry. A second concern was that China's massive state-supported subsidies programs could overshoot, leading to supply gluts in industries globally, as had happened earlier with solar panels and steel. With at least 98 billion yuan of investments in electric-car factories announced, for example, China's capacity in the new-energy vehicles had already reached 2.9 million units by 2017—six times the number sold in the country the previous year, data by Bloomberg showed. "The worry that people have is China Inc. on steroids is going to kill profits, not only for companies but for industries as a whole," said Scott Kennedy, director of the Project on Chinese Business and Political Economy at the Center for Strategic and International Studies in Washington.[42] In response, Chinese officials had begun to downplay the importance of its industrial policy, with state media instructed to stop mentioning it.[43] "China got rid of their China '25' because I found it very insulting," President Donald Trump told reporters in November of 2018. "I said, China '25 is very insulting, because China '25 means, in 2025, they're going to take over, economically, the world. I said, 'That's not happening.'"[44]

Few serious observers believed that Xi had any intention of backing off from national ambitions to build a high-tech economy, however.

While in public statements officials may minimize the importance of these plans, the reality is that the aspirations to upgrade China's system go back decades, and indeed it would be surprising if any country with means didn't have such goals. Indeed, the speed at which the program continues has some officials and economists worrying that overly rapid factory automation could start to cause labor problems. A World Bank report has predicted that more than three-quarters of all jobs in China could be threatened by 2030 because of automation.[45] China is so large that even while one region might still be facing worker shortages, other parts could easily see high unemployment. And even as the Chinese workforce shrinks, it is still huge—close to one billion sixteen-to-sixty-five-year-old people in the working age population. These were the realities that began to cause anxiety among the robot skeptics. Even China's premier had voiced a note of caution: "Will the extensive application of artificial intelligence and robots deprive people of their jobs? This is indeed a question, and it is already happening in some industries," Li Keqiang said in a speech in 2017 to the World Economic Forum in Dalian.[46]

One of China's top labor economists, Cai Fang, longtime head of the Institute of Population and Labor Economics in the Chinese Academy of Social Sciences, had been warning of the economic risks of labor shortages for the last decade. It was Cai who first wrote about the Lewis turning point, introducing the concept to a generation of Chinese economists and officials. But now the soft-spoken Beijing native was concerned that too-rapid automation might lead to unemployment. "We must cap the speed and restrict the direction of robotics' development to avoid any bad effects on human beings," said Cai, now serving as vice president at the academy, in an interview with the *South China Morning Post*. "Demographically, China is in two races against time," Cai said. Indeed, more robots were necessary to boost productivity as the workforce continued to decline. But at the same time, China must "figure out in what aspects human beings are better than robots—emotional quotient, judgment or creative thinking? Then we can make a plan to compensate the weakest group of people—workers replaced by robots and those who will never get another job."[47] But even as Cai called for steps to ameliorate the adverse effects of automation on migrants, most company managers and officials seemed little concerned. When I had asked Midea's and Guangzhou Auto's CEOs what steps their companies were taking to prepare employees for a future world of "intelligent manufacturing," both responded with general comments about training for the new jobs to be generated, running and repairing the robots. But when asked what would happen to the majority who would likely lose their jobs they seemed nonplussed. How was that their responsibility?

Later that evening I met an old friend, Dee Lee, who, after studying in England, now ran his own small labor consultancy in Guangzhou. Dee, who combined a love of Scotch and wine with vegetarianism and who played a serious game of squash, had chosen one of the city's cool cocktail bars to meet at. POP was located on the second floor of a slightly run-down department store above a McDonald's, but stepping through its door was to enter the world of hip young and monied urban white-collar China, its customers mainly working for sharing-economy internet start-ups or blockchain technology plays. The room had a stylishly unfinished look, with exposed ventilation pipes on the ceiling, and rough cement walls; it was dimly lit but with yellow light shining in upside-down triangles from the underside of the polished bar, illuminating the leather-topped stools along its length. On the wall behind the bottles of high-end whiskey and vodka, a video of a pulsating blob constantly forming new shapes in new colors was being projected, looking like the liberated contents of a lava lamp, perhaps after someone had taken some LSD.

Were workers in Guangdong starting to protest or push back against the Robots Replacing Humans policies? I asked him. What signs was he seeing that the rush to automate was causing new labor problems? Dee's company ran staff grievance hotlines in some of the larger factories of the Pearl River Delta, paid for by the big international brands who sourced from them. His company had run one for Adidas's supplier Yue Yuen, including when its factories in Gaobu had erupted with tens of thousands protesting. Dee looked at me with an odd little smile that seemed to say I really didn't get it at all. "Dexter," he said in the Oxbridge-accented English he had picked up from his years in the United Kingdom, taking a sip of his single-malt whiskey. "You have to remember something. These workers don't want to be here. They don't want these jobs. The last thing a worker really wants to be is a factory worker."[48]

6

Going Home

Returning geese revitalize Guizhou.

—PARTY SLOGAN ENCOURAGING MIGRANT
WORKERS TO RETURN TO THEIR HOMETOWNS

Poor and backward isn't honorable
Eating well and being lazy is even more disgraceful
Returning to the village and working is much more
    advantageous
Reduce tiredness and avoid rushing about
Only the industrious aren't impoverished
If you want to escape poverty, then act vigorously.

—BANNER ON A GUIZHOU RURAL CONSTRUCTION SITE

By the summer of 2016, the normally sleepy Binghuacun had an expectant air. As manufacturing costs relentlessly went up along the coast and factories shut or moved abroad, a handful of migrants had recently come back to the village, and there was talk that more would soon return. Their intention this time was to stay. They would start their own small businesses in their hometown, serving a hoped-for booming local tourism industry, perhaps finally breaking the village's multiyear slide into obsolescence. The elderly who sat on their porch steps, men and women alike smoking brass pipes tamped with local tobacco or cheap cigarettes, almost had a jaunty air. They talked about whose children had plans to return and whether they would start a guesthouse or perhaps a fish farm. And they gossiped about which households were slated to get funding to restore their traditional wooden houses, and how they might spend that windfall, compliments of a special fund arranged by the prefectural government in Libo.

In the new section of Binghuacun, a long walkway with benches down its length had been built. With a stretch of Chinese arched roof crowned at its midpoint with a cement reproduction of a bull skull with horns—supposed to be an ethnic Buyi touch—the walkway was near a new parking lot, no doubt built in expectation of eventual tourists but now usually empty. While parts of the road running to the village had been paved, it was still mainly one lane, but it would be widened soon, the villagers said. With Guizhou's dramatic mountains, dozens of ethnic minorities with their own dress and customs, and spicy local cuisine, planning officials in Beijing had chosen the province as a favored travel destination for the fast-growing rural-travel industry; the Qiannan Buyi and Miao Autonomous Prefecture, home to Libo and Binghuacun, had also been singled out for more development, and UNESCO, the United Nations organization, had included it as part of its South China Karst designated World Heritage site, a decade earlier. Xiaoqikong—literally, "small seven openings," a stone bridge with luxuriant tufts of ferns growing from its arches in a dense forest just south of Libo—had been built in 1835, part of a key trading route between Guizhou and Guangxi provinces. Sitting over turquoise waters, it had become a top draw for Chinese tourists.

When people had first come to live in Binghuacun over five hundred years earlier, they had chosen the location carefully. The small hill tangled with bamboo groves, Chinese yew, and gingko trees that sat at a turn in the green waters of the Jialiang River was shaped in what was a rough approximation of a dragon's head and that is what the settlers had anointed it. Looking from the opposite bank, one could see the creature's face, if one squinted one's eyes. On the far side of the valley of gently terraced rice fields was a second small mountain range—the dragon's spiky back, the villagers had explained to me. It all made for very good feng shui—a mountain behind, trees tumbling down its sides; water, the river, in front, before it looped off across the fields. And on the mountain was the auspicious place to build their homes. That special topography had saved Binghuacun from the crass "upgrading" that had destroyed so many Chinese villages. When locals had become better off, mainly on the remittances sent home from migrants, and it came time to build larger farmhouses—invariably ugly, several-story boxlike cement structures—the flat high bank across the river that had always been empty of residences was the natural place to choose. So rather than Binghuacun being torn down and redeveloped, the empty riverbank had become the site of the characterless new town built in the mid-2000s, some years after my first visit. That left the nearly intact, if crumbling, traditional Buyi village built above the river untouched. Many of the two-frame wooden farmhouses were centuries old, with ancient paths of paving stones winding up the hill among them. Because so much of the village was still there, Binghuacun had won special designation as a AAA historic tourist spot worthy of preservation, the decision made by cadres in Libo. The villagers had been told to stop cultivating corn and peppers in the surrounding mountains, and plant them once again with trees, returning them to something close to their original state. Tossing lit firecrackers into the river— the crude and popular form of fishing where explosions momentarily stunned the fish, which helpfully floated to the surface to be scooped up in nets—had been banned, too. The rice paddies could stay, as they had been deemed scenic and tourist-friendly. Above all, villagers could not make additions or improvements to the old houses, a policy that had caused grumbling among some who wished to update them with modern amenities like flush toilets. Those were the trade-offs that would help give Binghuacun an edge in the province-wide competition for tourists, or so the villagers hoped.

All told, the plan was to radically transform Binghuacun's future. The centuries-old reliance on subsistence farming was to end in favor of an economy built on a "modern service industry," the classification now officially granted to Guizhou's travel business, or what was called within the province "mountain tourism." Rather than Binghuacun being home to only elderly villagers and toddlers, the "empty nest" phenomenon plaguing rural China, more and more migrants would return and become entrepreneurs, starting small businesses to serve the new industry. They would open bed-and-breakfasts in the traditional houses, run river-rafting and mountain-biking operations in the rivers and hills, and raise "green" ducks, eels, pigs, and mountain rabbits, all to cater to the wealthy urbanites who would come seeking escape from their busy lives. That there was virtually no heavy industry to speak of in this part of Guizhou (and, indeed, in much of the province), and so the water was clean and the air was free of the smog that torments much of China, would be a further draw, luring vacationing city folks with cash to spend. And as was the case in villages across the country, the transition on the ground was to be managed by the local party organization, in Binghuacun run by Mo Bochun, a forty-five-year-old local who had already been in the job for nine years when I met him. It was his task not only to convince villagers that the radical changes would be good for everyone, but also to host visitors from afar, including foreign journalists. (For him and many other Chinese officials and enterprise heads, being mentioned in a business publication was seen simply as marketing, getting the word out to potential investors or partners.)

Among Binghuacun's 968 residents, twenty-five were party members—that was how the organization chief chose to begin his introduction on one hot July afternoon. While it seemed an odd start, I reminded myself that managing those couple of dozen members was his responsibility and that this group was no doubt supposed to be the vanguard, who through their example and counsel would demonstrate to the nonbelievers why they should get on board with the changes ahead. We were sitting in a small room in the party's organization department, me facing Bochun across a long table. His deputy had joined him while several returnee villagers had been assembled to explain to the foreigner why they had decided to give up their lives as migrants. At the head of the room, hung on the wall at a height to give them prominence, was a poster showing the pantheon of Communist leaders: Marx, Engels, Lenin, Stalin, Mao, and Deng Xiaoping; below them were images of Xi Jinping and his two predecessors, Jiang

Zemin and Hu Jintao, all looking bemusedly down upon us. Meanwhile, Bochun seemed distracted by more immediate concerns: while his daughter was already in college in Changsha, Hunan, the neighboring province, his son had just taken his college exam, the *gaokao*, in Libo. "We don't even know his test results yet. If he did well, he can get into a good college. Otherwise, we don't know where he will go," he said with a worried smile breaking across his face.[1]

Meanwhile, for most families in Binghuacun, college, good or bad, was not a concern—just finishing high school was an accomplishment for their children. Instead, they worried whether the planned transformation of the village would succeed. This was a particularly important question for one recent returnee, thirty-six-year-old Mo Wangqing. After coming back a year earlier, the distant cousin of Rubo's had invested 500,000 yuan, his entire savings plus some borrowed money, into a fish farm of 80 *mu* (13 acres). (His WeChat photo showed him beaming as he held up a twenty-four-inch-long silvery fish with two hands.) After leaving Binghuacun when he was eighteen, Wangqing had worked in electronics factories in Fujian Province and in the provincial capital Guangzhou, and had run a small clothing shop, also in Guangdong's capital, before getting his last job, in a wall-paneling facility, in the city of Guigang, a lumber-industry town in the neighboring province of Guangxi, which sat just south of Libo. That was also where Wenzhi, the cook I had met in Dongguan many years before, reportedly now was a manager, also in a wood-processing factory. I was not able to overlap with him on my various visits to Binghuacun. Similarly, despite repeated attempts and occasionally speaking with her father, who still lived in Binghuacun, I was unable to meet Meiquan again. As was the tradition in China, after she married her husband she was formally part of his family rather than the one she was born to. She had left factory work and was now living with her husband and their son in a village not far from Binghuacun, she told me via text. But she was too busy with her family to meet.

"I was there for a year and eventually became a line manager. That was where I first saw people running fish farms and decided I wanted to have one, too," Wangqing, a dark-skinned father with a fourteen-year-old daughter and twelve- and ten-year-old sons, told me, adding that the high cost of children's education in the city had also influenced his decision to come back. "I thought I could make and save more money and enjoy my life and new vocation here much more," he said with a broad smile. "When you work as a migrant worker far away, you often feel lonely, and you can't easily visit your family and friends. As a returnee in your hometown, you can see them anytime. And you can go wherever you want, as you like. It's not like when you are working in the factories and you feel stuck there," he said in a rush. "I want to develop my business here and stay forever. My next plan is I want to open a fish restaurant here for tourists. I am very happy to be home in my village again, but I do feel the pressure of running my own business."[2]

Binghuacun's success was impossible without migrants like Wangqing willing to return home and start businesses, the party organization chief explained. And it wasn't just about bringing back working age people who weren't elderly or still children, like most village residents now. He hoped that after years on the coast, the returnees would pick up skills and knowledge unavailable in the Guizhou countryside. "Our migrants can bring many benefits with them when they come back. First of all, they can help the older people who are here by giving them jobs in their new companies. But they can also bring back new ideas like e-commerce and business practices that they may have learned in the cities." Eight migrants including Wangqing had already returned, and eventually almost all would move back, he confidently predicted. To further entice them, banks in the nearby township of Jialiang had begun to offer cheap loans to returnees starting their own businesses, and the local commerce bureau had set up an online sales platform on which they could market their products, whether they were rustic lodgings or chickens raised without antibiotics. "Before we relied on agriculture, planting rice, corn, and peppers," the chief explained. "Now we plan to develop our old village into a tourist spot. We will let people stay in the old houses, eat our fresh food, and have them go rafting in the reservoir, enjoying nature," he said, listing off the three characteristics that every local resident now knew to be Binghuacun's advantages. Several years earlier, the county finance office had awarded the village 2.8 million yuan to restore the traditional dwellings; now locals were expectantly waiting for word on whether their request for an additional 3 million yuan had been approved or not. "We will use that money to finish renovating the inside and outside of those houses in the old village," he explained. "We will fix them so the water doesn't leak in when it rains. Also, we plan to make a fishing platform next to the river for our visitors."[3]

While one village in Guizhou tried to lure back its migrants, China's entire workforce was facing a shift with far-reaching implications for the economy and the world. Breaking a growth trend that extended back decades, the population of sixteen-to-sixty-five-year-olds had peaked at around one billion in 2015 before starting to decline. Today fewer than fifteen million new workers enter the labor force every year, down from almost twice that number three decades earlier.

By 2018, China's migrant population was barely growing, up only 0.6 percent over the previous year to 288 million.[4] According to another survey, the number had already begun to shrink in 2015.[5] The decades-old expansion of China's *nongmingong,* on which the country had built its manufacturing rise, was now ending.

Why that was happening was at its most basic the result of a simple demographic equation. Chinese women of childbearing age on average were having 1.6 children, well below the replacement rate of 2.1 needed to maintain a population, and down from a high of six in the 1960s, before the one-child policy and other birth restrictions were instituted. In simpler terms, births were not happening fast enough to keep up with mortality. Despite a relaxation of the rules on allowed births in 2015, Chinese women had reached a level of income and education where they naturally wanted small families, and birth rates remained stubbornly low. In early 2019, the Chinese Academy of Social Sciences came out with a new report predicting that China's total population would peak at 1.442 billion in 2029, three years earlier than had been expected. By 2050, it was supposed to drop back to 1.36 billion, and continue falling, to 1.17 billion by 2065.[6]

But beyond just the reality of fewer births, there were other factors affecting the number of migrants and where they worked. As China's floating population became older—the percent of workers over fifty grew from 15.2 percent to 21.3 percent from 2013 to 2017, while the proportion of sixteen to twenty years old dropped by over two percentage points, to only 2.6 percent—there were also fewer inclined to leave home and travel far. A survey by the Chinese Academy of Social Sciences in 2016 showed that one-half of all rural Chinese were no longer interested in moving to the cities, saying they felt they were too old, they needed to take care of parents and children, or they were unfamiliar with urban life. The same study showed that of those who still planned to migrate, two-thirds said they definitely planned to later return to their villages. The discriminatory *hukou* policy that made life in the city almost impossible also definitely was playing a major part. Meanwhile, years of infrastructure development, including better roads and high-speed rail across Western China, had drawn more factories and other opportunities to the interior, providing better jobs for people who were returning home. So, while for years China's wealthier and more developed east had been by far the most popular destination for the migrants, now the western region was catching up, with 20.1 percent working in China's interior in 2017, up 4.9 percent over the previous year, compared to 55.8 percent in the east, up a tiny 0.2 percent. Central China also outdid the east in growth, drawing 20.6 percent of all migrants, with growth up 2.9 percent. In the beleaguered Pearl River Delta, the number of migrants fell by 450,000, a drop of 0.9 percent.[7]

Another change with far-reaching implications was that migrants were now finding new kinds of jobs; in particular, far more were working in the service or tertiary sector, including in restaurants and the logistics delivery business, rather than in factories or at construction sites, the traditional places of employment. That trend not surprisingly followed the larger shift of the economy, which was slowly moving away from manufacturing, to one much more reliant on services. Again, 2015 was a milestone. In the first quarter, for the first time ever, service industries made up more than half of the economy. From the planning officials' perspective, this was a desired change. Service businesses generally used less energy and didn't harm the environment in the same way that factories did. They also provided more jobs for the same amount of GDP, compared to capital-intensive manufacturing and construction industries. And according to commonly accepted economic theory, these tertiary jobs would pay better. (The reality in China, as it would turn out, was different.) If that were the case, a more service-oriented economy would also help in the national goal of boosting personal consumption, still at a low of around 40 percent of GDP, well below the roughly 70 percent proportion in the U.S.[8]

In 2017, the proportion of migrants employed in factories was 29.9 percent, down 0.6 percent over the year before, continuing what was by then a well-established declining trend. Those working on construction sites had also fallen slightly, to 18.9 percent, down 0.8 percent. Meanwhile, the proportion of those employed in the service sector that year reached 48 percent, up 1.3 percent over the previous year.[9] That contrasted with when, in 1978, at the dawn of reforms, 70.5 percent of China's labor force was employed in agriculture, with only 12.2 percent in services.[10]

These shifts fit nicely with the party's wishes. Plans to push Made in China 2025 and automate factories along the coast mean ever-fewer manufacturing jobs for workers. And ambitious plans set during the November 2013 Chinese Communist Party's Third Plenum meeting to loosen *hukou* policy and allow migrants to more easily settle down where they wished had been largely cast aside in the last few years, in favor of even more stringent population controls in many larger cities. Authorities had, however, stuck with a pledge to convert one hundred million more people with rural registration into city residents complete with urban *hukou* by 2020; once again, it was a sweeping central policy with few specifics, but hewed to the belief that urbanization would boost consumption. Rather, however, than let migrants themselves decide where to go, China's planners wished to guide them into smaller cities, particularly those which had been officially designated for population growth. Each city, as per China's tradition of five-year plans, set its own population targets and then went about trying to meet them, with either the carrot or the stick, depending on how much growth was viewed as appropriate: preferential policies, including offering low-interest loans to lure back migrants, in some; orders shutting migrant children's schools and evicting workers from their apartments in others, including the showcase cities of Beijing, Shanghai, and Shenzhen, and many provincial capitals, too.

On November 18, 2017, a fire broke out in a run-down two-story building honeycombed with apartments on the southern outskirts of Beijing. Nineteen people, including eight children, died in what had been called the "Gathering Fortune Apartments."[11] It was a disaster that would set off an even larger one, when first Beijing, then other cities across China used the tragedy as excuse to evict tens of thousands of migrants and their families from their homes, forcing them to return to the countryside. Over the past years, Xinjiancun, in Beijing's Daxing District, had become home to a swelling community of workers, many from Hebei and Zhejiang provinces, who worked in unregistered textile factories and, more recently, as motorcycle delivery workers. The fire started because of a short circuit in the cold-storage unit in the basement, igniting insulation, which quickly sent toxic smoke and flames through the building's tiny flats, each of which housed three to four people. The city's work safety committee launched a forty-day campaign to raze unregistered apartments across the city. As temperatures fell below zero,[12] teams of security guards entered apartments, forcibly evicting those tenants who refused to leave. The narrow streets of Xinjiancun became clotted with clothes, books, and furniture of residents who had to leave so suddenly they were unable to take all of their belongings. Many buildings were bulldozed into rubble.[13] In official documents ordering the evictions, the migrants were referred to as *diduan renkou,* or "low-end population," which contributed to wide outrage over the evictions. "They say they want social stability, but then they carry out a mass operation that is inherently destabilizing," said Beijing scholar Zhang Lifan, who was part of a group of academics who wrote an open letter to the Chinese Communist Party's Central Committee criticizing the evictions. "It is discriminatory to target the low-income population."[14]

The purge of migrants coincided with an earlier order to strip Beijing of "functions nonessential to its role as the capital," as it was described in party bureaucratese. That meant shutting down huge wholesale markets selling everything from clothes to furniture, effectively depriving the thousands who worked in them of any income. Similar crackdowns followed in Shenzhen, Guangzhou, and Shanghai in the following months. At the same time, a new wave of closures of the private schools catering to migrant children swept China's major cities, further demonstrating how unwelcome they were. In 2017, China's National Bureau of Statistics had announced that the population in the capital (only including those who had lived there for at least six months) had actually shrunk for the first time since 1997, falling by 22,000 over the previous year; in 2018 it fell an even more substantial 165,000, to 21.5 million people. Shanghai saw its population shrink, too, falling 13,700, to 24.18 million, in 2017.[15] "The reason for migration in China is economic benefit. People are always willing to go to places with better pay, better economic benefit, better opportunity. But the government is stopping that. They don't want to share real benefits with all these people. So they block them from migrating where they want to go, by using the *hukou*," said Ernan Cui, an analyst at Gavekal Dragonomics in Beijing.[16] "The government for years has been trying to push migrants into smaller cities and towns rather than the big major urban cities, like Beijing and Shanghai. But it is very hard to encourage migrants to come to a particular place," said Mark Williams, chief Asia economist at Capital Economics.[17]

Xi Jinping, who had grown up in Beijing in an era when migration was strictly controlled and the city's population was less than a quarter what it is today, was clearly behind the hard-line stance on migrants. In the fall of 2017, at the 19th National Congress of the Communist Party of China, Xi announced a "Rural Vitalization strategy," whose most concrete policy was the decision to extend rural land leases another thirty years, and which expressly aimed to direct migrants back to the countryside. Midway through a marathon 205-minute speech on October 18 to the assembled twenty-three hundred party delegates in the cavernous Soviet-designed Great Hall of the People, just off Tiananmen Square, Xi outlined his broad vision for rural modernization. While emphasizing the importance of a richer countryside to boost consumption as an economic driver, Xi also showed his conservative tendencies. He emphasized the continuing importance of food or grain security for China, a policy many economists view as old-fashioned in today's world of commodity trading. While stating that China must "safeguard the property rights and interests of rural people," Xi also said China must "strengthen the collective economy," in effect ruling out any possibility of giving farmers real rights to their land.

"Issues relating to agriculture, rural areas, and rural people are fundamental to China as they directly concern our country's stability and our people's well-being," Xi said in the seemingly never-ending speech. "Addressing these issues should have a central place on the work agenda of the Party, and we must prioritize the development of agriculture and rural areas. To build rural areas with thriving businesses, pleasant living environments, social etiquette and civility, effective governance, and prosperity, we need to put in place sound systems, mechanisms, and policies for promoting integrated urban-rural development, and speed up the modernization of agriculture and rural areas. . . . We will promote the integrated development of the primary, secondary, and tertiary industries in rural areas, support and encourage employment and business startups there, and open up more channels to increase rural incomes." Meanwhile, Xi stated, "we will relieve Beijing of functions nonessential to its role as the capital," thus signaling his continuing support for reducing the population.[18]

Xi's strategy was just the latest effort by China's leadership to resurrect the lagging countryside, in part to ensure that migrants would eventually settle down there. His predecessor, Hu Jintao, had pushed the New Socialist Countryside policy, launched in 2005, which had pumped vast quantities of government funds into improving rural health care and education but failed to reverse the gap between city and countryside. (The end to the centuries-old agricultural tax on January 1, 2006, also under his rule, had a positive impact on farmer incomes and welfare.) Before him Jiang Zemin had continued policies supporting the growth of so-called township and village enterprises, or TVEs, the quasi-private businesses that villagers had started in the years after reform and opening, and that had been key to increasing wealth in the countryside. And under Deng, the household responsibility system, in some ways not a policy in that it simply recognized what was already happening—farmers quietly dismantling the collective-farming system to till their own plots—had no doubt contributed much more to rising living standards in rural areas than the grandly named policies that were to come later.

Earlier, Xi, too, had pushed countryside-improving initiatives, policies he called "Beautiful China" and "Ecological Civilization," which aimed to "alleviate environmental and social crisis" and "reduce the disparities in urban-rural development, in development between regions, and in living standards," as some Chinese scholars described them. Now the Rural Vitalization strategy was a far more ambitious master plan for managing the migrants' future: deciding where they would go and what they would do.[19] Migration back to the countryside, whether voluntary or not, was seen as necessary: workers would revitalize forgotten communities and jump-start stagnating local economies by starting businesses, buying homes—all the while, simply by their absence, alleviating the overburdened roads, hospitals, and schools of China's crowded cities. Their sudden departure, too, would initially be widely welcomed by urban residents. Only later would it become apparent how much the cities and their urban residents had depended on them as restaurant cooks, waiters, and dishwashers, delivery people, drivers of Didi Chuxing (China's version of Uber), proprietors of small shops and hairdressers, and household cleaners and nannies.

Not surprisingly, how the migrants would make a living, after departing the cities and returning to the countryside, was an issue of great concern for policymakers. Inspired by 2006 Nobel laureate in economics Edmund Phelps's 2013 book *Mass Flourishing*, Premier Li had begun to tout a theory he called "mass entrepreneurship and innovation," which argued at its core that by simply encouraging people to be adventurous and start their own businesses, China could create a new, sustainable model of economic growth, replacing the state-supported, investment-heavy one of before, as well as the decaying agricultural one in the countryside.[20] Given the right mixture of supportive policies, including tax breaks, cheap loans, and training, China's migrants, too, would rush to start their own businesses in the villages, serving others who were moving back and hungry to replicate the standard of living in the cities, thereby igniting a virtuous circle: migrants return to villages; they demand goods and services; more returnees open businesses to serve them; local economy flourishes; more move back.

Policymakers, too, were confident that the newly rejuvenated countryside could also provide products and services meeting the needs of the cities and become an important part of the national economy. And they had a new weapon to ensure the migrants' success in China's far-flung villages: the internet, and specifically e-commerce, which had exploded in use in recent years. According to their understanding, the countryside is full of rich resources, including fresh fruit, organic tea, and free-range poultry and pork, not to mention more exotic fare like Tibetan caterpillar fungus and tie-dyed ethnic Miao batik cloth. Returnees were opening bed-and-breakfasts and starting small factories producing sports apparel, shoes, and bags. A lack of salable products was not the problem. Instead, the challenge had been getting goods to customers across the vast geographic reach of China. That is where online sales came in, able to link a remote farmer who harvested mountain morels to an upper-middle-class white-collar worker with a yen for obscure fungi, or offer a rafting adventure to a risk-seeking urbanite.

So most local governments had set up online business platforms, often working together with China's e-commerce giant Alibaba, already the world's largest web sales service for farmers through its Rural Taobao program ("*Taobao*" chosen for its meaning: "to search for something precious"), or with JD.com, which runs a similar rural online business. By sheer volume, it has been a success. By the end of 2017, online retail sales in the Chinese countryside reached 1.24 trillion yuan ($180 billion), up almost 40 percent over the previous year. That amounted to about one-quarter of all web sales in the U.S. The number of online shops in rural China reached 9.8 million, up 20.7 percent, with e-commerce generating 28 million jobs, according to the Ministry of Commerce. And while online sales in urban China still remain multiples larger and continue to grow fast, they have not kept up with the torrid pace of the countryside.[21]

The development has been so rapid that a new phenomenon has

emerged over the last few years: Taobao villages, where a cluster of factories are opened outside the cities to make a similar product, often clothing, shoes, and bags. Rising costs had made the countryside more competitive than the coast, and with the flexibility of the internet, buyers did not always have to be close to production. And as orders had become smaller in size, with faster turnaround times, the new, often tiny production facilities proved particularly well suited for the business. In 2016, when I had visited "empty nest villages" in Hebei, I had been told by aging farmers how the population had begun to vary by the season. Many of the residences, empty after the younger folk had migrated to the cities, now had a new use. They were filled with simple sewing machines that were sometimes idle but then thrummed busily when migrants returned temporarily to make handbags and clothing during the high season, in the months before Christmas when orders from America and Europe took off. When the young people returned for work—often mothers who wanted to breast-feed their infants for their first several months, before leaving them with their grandparents and returning to coastal factories—the village population could easily triple overnight, they explained.

According to the World Bank, which, together with Alibaba, has studied the phenomenon, Taobao villages are spreading so fast that they have the potential to rejuvenate huge swaths of China's countryside. These villages, defined as those having annual transaction volume of at least 10 million yuan, and at least a hundred online shops, have grown in number from 20 in 2013 to 3,202 in 2018, their research shows.[22] Then World Bank president Jim Yong Kim waxed rhapsodic on Twitter, after making a trip to some of these manufacturing clusters in Guizhou in 2017: "I saw how Taobao villages empowered new online entrepreneurs, allowing their young families to come back home and take care of their relatives, while enabling farmers to get a better price for their products. This paves the way to a new development path—I hope many will learn from Guizhou's example."[23]

Having anyone call Guizhou a positive model for development was unthinkable when I first visited, in January of 2000. President Jiang

Zemin had just announced a massive infrastructure investment strategy to help China's interior catch up with its coast, the Develop the West plan, and I had come to visit the place that stood out as backward even set against the low standards of the region. Other than Tibet, Guizhou had the lowest average income and highest level of poverty among the ten or so provinces and autonomous regions included in the scheme. Much of the economy relied on just two products: distilled Chinese liquor made from fermented sorghum, and tobacco. As in other provinces, investment into roads and electricity was supposed to jump-start its economy. Of Guizhou's more than fourteen thousand villages, about a third still did not have proper roads or regular power. Bringing this basic infrastructure to the countryside was key to improving life, including for its 3.87 million officially impoverished residents. But with its mountainous terrain and rainy clime, the province presented particular challenges. With less than 10 percent of its land level, fields suitable for crop growing were scarce. And limestone mountains, the dominant geologic structure, were especially vulnerable to erosion, which could destroy crops or even cause landslides, wiping out farming communities, explained Xiao Xintian, a director in the local poverty-alleviation bureau in Guiyang. In normal years, some 10 percent of the province's 36.3 million people—the vast majority of whom were still farmers—might fall back into poverty. In years with bad weather, the proportion could grow to 15 percent. One solution: move whole villages out of the mountains, resettling them in state-provided apartments in less remote parts of the province, a policy that had been used for years already. Some 400,000 more impoverished farmers living in remote areas would be relocated to new areas in the coming years, Xiao explained. "We can say that the main reason for poverty in Guizhou is from our karst mountains or our landform. We must deal with this problem," he said.[24]

Heading west out of Guiyang, one first passes ravaged, scavenged hills of limestone and granite, trees gone and slopes pockmarked with stone quarries, holes dug so gapingly deep that it looks as if they might fall in upon themselves. It is raining, and the infamous fog, or "miasma of suffocating vapors," hangs over the land, curving about the peaks beyond. Boys push carts down the road loaded with wood for fuel, puffing on cigarettes. Dirty white geese preen in water-filled potholes as swaybacked water buffalo sidle along. The road through one village is lined with tired-looking men and boys as young as ten pounding with hammers on granite slabs or chipping them into grave-stones, clouds of white dust hanging in a perpetual cloud. Peering through huge protective glasses—their lungs rather than their eyes are what is at risk, I think—they look like displaced intellectuals who have been stuck in a penal colony. A kid sits on the open back of a put-tering truck and contemplatively sucks on a sugar cane. A little girl hawks and spits on the side of the road just like the elderly men who sit on doorsteps. A jeep with the white UNDP logo roars by. We stop at a Miao village called Dapo, to see a mountain-terracing project, funded by the provincial government. The sound of moving rocks is everywhere: sudden, sharp, shattering noises as dynamite explodes the mountain face; grinding screeches as a tractor pushes the broken debris at its base; cracking retorts as shards of stone are thrown into the back of tractors. The process is arduous but simple: dynamite hill, crush rocks, make walls for terraces, spread soil, plant corn (and, be-tween seasons, wheat, watermelons, and tobacco), and build water tanks to hold the runoff. "We are using a technique that our ancestors used," a local official explains. For Guizhou, fighting poverty seems a constant violent battle with its mountains.

While I did not make it to Binghuacun on that visit, or meet any of the Mos, later that fall I returned to Guizhou and was finally able to do both. A friend had passed me Mo Ruxuan's contact number, suggesting I should meet him. He was a young, ambitious local of-ficial, eager to bring attention to his hometown of Binghuacun, aware that China's recent entry into the World Trade Organization would bring foreign investors to China, and eager to talk to a business re-porter. Ruxuan was serving as deputy chief of the town of Mawei, some kilometers east of the village he had grown up in. That he was not in charge of Binghuacun made things simpler. Rather than having to go through the usual hoops of getting permission to host a foreign reporter, an often lengthy process that involved faxes and phone calls to the local propaganda office, Ruxuan had quickly agreed to take me on an unofficial visit. "With the new open-door policy, we welcome all investors," he had said, dressed in a rumpled dress shirt, with no tie or jacket, when we met for the first time, sitting in his little office in Mawei. He was eager to talk to me and surprisingly relaxed to meet a foreigner he knew little about. Outside it was market day, and Miao and Buyi villagers had poured into town from the surrounding mountains, many in their checkered ethnic headdresses. Bamboo cages on the street were filled with squawking ducks and chickens, which were pulled out and hung upside down by their feet from the balance scale to be weighed before they were sold. "All villages have to compete with each other to get money," he said.[25]

The next day he had taken me to Binghuacun, first in a jeep, then riding in a horse cart over the last stretch of muddy road. Ruxuan's hopes for growing the economy of his village all focused on planting crops that could be sold commercially, rather than the corn, wheat, and rice that were consumed by the farmers themselves. "While this year peanut prices are good, next year it will be something else. Our most reliable economic crops are chilies and oilseed rape. Our fruit industry, growing oranges, plums, and peaches, is not developed yet but eventually should be the backbone of our town. Before we only used natural fertilizers. Now we are using chemical fertilizers," he told me proudly, as he showed me around the village. After they made the transition to cash crops, the next step would be to try to find investors who would fund processing factories, probably first for chili paste, Ruxuan said. But to convince them to come, first the road would have to be improved, getting rid of the bumps, and widened. "Right now, no one wants to buy our products because it is so hard to get here. But now that we are part of the Develop the West project, we have great expectations for our future."[26]

Guizhou's infrastructure needs had been well served by the plan, and that seemed key to its economic development. As a U.S. diplomat based in Chengdu, Sichuan, a neighboring western province, had put it to me back in 2000, "The problem has always been transportation. How the hell do you get your products out." Now many years later, that question had been solved it seemed. Amid a massive build-out of infrastructure throughout Western China, Guizhou had not been left out. By 2017, its total length of expressway reached 5,833 kilometers, and high-speed railway extended 1,214 kilometers. Nine major airports had been built in cities including Guiyang, Zunyi, Anshun, and Liping. The provincial power grid produced 100 billion kilowatts. And indeed, Guizhou's economy was growing fast, up an annual average of 10.9 percent for the last five years. That had helped bring down poverty rates, from 26.8 percent in 2012 to 7.75 percent by 2018, with eight million fewer seriously poor.[27]

But, as is so often the case with China's planners, ensuring growth of what economists like to call the "real economy" was not grand enough. Officials wanted the next chapter of Guizhou's development to be in tune with the rapid technological changes related to the internet happening around the world, including the rise of e-commerce, social media, and video streaming. The plan called for making Guizhou into a big data storage center for the ever more plentiful information being generated, which needed a home somewhere on the Web. And in an ironic twist, this new high-tech version of Guizhou's future was supposed to benefit from some of the same characteristics that had been seen as long holding it back. The excessive rainfall that filled its rushing rivers gave the province rich hydroelectric power resources, which meant cheap electricity, key for storing data in servers that had to be kept at a low temperature. The remoteness of Guizhou made its land cheap. The climate meant there was less need for air-conditioning. Even the mountains, with their peculiar geology, proved useful. When IT companies including Tencent brought giant servers to install in a new business development park outside Guiyang, they realized they could expand the often naturally occurring karst caves into secure, long tunnels, and use them. The wind that blew through the giant cavities in the mountains provided a natural cooling system for the thousands of servers companies were to place inside the mountains.

After the central government had decided in 2015 that China should develop a "big data and cloud" industry, and looked to its remoter regions, with their affordable land and electricity, Guizhou had emerged successful in the unofficial multiprovince competition to lead the effort, in large part because of its extreme poverty; that hardship made it the most appealing choice, odd though this may seem, as a place desperately in need of development. For the same reason, Guizhou had long played a role as a testing ground for up-and-coming party officials. Before promotion to the top ranks of the leadership in Beijing, leaders were almost always required to first spend time working in one of China's poorer, more remote provinces. Xi's predecessor, Hu Jintao, had served in Guizhou, as had Lou Jiren, a former finance minister, as well as the head of the central bank, Guo Shuqing. (Xi had worked in rural Hebei and Fujian, as well as in the better-off province Zhejiang.)[28] So when the first government-organized China International Big Data Industry Expo was held in Guiyang in 2015, it was clear that the other early contenders, including the Hui Muslim–dominant province of Ningxia and Inner Mongolia, would never play as large a role in the country's cloud aspirations and would not receive the flood of central-government-provided subsidies and tax breaks on the same scale that Guizhou was to get.[29]

Xi, too, had seized upon Guizhou when he decided to make eliminating absolute poverty by 2020 one of the country's top priorities, a choice made official during the nineteenth party congress, in the fall of 2017, when he named it one of the "three tough battles" facing China. (The other two were preventing financial risks and fighting environmental pollution.) Xi and other leaders saw poverty eradication—defined by the government as ensuring that no person made less than 2,300 yuan a year ($335 or about $1-a-day, still far lower than the $1.90-a-day level used by the World Bank)—as crucial to bolstering the increasingly battered reputation of the Chinese Communist Party, in part by focusing on an issue that had been central to the idealism of its founding days.[30] (China's leaders, who claimed to have successfully reduced the number of people living in poverty from 82.39 million six years earlier to 16.6 million in 2018,[31] appeared on track to meet their goal of complete eradication by 2020.)

At the same time, they knew that successfully raising average per capita GDP to $10,000 by 2021, part of the national goal of creating a "moderately prosperous society" by the hundredth anniversary of the party, required higher living standards for China's poorest. That target had been set by Deng Xiaoping, and reaffirmed by every leader since, including now Xi. At the party congress in November, Xi had served as a delegate to Guizhou, a symbolic gesture that was meant more to show that he was serious about ensuring that all benefited from China's rise than to help any particular province. "Guizhou's achievement is an epitome of the great progress in the party and country since the eighteenth congress," Xi told the delegates, citing its reduction in poverty, environment improvements, and "good political environment." Guizhou's success showed that "the policies and plans set by the party center are completely correct."[32]

Guizhou's growth was really to take off after a Xi protégé, forty-one-year-old Chen Min'er, had been transferred there, serving first as deputy party secretary, then assistant and full governor, before later getting the top job as party secretary. Chen, who had previously risen through the propaganda department in Zhejiang and had once been a newspaper editor, had filled out his last job in that province as a deputy to Xi, when China's top leader had been the provincial party secretary. In his new role, the Zhejiang native oversaw the province's massive infrastructure expansion and the opening of the huge Guian New Area in January of 2014, to house technology companies.[33] Chen, too, had successfully wooed big multinationals to Guiyang, including Apple, which agreed to invest $1 billion in part into a facility to store its data, linking up with a company that belonged to the provincial government, Guizhou-Cloud Big Data.[34] Another key person in the province's rise was Chen Gang, who had previously been an official in Beijing, and now became Guiyang's party secretary. By the time the two cadres left in 2017—Chen Min'er promoted to the Politburo, China's top leadership body, and transferred to the party secretary position in Chongqing, the largest and most important city in China's interior, and Chen Gang now heading the Xiongan New Area project, Xi's ambitious effort to create a huge new innovative city in rural Hebei, just outside Beijing—Guizhou and its capital, at least in sheer investment and GDP growth, had been transformed.[35] Along with Apple, also Qualcomm, Huawei, Tencent, Alibaba, and China's state-owned telecom giants had invested billions of dollars into Guiyang. The growth rate of the digital economy in the province—the vast majority of it based in the capital—grew 37.2 percent in 2017, the fastest pace in the country, with software services growing 34.8 percent and e-commerce, 40 percent.[36] "Big data has become a new business card for Guizhou to go global," said an official at the provincial government.[37]

On a smaller stage, Ruxuan, too, had done well. After years serving in the Libo County government, including a posting in the finance office, a role that allowed one to disburse funds to villages, in 2016 he moved to Guiyang, his new position managing private enterprises in Guian. The respect his position earned among the villagers in Binghuacun was obvious. They lost no opportunity to mention his promotion to work in the provincial capital, and their voices suddenly became solemn when discussing his new role, the consummate local boy done well. Rubo had told me that the reason for Ruxuan's successes was because he had studied with a teacher who knew Li Keqiang, although I was never sure whether that was true or not. His brother Ruchun, for his part, seemed slightly bemused by the success of his younger sibling, as if wondering why he himself wasn't also a hotshot cadre who got to drive a black Audi A6 like Ruxuan. My repeated attempts to catch up with Ruxuan suggested just how busy he was, always departing on a plane or high-speed train to another booming western city right before I arrived in Guiyang: "Unfortunately, I'm so sorry, but I am not able to meet this time. I must leave immediately for meetings in Chongqing (or Chengdu or Xian). Call again on your next visit to Guizhou." But I knew the smaller private companies he was responsible for managing were not the main show. Those instead were the big state-owned telecom firms, and the multinational and Chinese tech giants, that were now flocking to the zone.

Forty-five minutes by car on a well-paved expressway outside Guiyang's downtown, one reaches the Guian New Area. The sharp hills start to look less wild and deciduous trees have been planted along the road. Billboards tout "Guizhou's Big Data Cloud Future" as one enters the vast complex that will eventually cover almost 1,800 square kilometers, now still mainly mountains, but many with "data tunnels" drilled into them. This is where the tech giants will store the massive and growing data that each is collecting and managing. Foxconn has recently decided to open a center here, along with production facilities for iPads and iPhones, and founder Terry Gou has come for the launch ceremony. A press conference has drawn dozens of Chinese and foreign reporters, eager to hear about what has convinced the country's largest private employer, with over one million workers, to come to Guizhou. In some ways it seems surprising. After all, we are 868 kilometers away from Shenzhen, home to its biggest iPhone and iPad production facilities and the world's largest electronics supplier network. Guizhou is not known for having skilled workers or engineers. And while Foxconn has been opening factories in China's interior to tap cheap labor, including in Zhengzhou, Henan, and Chengdu, Sichuan, Guiyang is far remoter and poorer.

Foxconn's founder looks unfazed by the frenzied attention he is receiving—Chinese reporters have surrounded him in a wild scrum of cameras and recording devices, yelling out questions as he enters the room. He has the stern smile he favors, and is dressed in a light blue suit with a blue-checked tie. His shoes are a well-polished shiny black. On his wrists are the two Buddhist bracelets he always seems to wear, one with big orange stones, the other dark brown wood beads. He steps up onto a small stage prepared for the event, and grabs a microphone. He is more than willing to explain why he has chosen Guiyang for his company's latest investment, and lists all the ways the local government has bent over backward to lure Foxconn. First, the Guiyang government built a new speedway directly from the airport to Guian, ending near Foxconn's facility. "We didn't want to go through the city, so they did that for us—they built the highway so it came to us. Good infrastructure is always key," he said. "To encourage the convergence of the big-data industry, they have done a very good job putting in a new fiber network, that all companies can utilize." As for the approval process for new operations, the city government had been so eager to ensure that it went smoothly that they had moved staff to the zone. "In fact, those government officials live on-site. Normally you would have to apply on your own in the nearest city. Here they moved the agencies right onto our site, to encourage our development."

Beyond the capital investment, taxes to be paid into local coffers, and prestige of getting a company like Foxconn to invest, for Guiyang and other cities a crucial payoff was always jobs. How many people did Foxconn expect to employ in the new facility, one person asked? The usually unflappable Gou seemed for the first time slightly agitated, curtly nodding his head no, as if to dismiss the question. "I hope that our commitment to this industrial park will not be shown by how many people we hire," he said, adding that Foxconn's model this time was different. "Once we build a foundation here—this takes time—maybe three to five years—then maybe we will [start to] use robots to make robots or robots can make a product. We don't want to go back to the traditional [model], labor-intensive, simple and boring. We don't want to just make this factory environment-friendly, but we are also interested in making it high-tech, engineer-intensive and skills-intensive. We want to build a foundation for that here," that can be rolled out across China, he said. "We don't know how many people will work here. So I can't give you this answer."[38]

Meanwhile, Guizhou's migrants were coming back. For a province that had been defined by outward migration, with the majority of its youth leaving to work, this was a sea change. In 2011, 520,000 workers returned from the coast, a number that more than tripled to 1.6 million by 2015. As did those in other provinces, Guizhou officials viewed the reverse migration as a good thing. Not only could the returnees bring new economic vigor to decaying rural communities, but there were unalloyed social benefits; migrants could now raise their own children, and take care of their ailing parents, ending the tragedy of left-behind children with psychological problems and learning disabilities, and ensuring that the elderly rural poor lived better. "Migrants returning to their hometowns for employment, on the one hand can not only help grow local economies, expanding the tax base, and enhancing the development of towns, they can also help villagers by promoting employment and lead us out of poverty," a Guizhou labor official explained. "They can also promote family harmony and social stability by contributing to . . . timely care for the elderly and children, so that more children can grow up healthy and happy."[39]

Under the colorfully named slogan "Returning geese revitalize

Guizhou," the provincial government was also taking steps to encourage the smooth reintegration of the returnees. And as was usually the case with party policy, an action plan was created, one defined by a series of numbers, as if making it sound like a mathematical equation would somehow ensure its success. The "Five 100s Project" called for Guizhou to set up one hundred industrial parks, one hundred high-efficiency agriculture demonstration zones, one hundred designated top tourist attractions, one hundred model small towns, one hundred model urban complexes, and five new industries, including the Big Data project; pharmaceuticals; pollution-free, organic "mountain agriculture"; culturally oriented "mountain tourism"; and low-carbon, energy-saving building materials. Training programs would be held across the province to improve the skills of rural laborers and provide instruction on being an entrepreneur. In each of the "100s"—parks, agricultural zones, tourist sites, model villages and cities—returnees would be encouraged to set up businesses with subsidies, tax waivers, and low-interest loans. As in the rest of China, using e-commerce to develop one's business was expected to be key to its success.[40]

For the cadres sitting in their offices in Guiyang and Beijing, the still-pastoral environment of the province was to be exploited in a new mountain-tourism industry. The aim was to build a travel business around the draw of stunning scenery; colorful ethnic minorities, long patronized as exotic savages by Han Chinese urbanites; and the spicy local food, which included many varieties of sautéed wild mushrooms and other forest plants. And as a new Chinese middle class started to spend more money, Guizhou had benefited. Over the five years ending in 2017, the annual income from tourism and the number of tourists both increased by about 30 percent. Overall services had become the largest contributor to the economy, accounting for 45 percent, compared to around 40 percent in manufacturing and only 15 percent in agriculture. (The majority of the population, however, were still farmers.) Ordered by the central government, wealthier municipalities and provinces had long been required to invest and send managers to Guizhou and other poor regions, including Tibet. Under the auspices of yet another number-heavy policy, "10,000 Enterprises Help 10,000 Villages," in Guizhou two of China's largest real-estate companies, Dalian-based Wanda and Guangzhou-based Evergrande, were building vast tourism resorts in the karst mountains.[41]

Still, the hope was that large numbers of returnees would open bed-and-breakfasts, and be the backbone of a new sustainable model for the villages and rural families. "Left-behind children are one of the biggest tragedies today in China. There is an invisible wall that prevents these kids from entering society," Sun Zhe, an academic turned entrepreneur who ran an online rural-tourism travel business from Guiyang, told me. His company had linked up with hundreds of villages in Guizhou that were trying to lure city folks to come vacation (although not yet with Binghuacun). "We want to make money, but also want to help families have the chance to go home." Sun himself was from a different class of migrant family: his father had come to Guizhou to assist the Third Front strategy in the 1950s, moving from Shenyang in China's Northeast to an impoverished town called Qinghong in northern Guizhou, to help develop its steel industry. While his family had never had the chance to return to live in their hometown, Sun hoped his company could help others have that chance.[42]

There were plenty of signs of the growing tourism boom in the county seat of Libo, where Binghuacun was located. A 3.2-billion-yuan ($480 million), 180-acre ethnic theme park, the Libo Ancient City, had been built just beyond a brand-new, bright red arched bridge over the Zhang River.[43] It was composed of two- and three-story gray brick buildings with sweeping Chinese temple-style roofs, housing tourist shops selling Miao-style batiks, factory-produced colorful minority outfits, and fake horned-ox skulls, and overpriced restaurants, opening onto new cobblestone roads. In its racist representation of minorities as crude but adorably colorful, it was similar to scores of other ethnic cultural-tourism sites built across China. A statue of three leaping bulls surrounding twisting dragons stood in a paved square: BUYI PEOPLE LIVES [*sic*] IN THE PICTURESQUE AND BEAUTIFUL YUNNAN-GUIZHOU PLATEAU WHERE THE HOSPITABLE PEOPLE CAN SING AND DANCE WELL AND THE TOTEM IS POPULAR. THEY THINK THE DIVINITY IS IN EVERYTHING AND EVERYWHERE, read a plaque in English at its base. OX IS THE SYMBOL OF POWER, DRAGON AND FISH HOVER OVER THE PHYLLOSTACHYS PUBESCENS ([*sic*]), EXQUISITE, HIGHER AND HIGHER, EMBODYING THE ENTERPRISING

SPIRIT OF BUYI PEOPLE AND THEIR LONGING FOR A BETTER LIFE. (*Phyllostachys pubescens*, also known as moso bamboo, is common in Guizhou.)

On the other side of the river, where Ruchun lived, were dozens of twenty-eight-story apartment buildings being built on reclaimed rural land, whose high value rested on speculation that the tourist industry would get bigger. Giant green billboards advertised MONA LISA TILES, showing a huge reproduction of that famous face. (As elsewhere in China, most buildings were finished off by affixing countless little glazed ceramic tiles to their exterior, and tile ads were a feature of the countryside.) Streets were lined with glowing faux-classical lampposts, a modern variation on the Soviet-influenced ones that went up in Chinese cities in the 1950s. Ruchun's building, another highrise, had one shop selling Haier-brand air conditioners and a second offering full apartment-renovation services. (Most apartments are sold in China as unfinished cement shells.) He had bought it several years ago, using some of the money he had earned as a labor broker in the Guangxi wood-processing industry. After working on wood-processing lines for several years, he had stumbled upon a lucrative business: He could scour the villages to find other migrants willing to work at low wages, a service that managers at the hundreds of mills across Guangxi province paid him well for.

The three-bedroom apartment that the fifty-year-old shared with his wife, son, and future daughter-in-law, on the tenth floor of the high-rise, felt worlds away from the drafty farmhouses in Binghuacun. The kitchen was fitted out with a giant new shiny red Midea refrigerator, while the living room had an ostentatious silver-colored sofa with brocaded doilies and overstuffed pillows, apparently unsuccessfully aiming for a classical European look, along with a matching coffee table. A self-dealing automatic electronic mahjong table sat in the corner. An enormous flat-screen television was mounted into a wall that was paneled with cushiony white fake leather. And a large open cabinet by the door was filled with all the drinks a guest might require: Moutai, the rice liquor that was perhaps Guizhou's most famous product, in its distinctive squat red-and-white bottles; Chinese Great Wall red wine; PURE MILK, as it was labeled, in little red cartons; and Yigancao herbal tea, a locally made drink that was said to repair one's liver. From the balcony one looked over a construction site, with yet more high-rises going up—the contractor, Ruchun had told me earlier, was Qin Jijie, the driver who had taken us to Binghuacun one rainy day, and had spent the drive pressing me to help him find an American wife.

I had stumbled out of the guest room, my head hurting from too much beer the night before, made myself an instant coffee from the satchels Ruchun had kindly pointed out to me, and planted myself in front of the television, hoping to overcome my headache before Ruchun got back from a morning walk. The program it was tuned to apparently aimed to provide advice to a new class of agriculturalists, in this case those who wanted to raise rabbits. Interspersed with flashy, loud commercials for mobile phones and energy drinks was a farmer—or was he a scientist—providing tips on animal husbandry, dressed in a blue laboratory smock and wearing rubber gloves. Standing inside a hutch, he grabbed a female hare by the ruff, expertly seized her two back legs, and flipped her over to see whether she was in rut and ready to mate. The show then cut to a scene featuring a nest of straw holding fuzzy baby rabbits. "You must always keep them warm. Give them as much food as they are able to eat," the narrator said solemnly.

As Ruchun had explained the night before, he was interested in something far more ambitious than raising rabbits. Over multiple cups of *maojian* tea and Snow Beer, the skinny, sharp-dressing former migrant had explained how he hoped to create a tourism business that would transform his home village. It all centered on the rice fields that fell in gentle terraces from the hills surrounding Binghuacun down to the banks of the river. With plans to transition to producing more value-added cash crops that could be sold elsewhere, the villagers would need far less land-intensive rice cultivation, he explained. By renting the plots held in long-term leases, or by bringing the farmers in as shareholders in the venture in exchange for use of their land, he planned to convert the fields into a resort plus newly planted orchards that tourists could pick fruit from. There would be a hotel, and a restaurant specializing in fresh river trout, wild edible herbs from the mountains, and yes, some locally raised rabbit meat; and there would also ultimately be a swimming pool—although the river was clean, some tourists would not want to take a dip in a river, he explained. His son, a pretty-faced twenty-two-year-old with a perpetual pout, came through the living room, on his way out. Ruchun looked up at him, then tersely ordered him to offer me a cigarette, the ubiquitous symbol of hospitality among men in China. The boy handed it to me without speaking and left. "He wants to be an entrepreneur, but he refuses to do business with me," Ruchun said with a rueful smile. "We didn't get to know each other, as I was away when he was growing up," he added. This was not the first investment plan I had heard from Ruchun; on an earlier visit he had told me about a planned cherry orchard for tourists on the hill above Rubo's parents' house, and even earlier he had outlined how he would create a consulting company for farmers turned entrepreneurs. None had come to fruition. A recent investment in one hundred cows he and his friend had purchased from a dealer in Shandong Province had ended badly; the cows never grew as large as had been promised, and they had sold them at a loss. "We got cheated. There is nothing we can do but accept that fact," he said.

One business Ruchun knew a lot about was lumber processing, and his latest project sounded potentially lucrative. With costs going up in Guangxi, he planned to break the semi-monopoly it had had in the region, and open a milling operation in Libo. The mill would also benefit from being close to Guizhou's rich tree-farm resources, he said. And even though it had become increasingly difficult to get permits to open factories, as the province pushed its plan of becoming a green-tourism destination, Ruchun had won approval before the recent tightening. He hoped to earn enough from that business to have seed money for what he really cared about: the Binghuacun development. Still, he would need investors from outside the region—people with real money—to help fund his village project. "You know, all this talk, and still we don't even have one hotel in Binghuacun. We don't even have a restaurant. There isn't even a store. Not one of the house renovations has been completed," he told me. "How can we convince anyone our village is worth putting money in? How can we know whether we will actually ever be able to make our village into a tourist destination?"

That was the same concern bedeviling Rubo. After years living in Dongguan, moving from one small rented apartment to another, he had finally begun to question his determination, settled upon long ago, to stay in the city. The high costs of paying for his daughter's education as a migrant child in the city, concerns about his elderly parents' health, and the perpetual grind of being an outsider who was not welcome had begun to weigh on him. He had moved back to Libo for several months a couple of years earlier, but had found he was too far from the Guangzhou factories that supplied him, and no Taobao operations he could source from had been set up nearby. Now he was considering building a guesthouse on the flat plot of land next to his parents' place. But that would work only if Binghuacun became the tourist destination villagers were hoping for, and there was no guarantee of that. "There are lots of things to do in Libo. From May to October the hotels and restaurants fill up, but not in our village," Rubo had said, showing me a Libo tourism website on his smartphone with a photo of white-water rafting and a little graphic with a plane, bus, and high-speed train, all supposedly transportation options for the region. The airport, however, was a run-down, scuffed white building that had recently won the dubious distinction of least-used terminal in China; the high-speed rail and a new road had not yet been built. "I will wait for more people to come before I consider building a small hotel there. But who knows if that will ever happen," he said.[44]

For migrants, returning to the villages is certain to be difficult. After spending most of their adult lives in cities, they often find the slower pace of life and limited choice difficult to adjust to. While e-commerce has made far more food and clothing products available, it hasn't had the same impact when it comes to leisure offerings, whether it is cinema or just a stroll in the park. Similar to the experience of migrant children who return to the countryside for middle and high school and, overwhelmed by the change and feeling like strangers in their own hometowns, drop out, not a few returnees are likely to fail. "I am already poor, and for people like me who try to start a business in the countryside, the risk is we fail and end up even poorer," said Yang Meng, a thirty-year-old migrant from Yibin, Sichuan, working in Shenzhen, whom I had met through other migrants.

Yang described how his parents had lost almost all their money, buying three hundred pigs and then being unable to sell them in the economic downturn after the SARS crisis in 2003. "Migrants' biggest challenge is they do not have the skills or ability to control the market. And after they have been in the cities for many years, they don't have *guanxi*. If they run into trouble, they don't know who to turn to," Yang explained. "The countryside can accommodate only some of us. Not all the workers can go home and expect to find a job."[45]

Back in Guizhou, there were indications that the "returning geese" weren't all being smoothly reassimilated. On the road between Guiyang and Binghuacun, long after passing the fancy new regional offices of technology multinationals and tall billboards proclaiming "Bright Future of Innovation, New Dream for E-Commerce," where the roads narrowed and run-down farmhouses and heaps of trash and scrawny village dogs began to once again appear, one could see walls painted with slogans exhorting returnees to find work and not slack off. Outside one village about halfway to Binghuacun, red banners were strung in two rows on a blue construction-site fence, with large white characters reading:

> poor and backward isn't honorable
> eating well and being lazy is even more disgraceful
> returning to the village and working is much more
>   advantageous
> reduce tiredness and avoid rushing about
> only the industrious aren't impoverished
> if you want to escape poverty, then act vigorously.

7

The Future

It would be a miracle for powers that are beyond people's
control suddenly to start serving the people. Miracles may
occur, of course, but they cannot be taken for granted.
In order to guarantee that the government will serve
the people, people will first have to check the power of
government.

—FEI XIAOTONG, *RECONSTRUCTING RURAL CHINA*, 1948

As the Lunar New Year of 2019 approached, Beijing had an emptied-out
feel, surprising for a city that still was home to twenty-three million.
One year after the great migrant evictions, once-busy commercial
districts were quiet, with shops boarded up, the red bricked-in former
doors and windows against gray-painted walls hinting at where there
had once been life, the visual equivalent of a "phantom limb," when
an appendage is cut off but the nerves still tingle. A new ban on setting off fireworks within the city's Fifth Ring Road, enforced in other
cities including Shanghai and Guangzhou, gave China's biggest holiday, ordinarily its most lively, an oddly lifeless feeling. The bleakness
was heightened by the dolorous economy. Twelve months into the latest trade war with the U.S., tariffs had begun to cause real pain, with
North America–bound exports starting to dry up, and factories laying
off workers. The economic strains due to a contracting population,

plus years of reliance on debt-fueled spending that was losing its efficacy, were ever more apparent, as grayness settled over the gray city.

China's fabled urban middle class—the creators of the world's best consumption story, the analysts had told us—were cutting back on spending, and sales of cars and smartphones had plunged. Even the fleets of motorcycle couriers that clotted the streets, the lifeblood of the city, rushing packages and home meals about its arteries of avenues, streets, and lanes, were fewer in number, and the tired drivers grimmer than before. When Xi Jinping went to "greet the people" (the traditional leadership display of concern for the less well-off during the New Year), he visited a *hutong* neighborhood that had first housed itinerant merchants and laborers more than a thousand years earlier.[1] The deliverymen looked nervous and uncertain. "You are the most diligent, like diligent bees, traveling here and there and being exposed to the sun and rain. It's not easy," Xi said to them, the show of avuncular benevolence broadcast that evening on the nightly news. "Will you go home for the holiday?" China's leader-for-life had asked.[2] They grimaced, answered yes, probably wondering whether they would ever return to this shrinking city, following their soon-to-come village reunions.

Less than two weeks earlier, in the run-up to the New Year, traditionally a time to straighten one's affairs—whether cleaning the house, getting a haircut, sharpening knives, or paying off debts and settling scores—Zhang Zhiru and Wu Guijun, two of China's best-known labor activists, had been pulled from their apartments two thousand kilometers south, in Shenzhen, and taken away by police. While both had spent the last years learning how to toe the line just enough to stay out of jail—foreign media reports that featured activists also made it tougher for the police to lock them up, Zhang Zhiru had told me earlier (censors had ordered Chinese media to avoid reporting on sensitive characters like Zhang and Wu altogether)—this time something was different: a handful of other worker activists who had also been detained in Shenzhen and nearby were quickly let go, but Zhang and Wu were not; instead authorities charged the two with "disturbing public order," the same charge as Zeng Feiyang and Meng Han four years earlier.[3] When Wu a year or so before had texted me on his phone, our last communication, his message had seemed a bit melodramatic. "Fortunately [this word was followed by a smiley-face emoji] it's work as usual. 'Drinking tea' has become my habit," he had written, using the common euphemism for when security officers tell people of concern to join them for a drink, the real point being soft interrogation. *Ah, I'm sure these meetings must be intimidating,* I had thought, *but at least Wu and Zhang know how to keep out of jail.* Zhang's and Wu's WeChat moments, not surprisingly, had both stopped; the two had been prolific posters. (Zhang's former deputy, the one who had once vainly tried to open an office for Chunfeng in Dongguan and more recently was running a day care for workers' children, was keeping a low profile but still active on his WeChat stream. One could see he had recently become interested in New Confucianism; his We-Chat moments showed him kneeling in front of a shrine to Confucius and lighting incense, with the message, "Keeping up with the heart, the New Year is with the ancestral sacred ancestors.")

Their arrests had come during the most far-reaching crackdown on worker activism in China in years. In the spring of 2018, workers at a welding-machine factory in Shenzhen owned by Jasic Technology had organized to protest against unpaid wages and to call for the creation of an independent union to protect their interests. Authorities had responded with typical harshness, arresting twenty-nine factory hands in July, no doubt counting on their heavy-handed approach to put an end to the matter. Then, in what was for the leadership a deeply alarming new twist, the issue had caught the attention of left-wing students and recent graduates at some of China's top universities, including Peking and Tsinghua universities in Beijing. They had traveled to Guangdong to help the workers, renting an apartment in a crowded district of Huizhou, north of Shenzhen. Shortly after arriving in late August, the students had released a video where they explained their decision to support the protests, showing themselves raising clenched fists while dressed in identical white T-shirts, each featuring an image in black of five young workers, below which was written in bold red characters, STRENGTH IN UNITY, socialist-realist style. Just a day later came the crackdown. In the early hours of the morning of August 24, riot police, wearing projectile-resistant plastic masks and shields, had forced open the door of the apartment they were staying in, swept through swinging batons, and taken away some fifty students and workers. While some were forcibly returned to their hometowns by police and handed over to their parents, others were held much longer.[4] The suppression continued, with simultaneous abductions of more students and activists in five cities, including Beijing, Shanghai, Guangzhou, Shenzhen, and Wuhan, that November, and then more abductions again in December and in May 2019. "They hit him hard, and quickly got [him] under control," one eyewitness told a foreign journalist, describing how a recent graduate of Peking University had been grabbed and beaten on the campus by around ten men dressed in black, then forced into a car and driven off.[5] (In an irony perhaps missed by the authorities, the latter abductions happened on December 26, the 125th anniversary of the birth of Mao, and May 1, celebrated as International Labor Day in China and other socialist countries.)

While it was unclear whether the arrests of Zhang and Wu were related to the Jasic protests—neither had publicly aided the workers—it was obvious what message their harsh treatment aimed to send. It was a warning of what would come to others who considered helping China's beleaguered workers, as a new wave of strikes rolled over China. The demonstrations now were no longer limited to factories and construction sites. Instead, many of the more than 1,700 labor actions counted in 2018, up from 1,255 the previous year, were happening in the service sector, including in the new fast-growing and dangerous profession of delivery workers, which now employed more than three million migrants. (The protest numbers, too, probably underestimated the actual scale of unrest; collected by China Labour Bulletin, the Hong Kong–based organization founded by the former Tiananmen Square worker leader Han Dongfang, they included only the actions his small organization was able to document.)[6]

The poorly paid couriers were playing a supporting if usually ignored role in what was now being heralded as the latest chapter in the world's best consumption story, the explosive growth of e-commerce. And while internet sales, whether they were for home-delivery meals, groceries, office equipment, or gifts of flowers, were occurring all year long, no single date was as important in supporting the awe-struck narrative of the Web's transformative magnificence as Double Eleven Day, so-named because it fell on November 11. Initially created as "Singles Day" (for the multiple "ones" designating the date: 11/11), a wry alternative to Valentine's Day for those who did not yet have a mate, it had exploded into the biggest shopping event of the year, a twenty-four-hour-long orgy of consumerism. On Alibaba's web platform alone, sales of brands including Apple, Adidas, Nike, and Xiaomi exceeded $30 billion, more than all of Black Friday and Cyber Monday in the United States combined.[7] Less discussed was its obvious cannibalistic effect—how the holiday's surge in business replaced sales on other days and helped in the gutting of retail outlets, whether malls or mom-and-pop stores—which in turn had laid off countless salespeople.

Double Eleven had become not just a festival of materialism built on the wreckage of China's brick-and-mortar businesses, but also a star-studded event paying homage to the glorious sway of technology. The maestros of Double Eleven were the billionaire founders of e-commerce companies, including Alibaba's charismatic implike boss Jack Ma, who in his youth had accosted foreign tourists at West Lake, in his hometown of Hangzhou, offering to be a tour guide for free, in order to practice his English. At Alibaba's gala, held in Shanghai, Mariah Carey sang and acrobats of Cirque du Soleil performed, while robots served cocktails and cappuccinos to the guests,[8] all mesmerized by a giant digital screen, totting up the sales in real time (each year the attention was on what new record of extravagant spending would be set).[9] But on the streets of China's cities, Double Eleven was notable for its bleakness: workers had to deliver as many as a thousand packages, five times the usual number, and as was always the case, could be forced to pay fines ranging from thirty yuan to two hundred yuan for a late delivery or a customer complaint.[10] And while the festival was always a day of discomfort and deep stress for the migrants on which it relied, the rest of the year wasn't much better. Forced to work long hours to meet a quota of deliveries and make enough money to live on, couriers had no choice but to limit any time taking breaks, including to eat or relieve themselves, and always drive faster. Workers, who were usually clad in bright yellow or blue in order to make them more visible in crowded traffic, became both the cause of and victims of ever more traffic accidents. In Shanghai alone in the first half of 2017, seventy-six couriers died or were seriously injured while delivering food, according to the municipal police.[11] And while China's biggest internet firms bought stakes in or acquired outright the most popular delivery platforms, including Tencent in Meituan Dianping and Alibaba buying Ele.me, this had little impact on the conditions in which the couriers worked; the vast majority of drivers had no relation to the giant companies and were instead freelance drivers or hired through third-party companies, and so had few guarantees of labor protections and often no contracts.[12]

The difficult conditions under which couriers worked, although bad, were in ways not unique. They mirrored a larger trend of low-wage, low-skill employment, common to most professions in the new service sector. This certainly was not what China's planners had envisioned. Instead, they had seen the rise of an economy more reliant on the tertiary sector, as one in which workers would earn more money, develop more skills, and be able to produce goods suitable to their vision of a higher-value-added economy. That, too, was where their plans for a large expansion of vocational education came in. Li Keqiang had mused in 2014, "Imagine the scale and level of Chinese products and services if most of the 900-million-strong labor force can be trained to master medium- and high-level skills." By 2016 the majority of Chinese were employed in services, rather than in manufacturing or agriculture. But most of the new jobs were not remotely close to the mobile-app-programming and AI-engineering jobs that planners had been hoping for. Far more jobs were being generated in restaurants, hotels, retail, and delivery. Over the last five years, education and government jobs, most of which had drawn college graduates, had fallen from about one-half to a third, research by Albert Park, the Hong Kong University of Science and Technology economist, showed.[13] "The higher-skilled sectors—telecoms, information technology, computers, finance, and business services—are still not a large share of the total service industry," he said. "And while some are growing, they aren't growing very quickly."[14]

The other plank that was to support workers in the new economy, of course, was entrepreneurialism, supposedly leavened by innovation, although it was never really clear what was meant by that. In China, as in the rest of the world, "innovation" seemed to function as a catchall term for whatever the capitalist zeitgeist viewed at the time as cutting-edge and good. In a measure of how important private business was viewed as being, Liu He, the gray-haired economist close to Xi, had begun using the term "56789" to describe it. That referred to the fact that private business already generated 50 percent of all tax revenue and accounted for 60 percent of GDP, 70 percent of all innovation produced, and, crucially, 80 percent of all jobs in the cities. (The 90 percent was the proportion of the total registered companies.) The reality, however, was that small and medium-size private companies, despite their importance, were still suffering under a deeply unfair system. Most bank credit, not to mention government contracts, had long gone to state-owned companies rather than private ones. This was hardly surprising, given that the banks themselves were all owned by the government, and quite naturally were more inclined to provide loans to other state-owned firms; that officials usually didn't want to see state companies go bankrupt, and so might come in to bail them out if times got tough, also made them more attractive when lending. And under Xi there had been a clear resurgence in the favored status of state firms. Nicholas Lardy, an economist who had long argued that the private sector was stronger and faced less discrimination than other economists had claimed, reversed his stance in early 2019, in his provocatively titled book *The State Strikes Back: The End of Economic Reform in China?* His previous book, published four years earlier, had by contrast been called *Markets over Mao: The Rise of Private Business in China*. In a meeting with other officials in Beijing in January of 2019, Premier Li Keqiang once more called for banks to change their longtime bias against private companies, something officials had been pushing for with little success for years. As reported in *China Daily*, "Li said stable employment relies on millions of small enterprises, and that the support of financial institutions is indispensable to their development. He called on State-owned banks to provide better services for small businesses and maintain market vitality."[15]

Worries about unemployment, always a concern of the leadership because of its link to social instability, were growing even stronger. By the end of 2018, China's economy was expanding at its slowest pace in almost a decade.[16] Over the last twelve months, 2.8 million industrial jobs had been lost, a national survey of large companies showed.[17] In December, the State Council announced that, in order to avert layoffs, companies would be reimbursed the cost of unemployment insurance if they didn't fire workers. Rules on starting new companies were being relaxed. And now the so-called gig economy—less grandly described as freelance or temp work—was also supposed to play an important part. As businesses saw profits squeezed and continued to shed staff, policymakers hoped that self-employment—in its capitalistic purity free of health insurance, pensions, or any kind of job security—would provide livelihood for workers. China's government would support "new industries, new formats and new models, forming a wide range of commercial applications, and effectively promoting the expansion of employment," China's state media reported, citing a symposium chaired by Premier Li held in Beijing.[18] According to one estimate, from 2015 to 2017 this new informal economy may have employed as many as 33.37 million workers who had had to leave industrial companies.[19]

But already there were signs of trouble. Opportunities for self-employment were shrinking in the face of new regulations on ride sharing (some cities were beginning to require that drivers have local *hukou*—a huge challenge in Shanghai and most other cities, where the vast majority were not locals); an e-commerce law that required online sellers to register as companies and pay taxes; censorship of live streamers, involving any content that was remotely racy or political; and, above all, the weakening economy. The gig economy "safety valve for the job market is not working" as before, warned Gavekal Dragonomics's Ernan Cui in early 2019.[20] Not long after, Didi Chuxing, China's largest ride-hailing service, announced that it was laying off two thousand workers, or 15 percent of its workforce.[21] And there was little reason to assume that returning migrants would succeed in the countryside, or that jobs they might find would be better. Even as small factories relying on e-commerce were set up in the hinterlands—the Taobao-village phenomenon touted by the World Bank's director—many seemed to be a throwback to the sweatshops of the 1990s: workers with no contracts, forced to work long hours, in conditions that threatened their health and safety. The new survival skill is to be "under the radar," and so free of profit-squeezing environmental and labor regulations, one such factory owner explained to me.[22]

In 2018, more than half of China's provinces grew more slowly than expected. Even Guizhou, one of the biggest beneficiaries of the push to expand western infrastructure and key to Xi's anti-poverty drive, had missed its target.[23] The possibility of far more layoffs, what could be a third wave of society-wrenching mass unemployment following the state enterprise restructuring of the late 1990s and the tens of thousands of factories shuttered during the global financial crisis a decade later, raised the specter of widespread discontentment. Whether that would finally put an end to people's faith in the center, that ancient piece of holy writ that has protected the leaders in Beijing from the people's wrath and ensured the party's future, was unclear.

Even without the challenges posed by rising unemployment, China's economy had rot at its core. Depending on who you talked to, China either had one of the most unequal societies on earth, or, alternatively, might be the most inegalitarian major economy of all.[24] Research by Thomas Piketty—French author of the bestselling *Capital in the Twenty-First Century,* which had focused the world's attention on inequality when it came out, in 2013—and Berkeley inequality economist Gabriel Zucman found that China's wealth inequality was roughly equal to that in oligarchic Russia, and midway between that in France and that in the U.S. More important, it showed an alarming rise, with the top one percent's portion of total wealth almost doubling from just over 15 percent in 1995 to 30 percent in 2015. (Similarly, the richest in Russia had seen their share almost double to 43 percent over the same period. The top 10 percent in the two countries held similar amounts: 67 percent in China and 71 percent in its northern neighbor.) "In China and Russia, the available evidence reveals a huge increase in wealth inequality over the last two decades," wrote Zucman.[25] Even more alarming were the findings of economist Gan Li, who had received his Ph.D. at Berkeley and now splits his time between Texas A&M and the Southwestern University of Finance and Economics in Chengdu, Sichuan. From the Survey and Research Center for China Household Finance, in Chengdu, which he had founded, Gan oversaw one of the largest national surveys done regularly in China. According to its findings, the Gini coefficient (a measurement of inequality created in 1912 by Italian statistician Corrado Gini) in China had reached 0.61, the highest of any major economy and well above the 0.4 level widely considered to be socially destabilizing.[26]

The central question facing China is whether that gap could derail the country's future. After he launched economic reforms more than forty years ago, Deng Xiaoping famously declared that it was important to "let some people get rich first," arguing that after the coasts, initially, became prosperous, the wealth would eventually trickle down to the interior. And there was an economic theory to support his slogan: the Kuznets curve, which said that after initially seeing wealth polarize, an economy would gradually become more equal as the economic benefits generated by the wealthy began to spread to all in society. Harvard University sociologist Martin Whyte later came out with research suggesting that China's least well-off were the biggest supporters of the unequal status quo, their attitude a backlash against radical and often unfair efforts to level people's fortunes in the Mao era. Whyte coined the phrase "the myth of the social volcano" to describe how China's disadvantaged were unlikely to take action against rising inequality.[27] (Others later strongly disagreed with his findings.)

Other scholars noted that people were usually more concerned with comparing their lot to their peers', rather than to the lot of those from other social backgrounds. And there was no doubt that China's poor were becoming better off, even as the rich got richer. Still, rising living standards for all could cause frictions, too, many believed. For years, social scientists and foreign journalists covering China—in a nod to modernization theory, which argues that with rising living standards and education, demands on government will inevitably rise—had predicted that revolution, were it to come, would arise from a new Chinese middle class that would force the party to reform or step aside. As so-called NIMBY—not in my backyard—protests began in the 2000s, with urbanites protesting against polluting factories or shoddy construction in their newly purchased apartments, this argument gained credence. And while more than three-quarters of Chinese reportedly believed they were better off in 2015 as compared to five years earlier, 75 percent also said the gap between the rich and poor was a big problem, and were split in their opinion of whether it would get worse or better going forward.[28]

But by that same year, as Xi Jinping forcefully moved to consolidate the party's power and crack down on social dissent, it looked as if the middle class were not going to drive much change after all. Interestingly, when urbanites did protest, often it was so their children would not have to share educational resources with migrant or rural families. When the central government decided to change the unequal points system in the *gaokao* so that it would not discriminate as much against children from the countryside, and to make it easier for them to go to good universities—thus also making it even more competitive for urban children—parents from cities organized demonstrations outside provincial education offices. Later, in Guiyang, Han Chinese parents protested an affirmative-action program that allowed minority students with lower scores to get into colleges.[29] That China's middle class were not the radicals some had assumed, but instead a conservative force, was no surprise, argues political scientist Lynette Ong. In fact, her research shows that the opposite is true. "Higher cost of reprisal in authoritarian states implies that those with higher income and education levels have considerably more to lose than the impoverished and poorly educated. In other words, the opportunity cost of participating in protest actions, a high-risk activity in authoritarian states, rises as one progresses up the social ladder. The cost could take the form of forgone income, loss of social status, or even loss of personal freedom," she wrote in a paper outlining her findings.[30] In a 2019 interview, she explained, "If you define modernization in its broadest term, i.e. as the income per capita increases, a country will likely democratize because citizens demand greater accountability (or protest to get what they want), then yes, the theory has gotten China wrong. Our findings show the more educated and wealthier people are, the less likely they will protest."[31]

By contrast, workers in poor-paying jobs—or, worse yet, those who have been laid off—have little to lose. As migrants, they get to see how urbanites live, and how they are discriminated against. A field of social science that measures happiness, in part by asking whether people are satisfied, provides some insights. Not surprisingly, surveys have shown that the migrants report levels of happiness or life satisfaction significantly below those people living in the cities who hold urban *hukou*. Perhaps more surprisingly, they also are not as happy as people who have stayed in the countryside—that's true even though their incomes on average are more than twice as high than those in the villages.[32] Dee Lee, who has spent most of his career trying to understand the concerns of migrants, put it bluntly. Through their years working as an underclass in the cities, as well as through the images they see in media—Lee mentioned a South Korean soap opera that was popular among younger migrants—they become convinced of how badly they are treated and how miserable their lives are. "Sometimes they even exaggerate how good city kids' lives are. They think they are all rich and always having a good time, like they see on TV. But that doesn't matter. They know their lives aren't as good and they are angry about that," he told me one afternoon as we sat in a coffee shop in a high-rise in downtown Guangzhou.[33] That helps explain the surge in worker protests.

But despite the anger, migrant activism has long tended to be fragmented, narrowly focused on one group's concerns, usually at a single factory. And for protesters to have a lasting impact they would have to link up across industries and regions, thus creating a real, national movement with its corresponding power, labor scholars had explained. As Karl Marx put it, workers who first are simply a "class in itself," aware of and unhappy with their mistreatment, must become a "class for itself," realizing that they are discriminated against, separate from others in society, and then work together to try to change their collective lot. That shift may already have begun.[34] Along with the Jasic movement, which brought together workers, activists, and students from across China, in 2018 first truck drivers and then later construction crane operators coordinated parallel national strikes in scores of cities. The crane operators, who timed the demonstrations for just before May 1, International Labor Day, called on "all fellow workers [to] proactively participate and make our voice known to the whole of society," via an open letter they published on WeChat. "This instance of a simultaneous mobilization of crane tower operators in dozens of cities across the country has every qualification to be considered the beginning of a historical inflection point in labor in China," Wang Jiangsong, a scholar of labor relations in Beijing, predicted at the time.[35]

For years, China's leaders have had an unspoken agreement with the people: they guarantee rising living standards and, in turn, the populace tolerates control by a nondemocratic and often unresponsive party. Four-plus decades of rapid economic growth drove a rapid rise in living standards that is without question impressive, and Chinese benefited tremendously from that. At the same time, most people seemed ready to accept that civil liberties were not expanding in tandem, and the minority that demurred were harshly dealt with. There are fatal problems with that equation today. Growing inequality means that a large proportion of the population could decide that the party no longer is fulfilling its side of the bargain, and begin to demand changes. And despite China's Great Firewall of internet censorship, people today are far more aware of the rights granted to others around the world, including the power to vote out those leaders you don't like. Just as serious a challenge will be posed by the future state of the Chinese economy. For years, the country has reaped the benefits of a reform-oriented path to development, which in some ways only required the government to step out of the way. By opening up a planned economy once reliant on inefficient state enterprises to more competition, by allowing private companies to grow and foreign enterprises with capital and technology to invest, policymakers unleashed a productivity surge that drove decades of growth. Similarly, the migration of people from farming to manufacturing or services, with each new worker generating several times as much output as when tilling fields, provided a huge boost to the economy, adding on average one to two percentage points to annual GDP growth.[36] That followed the earlier move to allow farmers to decide what to plant and where to sell it, unleashing agricultural productivity.

But now that formula seems to be no longer working. As the economy continued to slow in 2019, officials did what they have done every time growth slipped over the decade since the global financial crisis in 2008: They ordered the state-owned banks to pump liquidity into the economy. In January, banks issued 3.23 trillion yuan ($477 billion) in new loans, the most ever in one month. That enormous surge, however, suggested just how serious things have become, and risked China digging itself even deeper into its debt hole, estimated to be around 300 percent of the economy, an elevated level at which other countries have experienced crises. Even if the state's control of the banks continues to make a financial meltdown unlikely, the country's years of reliance on a ready flow of capital to keep things humming means that more and more money has been pushed to companies and projects that don't necessarily know how to, or need to, spend it. This, combined with a drying up of the worker flow from countryside to city, and the end to the earlier returns from adding technology and building better supply chains is behind the worrying drop in total-factor productivity—a measure of how efficiently an economy runs—which had fallen from, on average, 2.6 percent a year in the decade ending in 2007 to almost nothing in the years since. And while falling productivity is common as economies mature, China's drop has been unusually abrupt, even lower than in the U.S., where it had dropped from 1 percent to about 0.5 percent over the same period.[37]

China benefited from decades of reform, including the creation of township and village enterprises in the 1980s, the marketization of state enterprises in the 1990s, and entry to the World Trade Organization with the flood of foreign investment that brought in the 2000s, but now perhaps they have all run their course, meaning an end to the easy economic gains they brought. "Now China needs a new set of policy reforms, to try to sustain [future] productivity," says University of Toronto economist Loren Brandt.[38] Andrew Batson, research director at Gavekal Dragonomics, wrote in a report, "The government's repeated use of state-owned enterprises to stimulate short-term activity has weakened the private sector and lowered productivity growth." As a result, China is "increasingly locked into a slower-growth future."[39]

The other obvious challenge facing the country is successfully navigating away from the cheap manufacturing model that helped drive export and economic growth for decades. As factories have moved or shut with rising labor costs, the economy has slowed; so, too, has growth in income. And Made in China 2025, as much as it is a push for national technological greatness, is also about finding a new development path, one that allows China to avoid the middle-income trap, which has seen countries stall midway to developed status, as did South Africa and Brazil. But China faces tremendous difficulties going forward. Its plan to develop its own technology, key to creating a value-added economy rather than the labor-intensive and low-cost one of before, requires moving to a far more open system, one that doesn't cut China off from academic exchange through a heavy-handed system of censorship. Its aging population is also bad news, as older workers are less likely to take risks and experiment with new ideas, research has shown.[40] The deeply unequal education system, which is driving a growing school dropout rate among rural Chinese, is a huge obstacle to making the transition. "The lack of a skilled workforce has been identified as a main obstacle to China's drive for 'intelligent manufacturing,'" writes Hong Kong University of Science and Technology sociologist Huang Yu, who for years has studied the impact of robots on workers in Dongguan.[41] And its restrictions on migration through the *hukou,* as well as an economic system that still favors state-owned or state-affiliated companies over private firms, are drags on productivity.

The timing of China's efforts to make this economic transition is about as bad as imaginable. Just at the point where its access to the world's cutting-edge technology will become even more critical to its future, it is facing a global backlash against its longtime mercantilist policies, including requiring technology transfer as the price of market access. The trade war with the U.S., more than just disagreements over tariffs and deficits, has become an existential battle, with China aiming to replace the U.S. as an economic and technological power, and Washington determined to stop it. And the challenge isn't just about getting overseas companies to continue to invest and bring their expertise; it requires stanching the corporate exits already happening. While many companies are in China not just to manufacture, but also to sell to its consumers, and likely will never leave, others may eventually decide to depart for good. Over the previous year, 37 percent of foreign companies had already moved some of their manufacturing out of China, often the lower-end final assembly, citing the trade war as their biggest reason, as well as rising land and labor costs, and stricter enforcement of environmental regulations. That trend is expected to continue, with another one-third planning to follow suit over the next six to twelve months, showed a survey of two hundred American and European manufacturers, released by Swiss investment bank UBS in early 2019.[42] And while labor-intensive industries like furniture, toys, and clothing began relocating to places like Vietnam, Cambodia, and Thailand years ago, now companies in China's higher-end-electronics supply chain, key to its rise to global export power, are beginning to scale back their operations as they grow elsewhere. Apple assembler Pegatron is moving some of its networking-equipment production to Indonesia, as well as looking at India and Vietnam.[43] And Foxconn is considering cutting 10 percent of its blue-collar workforce for the iPhone, and reducing expenses by six billion yuan, even as it expands production in India.[44]

After meeting several times at the White House with U.S. president Donald Trump, Foxconn's Terry Gou announced that his company would invest $10 billion into a state-of the-art facility in Mount Pleasant, Wisconsin, that was to hire thirteen thousand U.S. workers to make LCD panels for televisions.[45] Foxconn's decision to open its first-ever plant in the U.S. was quickly touted as a political victory by the president, who joined the groundbreaking with Gou, then House Speaker Paul Ryan, and Governor Scott Walker. "Terry is a friend of mine," and together "we're restoring America's industrial might," Trump triumphantly crowed during the ceremony, which had the president clumsily wield a shovel at one point.[46] The deal has now been criticized as giving over $3 billion in tax breaks, the biggest-ever tax giveaway to a foreign company in U.S. history, and it is now unclear how many workers actually will be hired or if much will ever be produced there (it could end up primarily a research and development center and have few if any blue-collar employees, Foxconn's Louis Woo suggested in early 2019).[47] Still, Foxconn's consideration of a major investment in the U.S. suggests a future where China is expected to become less and less important to the Taiwanese company and probably many other global manufacturers.

At the Fortune Global Forum in Guangzhou in late 2017, several months after signing the Wisconsin deal, Terry Gou was his usual rambling self when he participated in a question-and-answer session attended by other CEOs and the media. He described his impressions of Trump ("He is a very straightforward—if he likes you, he likes you, if he doesn't like you, [you know] he doesn't. He is a businessman, he uses direct, simple language.") and talked about how much he missed Apple's Steve Jobs, who was a "great thinker," mentioning that he was one of the only Chinese to attend Jobs's funeral, which had included a tantric ceremony—"yellow tantra, not black tantra," Gou said. After bragging about how governors from ten states had approached him seeking Foxconn's investment before he chose Wisconsin, Foxconn's founder veered into a riff on how good his company had been to laborers in its many years in China. "Those poor workers previously couldn't get access to meat or eggs, but then we provided them good meals. After twenty years of business in China we had a gathering with them and they brought their kids, and we found out they were all fat and chubby," Gou said. "That's what I learned from the U.S. If you eat an egg every day you will get chubby. We have over 1.2 million workers in China. We have a lot of workers, and we have trained a lot of people through our management training system. They were able to learn from Foxconn, and I think we contributed to the whole process [of the development] of China."[48]

China's premier scholar of the countryside—from a privileged gentry family and educated at the country's best universities before getting a Ph.D. in sociology at the London School of Economics—might never have studied the Chinese village if it had not been for personal tragedy. Shortly after marrying, Fei Xiaotong and his wife, also a sociologist, set out to do field research on the Yao minority who lived in the rugged mountains of Guangxi, just south of Guizhou. While the two of them were walking alone on a narrow mountain path, Fei stepped into a tiger trap and was badly hurt. His wife left to seek help. A week later her body was found floating in a rushing stream, in which she had drowned.[49] After painful months recovering in a hospital, a time when Fei struggled with whether he was to blame for his wife's death, in the summer of 1936 Fei went to Kaixiangong, where his older sister taught sericulture techniques in a girls' school. The village, in Jiangsu Province, located not far from where they had been born, had a tradition of silk production but was struggling from new competition from the more competitive Japanese industry. It was there that he carried out a meticulous observation of local life and its economy, research that would become his dissertation thesis and seminal work, *Peasant Life in China: A Field Study of Country Life in the Yangtze Valley* (1939). In that book and in *From the Soil: The Foundations of Chinese Society* and *Reconstructing Rural China,* both published in 1948, Fei laid out in detail the then-radical belief that any viable future for the Chinese countryside would have to give agency to its poor and discriminated-against farmers. In understanding the countryside and what lay ahead for them, Chinese scholarship, too, should find its own way, not indiscriminately borrow from the West, Fei argued.[50]

Fei was a revolutionary of his time, but many of his ideas for China are still surprisingly applicable today. China's rural economy suffered from stagnation. China needed to reform the ownership of land and develop a local economy in the villages that in part relied on small family businesses and small-scale industrialization, possibly organized as cooperatives. He hoped that a more vibrant village economy with new enterprises would then lure back those villagers who had left and received an education, an outlook not dissimilar from today's "returning geese" policies. Influenced by famed Polish social anthropologist Bronisław Malinowski, whom he had studied under in London, Fei internalized Malinowski's theory of functionalism, that people acted to satisfy their own needs, rather than for society—a view, as it would turn out, deeply antithetical to the country's future Communist leaders. Politically, that meant rural Chinese would need to break free of excessive and ill-informed control by the central government, in part by developing some form of grassroots democracy, in which educated villagers could play a role. The details the sociologist largely left unexplained, although he wrote that traditionally some local autonomy was guaranteed by a "gentry buffer," a class of wealthier rural landholders that in theory would deflect some intrusive policies from the center, and who he thought might be key to some form of local democracy. He also recognized, however, that this rural gentry class, from which his own family came, was usually more interested in securing its own power and interests. "After the economic base is stabilized, political freedoms and other such rights that are secondary to sheer survival could be discussed and enacted, but it would be very lucky if this happened in such a country because it would be a miracle for powers that are beyond people's control suddenly to start serving the people," Fei wrote in 1948. "Miracles may occur, of course, but they cannot be taken for granted. In order to guarantee that the government will serve the people, people will first have to check the power of government."[51] After the founding of the People's Republic one year later, Fei, although not a party member, initially won acclaim for his prolific writings and was treated well by the new Communist officials as they tried to woo intellectuals to their cause.

That was to abruptly change in 1952 as the Communist Party solidified its control. In an irony probably not lost on Fei, the Western ideology of Marx, as filtered through the Soviet experience, became the only acceptable lens through which to view Chinese society, and the field of sociology was dismissed as "bourgeois pseudoscience." Fei was shifted into full-time research on ethnic minorities, which was viewed as important by the new leaders, but also had to be done within the parameters of a Marxist viewpoint.[52] He was to spend the next several years between Beijing and China's southwest, including Guizhou, before once again falling victim to China's politics.[53] Fei was outspoken during the Hundred Flowers Movement of 1956–57, when Mao briefly encouraged intellectual freedom, but then condemned as a rightist, when the chairman later reversed course. Fei spent the next twenty years out of academia and in exile; at one point his assigned job was keeping all the toilets clean in a building. Only after the death of Mao, in 1976, was Fei rehabilitated and chosen to help reestablish the field of sociology. In 1979 he was sent to the U.S. as part of a delegation to reestablish scholarly ties, where one American academic described him as "roly-poly, ebullient, outgoing, and invariably smiling."[54] But, no doubt chastened by his years in exile, Fei never again advocated for the political rights of China's rural people. Fei died in 2005.

Eighty years after Fei Xiaotong first wrote about China's countryside, it is still struggling. Despite years of economic reforms and billions of dollars spent on roads, rail, dams, and social-welfare programs, it badly lags urban areas. Rural incomes—including those of migrant workers—remain at about one-third those in cities. While coastal provinces Zhejiang and Guangdong have GDPs as large as Australia and Spain, both in the top fifteen global economies, Guizhou's is smaller than Bangladesh's,[55] even with huge transfers from Beijing. Vast differences in the quality of education define the country, with four times as much spent on Shanghai elementary school students as on children in western provinces. Young people from the villages are far less likely to finish high school, and far fewer yet ever make it to university. The gaps in resources put into education are mirrored in health care, with life expectancies in much of the interior below the national average. Despite years of effort and huge sums spent (in 2018, 1.2 trillion yuan, or $180 billion was spent on poverty alleviation),[56] millions of people are still poor with the majority of them in the countryside. And much of the divide ultimately can be traced to the continued force of the *hukou* and land-tenure policies that limit where people can live and how they use their land. After sweeping reform plans that aimed to eventually end the decades-old restrictions were announced at the Third Plenum in 2013, little has been done. Instead, those places that are starting to allow migrants to settle down aren't the cities they want to go to. Changes to liberalize land ownership outside the cities are piecemeal and often aim to encourage land consolidation or "scale agriculture," usually benefiting local officials and wealthy businesspeople from outside, rather than local farmers.

China's leaders continue their obsession with massive top-down, government-mandated schemes. It is a tendency going back to the Great Wall, first built in the third century BC and on display more recently with the Three Gorges Dam, finished in 2012, that cost $37 billion, including paying for the resettlement of 1.3 million people. The $76 billion South-North Water Diversion Project, which runs through ten provinces and supplies Beijing and Tianjin with water from the Yangtze River,[57] shows a similar mind-set. Even as cities in Guangdong add robots to their factories and run out migrants, the central government has announced, with great fanfare, a Greater Bay Area development plan, which is supposed to lure white-collar workers and professionals with tax breaks, and aims to link Hong Kong, Macau, Shenzhen, Guangzhou, and multiple cities of the Pearl River Delta, including Dongguan. What would be the world's largest economic growth zone is supposed to eventually surpass Silicon Valley, in its innovation and technology output. How planners intend to unify the different legal systems, customs control, and currencies of the region is still unexplained. (The massive protests in Hong Kong that started in 2019 against mainland Chinese control, also suggest how far-fetched the plan is.)

China's inland provinces, to which many migrants are returning, are afflicted with the same centrally planned megaprojects. Guizhou, for example, is fixated on building its Big Data Cloud base, while to the south, $184 million of central and provincial funds have been spent on the world's largest radio telescope, which is five hundred meters across and covers an area equal to thirty football fields in the karst mountains. Building that device, which it is hoped will facilitate the world's first contact with aliens,[58] required relocating nine thousand farmers,[59] many of them Miao and Buyi. Xi's poverty-alleviation goals, too, continue to rely on large forced population transfers. In just the northwestern province of Shaanxi, officials are relocating 2.4 million poor from their homes in remote, often mountainous regions to newly created villages.[60] Sometimes the relocations, too, are driven by the profit motive, where local officials are intent on converting the now-vacant land into industrial zones or commercial real estate. And whether the new resettlement communities will do well or sink into economic decline, as could well happen with Chongqing's new model village of Daling, is unclear. The danger is that China's west could become riddled with new, denser, and larger settlements of people, many without work, and all at risk of slipping back into poverty; people who once lived in dispersed villages in remote regions, but ultimately could feed themselves through subsistence farming, might become part of these newly created communities, which often have no means of livelihood beyond state handouts. Meanwhile, in the cities, fewer and fewer factories will want to hire workers, and those who stay could get stuck in dead-end, low-level service jobs or, worse yet, become unemployed. What the farmers and migrants actually want seems largely irrelevant to China's planners. "If workers are displaced by robots but have no land to return to, China might soon see the rise of urban ghettos and mounting social problems," warns sociologist Huang Yu.[61]

How all this will unfold in China is still unclear. Will planners be able to continue on the same course they have pursued through previous slowdowns and simply shovel money toward reigniting growth, even if it requires ever more capital? That is likely possible for at least the near future. But in the longer term, the law of diminishing returns means China will suffer an ever more anemic economy with slower and slower income growth. That becomes a serious problem as inequality grows and China's disadvantaged become ever more aware of their meager lot. And if China continues to clamp down tighter on migrants who want to settle in the cities, it could eventually spark serious protests. Research has shown that the ability to change one's social status by converting to an urban registration has been important in strengthening public support for the government, even when jobs and wages don't change. "Upward mobility defined by *hukou* status changes also significantly increases citizens' trust in the government. It implies that the slowdown of China's economic growth in recent years won't immediately result in political instability if the paths for upward mobility are kept open," notes one scholar.[62] But that route is facing resistance not just from officials, but also from urbanites who don't wish to share the cities' schools, hospitals, and streets, with migrants.

Stagnation or something much worse happening in China is bad
for the world. The argument that China's misfortune is another's fortune often doesn't pan out either: as jobs dry up in China, new ones
may grow in Southeast Asia but are unlikely to do so in the West.
While a too-powerful China is a threat to liberal values, a wounded
China could well drag down economic growth on a global scale. As
economies have slowed in developed countries, multinationals from
the U.S., Europe, and Japan have increasingly relied on China's rapid
rise. Since the 2008 financial crisis, China has been the largest contributor to global growth, a role some seem to assume will never end.
Perhaps that's because there is no other obvious country to step forward if China's upward rise stalls. (India, although potentially a future
driver of growth, faces its own set of problems.) Earlier predictions of
how large the country's middle class is set to become—McKinsey has
said that it will grow to 357 million by 2022[63]—now look increasingly
fanciful. Those bullish prognostications were all built on the assump-
tion that ever more people from the countryside would urbanize,
become well-off, and join China's ever-swelling and happily consum-
ing bourgeois. Now that counted-on spending power very likely will
never materialize. As international banks have spit out timetables for
when China becomes the world's largest economy—HSBC Holdings
says it will happen by 2030, when China's economy will total $26 tril-
lion, compared to the U.S. GDP of $25.2 trillion;[64] that's the same year
predicted by the International Monetary Fund—few if any are pos-
ing an important additional question: How long will its number-one
status last? It is entirely possible that China could become the biggest
economy in the world but then fall behind if things go bad at home.

That would have devastating consequences. A troubled China
where most people see their living standards plummet would expose
the yawning wealth gap in all its inequity, further fanning unrest.
Without a free press, an opposition party, or meaningful elections,
the people have few outlets other than taking to the streets. And while
the Communist Party long ago showed its willingness to crack down
brutally on its own people when threatened, it might well decide that
repression at home is not enough. A militarily powerful Communist

Party facing widespread dissension at home might well seek to distract its citizens by lashing out in a hot spot in the region, such as Hong Kong, Taiwan, or the South China Sea. While China's bottled-up system has far fewer pressure valves than the U.S. and other countries, and a brittleness they don't share, these countries are starting to crack under their own existential crises. A China that exported unrest could help "throw the spark into the overloaded mine of the present industrial system," as Marx predicted under different circumstances more than a century and a half ago.

While China's big cities now ban fireworks, the villages still revel in them. Lunar New Year, the one time of year when everyone comes back to their hometowns, is something of a festival of rejuvenation for the usually emptied-out countryside. The migrants who have saved a little money inevitably will set off their own collection of rockets, Roman candles, and long strings of exploding crackers; even if the townships are discouraging the practice, perhaps as part of an occasional environmental or safety campaign, the locals rightly assume they will turn a blind eye, and the villages reverberate with explosions, and wafts of acrid smoke hang in the air. It both fulfills the traditional purpose of scaring ghosts and bringing luck, and shows off the migrant's recent good fortune to fellow returnees and those who have stayed behind. The more one sets off, the wealthier one has become—that is the unsaid message, and everyone knows that there is no guarantee that their wealth will last another year. Residence doors have the ubiquitous red stickers with good-luck couplets. Pigs and water buffalo are slaughtered on the open-air charnel platform that sits on the little road just above the bridge that connects the old and new parts of Binghuacun. Each night is an occasion to eat hot pot together and drink the home-brewed *mijiu*.

One of my last visits to the village was during Lunar New Year, once again a chance to find its scattered migrants together in one place. Gathered around the low tables in Ruchun's parents' house, perched on the little stools and kid-size chairs seemingly favored everywhere in the countryside, we went through the rituals of toasting and exchanging cigarettes, and those who rarely saw each other talked of where factories were shedding workers, which were closing and where others might be opening, and what plans they had for the future. At one point in that long, drink-besotted evening, several men walked through, handing out small pieces of blank paper and well-worn pens to everyone, save myself and the driver from Guiyang in whose car I had come. Distracted by the hubbub, I didn't ask their purpose, and it was not until the next day that I found out I had witnessed an example of Beijing's long-touted grassroots democracy. It had been an election for the chief of the village committee, the less powerful counterpart to the village's party leaders. (China uses a two-branch system in the countryside, although often the committee-chief position and the party-leader position are held by the same person; the village's party leaders were chosen not by the village residents but by higher-rank party officials in Jialiang, the township overseeing Binghuacun and a handful of other villages.) Ruchun had pointed out a red poster roughly plastered on a neighbor's wall. On it were scrawled the names of the four locals who had competed for committee leader; the winner had received sixty-nine votes, each one counted in a stroke in the five-line character *zheng*, meaning "upright." When I asked Ruchun whether he was capable and would do a good job, he was deeply dismissive.

The new chief had never "gone out," as rural people referred to leaving the village to work, so had little knowledge of the world, Ruchun said scornfully. And regardless, the position had no real powers—the party head, Mo Bochun, appointed by officials in Jialiang, was the one who actually determined whether policies were carried out; he in turn, however, was relatively weak when compared to his bosses in the township, where the real power was held. The election really meant nothing. That was why he had not explained what was happening the night before. The new chief could do very little for Binghuacun, least of all help it develop into the new tourism village all were hoping for, Ruchun said. As for the road, the one I had first heard about in 2000—the two lanes of smooth asphalt that were to connect

Binghuacun to the township and on to the capital and then on to all the modernity of urban China—the new chief would have no role in overseeing its long-awaited completion. And indeed, Ruchun said, a look of pained honesty crossing his face, no one really knew whether a road would make much difference in Binghuacun's future.

Epilogue

In 2021, the Chinese Communist Party, already the world's longest-governing political party, will celebrate the hundredth anniversary of its founding. It will be a self-congratulatory event, cities hung with the bright red and gold national flag and banners featuring the hammer and sickle, and with Chinese media full of fulsome speeches given by senior party functionaries. Xi Jinping will no doubt proclaim success in meeting the first of the party's two centenary goals,[1] to "build a moderately prosperous society in all respects." That means eradicating absolute poverty, one of Xi's signature "three tough battles" (the other two, stemming financial risks and environmental pollution), and seeing average GDP per capita reach $10,000, both of which the country is on track to achieve. China will mark a second centenary in 2049, one hundred years after the country's founding. By that date the aim is to have transformed China into a "modern socialist country" that is both prosperous and strong and still firmly under the control of the heavy-handed benevolence of the party. But whether the CCP will be around then and leading China is unclear. The former Soviet Union, which had seemed stable and likely to long endure, quickly unraveled before getting to its seventy-fifth anniversary.

To make it through just the next decade, the party will have to find a balance between what has been described as "repression and responsiveness." That has long been the approach to governing used by Chinese officialdom, to both placate and control the populace, seen for example in its emphasis on ensuring ever higher living standards while harshly suppressing dissident speech and action. Using "repression and responsiveness" with China's migrant workers in particular has a long history. It was that group that Manfred Elfstrom, now an assistant professor at the University of British Columbia, was referring to when he coined this alliterative phrase.[2]

The strategy of punishment combined with conciliation was already obvious during China's first big industrial labor protests of the reform era, when in 2003 thousands of workers were summarily laid off after the ferroalloy factory in Liaoyang, Liaoning, in China's Northeast, was suddenly shut down. Then the Liaoyang authorities were ordered by their bosses in Beijing to pay some back wages and unemployment benefits to the unemployed workers, a few senior factory managers were publicly reprimanded, and punishment was promised for corrupt local officials. The strike leaders, however, were punished with harsh jail sentences, thus sending a warning message to other workers who organized for their rights. That two-sided approach of the carrot and the stick has continued to be part of the official playbook in dealing with workers' grievances ever since.

Today it has been updated for the digital age. Global attention has focused on the expanding and often frightening use of monitoring technology and social credit systems to reward and punish China's urbanites, as well as their horrific use in conjunction with the mass incarceration of mainly Muslims in the western region of Xinjiang. Less noted, the lives of China's migrants and poorest farmers, too, are the targets of new, more sophisticated forms of control. In cities like Dongguan, where factories increasingly struggle to make a profit, local officials are experimenting with social credit systems that punish bosses who cut costs by not paying employees full salaries and welfare benefits, barring them from borrowing from banks and buying plane or high-speed-rail tickets. China's Ministry of Human Resources and Social Security announced that it had blacklisted 180 companies for serious problems with wage arrears in just the first seven months of 2019.[3] The aim, of course, is to try to ensure that migrants get the salary and benefits Chinese law promises. This is how the party demonstrates responsiveness.

But repression, too, is expanding as strikes continue to grow in frequency. Facial and voice recognition is increasingly used to identify protesters, who often are punished with detention. Activist workers are also finding themselves blacklisted from future jobs and unable to start their own companies. What's changed from before is China's rapid rollout of "smart cities," where government agencies, including public security, transportation, banking, and commerce bureaus, increasingly can share information on any potential customer and, if they want, block them from receiving services. For migrants who have been involved in protests, that can affect their ability to borrow money, register a business, or even get their children into school. While previously these practices already existed, they often could be evaded by simply moving to a new city. Today that is less and less true.

In a disturbing example of China's new uses of digital authoritarianism, security officials are targeting the more vulnerable migrants in cities in an effort to develop larger, more sophisticated databases of China's citizens. (Old-fashioned physical documents like the *hukou* and the *dangan*, or personal dossier, have long been used to monitor and control China's people, of course.) But now local governments in provinces including Anhui, Shaanxi, and Guizhou are starting to use cutting-edge technologies to track their migrant populations, ordering them to submit to voice and facial recognition, fingerprinting, and blood tests for DNA sequencing, to help "construct a harmonious society," as police in Guiyang eerily put it, reported advocacy group Human Rights Watch.[4]

Even in the countryside where many migrants are now returning, one can see new uses of technology that aim to both improve lives and tighten control, the complementary aspects of stability maintenance. As part of his effort to end poverty, Xi Jinping has touted an improved form of "targeted" poverty alleviation. Rather than label a whole village as impoverished and provide all its residents with financial support, the previous long-standing practice, the aim now is to determine whether each family is poor enough to qualify for aid, a positive effort to ensure that money isn't given to those who aren't needy, while at the same time curbing the corrupt practice of local officials doling out money to their relatives or friends. To do that successfully, a national registration for poor households has been developed and is now being put into a digital database that multiple government agencies can access. Local officials have been gathering information in the countryside and have registered 128,000 villages and 29 million poor households in Guizhou, Hunan, Guangxi, Sichuan, Yunnan, and other provinces.[5]

The party also periodically surveys households to see whether they should continue to be eligible for poverty relief, including China's *dibao,* the minimum guaranteed income.[6] A huge amount of information is being gathered on rural residents, including their income, how much land they have, how many crops they grow annually, their education levels, any chronic illnesses they might have, and whether they have migrant relatives elsewhere, to cite just some examples. Authorities also check whether villagers have a computer or a pet or have enrolled their children in schools outside their neighborhoods, all defined as luxury items and so grounds for automatic disqualification from aid. Families find themselves barred from anti-poverty funds if they don't participate in what the government refers to as "voluntary" work, such as cleaning streets, taking part in neighborhood safety patrols, helping out older residents, and arranging and distributing donated goods. Increasingly, all of this personal data is available to anyone who wishes to use their phone to read it by swiping a bar code affixed to villagers' front doors;[7] the shame of revealing potentially embarrassing personal information to officials and their neighbors is causing some villagers to voluntarily opt out of the relief program. At the same time, authorities continue to push the use of rural e-commerce to boost farmers' incomes.

As the U.S.-China trade war continues on its hiccuping on-again, off-again course, the unwinding of manufacturing supply chains that have long tied the two countries' economies together is becoming a reality, what the pundits like to call "decoupling." Apple has encouraged its suppliers to consider moving manufacturing out of China,[8] and some, like Foxconn, have already begun.[9] A top executive from Li & Fung, the world's largest consumer-goods supplier (serving Walmart and Nike, among others), said that China factories are feeling "urgent and desperate." For the first time ever, Li & Fung's sourcing from China in 2019 fell to less than one half its global business, down from 59 percent in 2015.[10] Decoupling, too, seems to have become a key part of the U.S. government's trade strategy under Trump, while in China Xi Jinping increasingly touts the old Maoist policy of "self-reliance," or *zili gengsheng*,[11] while in reality seeking suppliers outside the U.S. for everything from soybeans to lobsters.[12] If the decoupling process continues between China and the U.S., each its biggest trading partner, more factories will lay off their workers, adding to tensions in both the cities and the countryside to which migrants will have to return.

As populist movements rise in reaction to economic and social disparity around the world, spurring unexpected outcomes—Brexit in the United Kingdom, right-wing politicians winning in Northern Europe, and Trumpism dividing and degrading American politics and society—one must wonder whether growing divisions in China could eventually force change, too. (The protests Hong Kong has seen, too, are in part driven by deep economic divisions.) While its leaders benefit from one-party rule, allowing them to push controversial policies that solidify their control, it also leaves them vulnerable, easily blamed for any and all problems the people may encounter. While they take credit for years of rapid economic growth, they also can be attacked for misrule when living standards deteriorate. The party knows this well, and so continues apace with its policies of repression and responsiveness, now updated with the latest technologies. The question is what happens if the millions of migrants like the Mos eventually decide that the carrot is insufficient, the stick unbearable. How would the party confront a sustained movement against its rule and would it ultimately survive? And could this derail China's continued economic and political rise? Those are real questions as the party struggles to navigate the end of an economic model that powered China's rise for decades, but still today doesn't provide a fair chance for one-half of the people in whose name it rules and is leaving them out of its grand visions for the future.

Acknowledgments

Twenty years ago I first met the Mos, young migrants working in the factories of Dongguan, and shortly afterward visited them in Bing-huacun, the remote village they came from in southwestern China. In the years that followed they were always open and welcoming to this curious visitor. For their generosity I will always be grateful.

I grew up in a household of books where writing was valued, and for that I have my parents to thank. My father, Dexter Roberts, taught me the importance of, as he put it, "looking from the lives of those not famous." My mother, Susan Boehner, read the manuscript of this book not once but twice, and helped improve its diction and grammar. Both always told me I should write a book, and not as an aspiration, but as something I simply must do someday, an attitude that helped in the long hours of writing before reaching the midway point. My stepfather, Bill Boehner, was always ready to discuss China with insight, and cut out and saved each article I wrote over the years.

In the struggle to produce a book that ranges across history I owe much to Steve Levine. Not only did he make sure references to Mao Zedong and the Chinese Communist Party weren't wrong, he also read the manuscript for infelicities of style, in the process helping make a better book. To my agent Leah Spiro, who was patient as I labored to get it done, and my editor Michael Flamini, I also owe a debt of gratitude. Without either of them, this book would not be.

I am particularly indebted to my former colleagues at *Businessweek*. Thanks goes to Mark Clifford, who one morning over breakfast in a

Beijing hotel told me it was time to write a book and sooner rather than later. Thanks to Bob Dowling, who found a place in *Businessweek* for the stories that introduced me to Western China, who long ago told me I should write about the people from the "Other China," and recently provided wise suggestions on the manuscript. I am grateful to Joyce Barnathan, who guided me through many an early story on China's economy; Brian Bremner and Chris Power, who later helped me with many more; and Pete Engardio, who was a generous writing collaborator. Greg Girard was along on many reporting trips, producing evocative images while always making traveling more fun. Also, very important were the researchers and news assistants that I worked with over the years: in particular I must thank Li Yan, Xiang Ji, and Huang Zhe.

As *Businessweek* became part of Bloomberg, Brad Stone lent invaluable advice as I navigated the complications of starting a book while working full-time as a reporter. Special thanks must go to Richard McGregor and Matt Pottinger, both of whom provided encouragement and helpful advice on writing a book, and Peter Wonacott, who gave me the contacts for a bright young official from Guizhou named Mo Ruxuan back in 2000.

Journalist friends in Beijing were always a delight to work and socialize with and it is impossible to thank them all. I, however, benefited from many conversations with Jonathan Ansfield, Rosie Blau, Rebecca Blumenstein, Andrew Browne, Chris Buckley, Zach Coleman, Mark Davey, Jason Dean, Paul Eckert, Gady Epstein, Haze Fan, Leta Hong Fincher, Jaime FlorCruz, Mei Fong, Matt Forney, Michael Forsythe, Hannah Gardner, Peter Hessler, Lucy Hornby, Charles Hutzler, Ian Johnson, William Kazer, Anthony Kuhn, James Kynge, Ed Lanfranco, Frank Langfitt, Christina Larson, Charlotte Li, Melinda Liu, Mary Kay Magistad, Mark Magnier, Peter Martin, Paul Mooney, David Murphy, Evan Osnos, Shai Oster, Jeremy Page, Philip Pan, Ted Plafker, John Pomfret, Brian Rhoads, Kirk Troy, Corinne Vigniel, and Jasmine Zhao. Thanks also to Brett Aaron, Mike Bauer, Bill Bishop, Duncan Clark, Colin Cowles, Ted Dean, Todd Ewing, Karin Finkelston, Greg Dalton, Jeremy Goldkorn, Trevor Hale, Jim Harkness, James Hawkey, John Holden, Fred Hu, Declan Kelleher, Scott

Kennedy, Elizabeth Knup, Lawrence Kole, Scott Kronick, Kaiser Kuo, Woo Lee, Robin Lewis, Phil Lisio, Bryan Lohmar, Alec McCabe, Matt McGarvey, James McGregor, Alex Pearson, Jack Perkowski, Mitch Presnick, Andrew Regier, Andy Rothman, Orville Schell, Joseph Simone, Tom Stahl, Anne Stevenson-Yang, Rose Tang, Didi Kirsten Tatlow, Corbett Wall, Evan Wonacott, Joerg Wuttke, and William Zarit.

For their knowledge of migrants' lives and work I am indebted to Dee Lee in Guangzhou, Sun Zhe in Guiyang, and Wang Kan in Beijing. Ben Schwall and Hayes Lou shared their voluminous knowledge and contacts in the Pearl River Delta manufacturing world. Han Dongfang and Geoffry Crothall at China Labour Bulletin, and Ian Spaulding and Aaron Halegua, helped me better understand worker-management relations. Li Ping introduced me to the basics of China's land system. I benefited immensely from the research of many economists, including Gan Li, John Giles, Louis Kuijs, and Albert Park, and the work of Arthur Kroeber, Andrew Batson, and Ernan Cui at Gavekal Dragonomics.

Deena Mansour of the Mansfield Center at the University of Montana provided me with a place to finish my book and continue getting intellectual stimulation, for which I am grateful. Finally, a heartfelt thanks goes to Sun Min, Ariana, and Jake the schnauzer, who were always there. My daily book-writing schedule often meant I was unavailable to talk, play, or be much fun at all, and for that they were mostly forgiving.

Notes

EPIGRAPH

1. Fei Xiaotong, *From the Soil: The Foundations of Chinese Society. A Translation of Fei Xiaotong's* Xiangtu Zhongguo, *with an Introduction and Epilogue by Gary C. Hamilton and Wang Zheng.* Translated and edited by Gary C. Hamilton and Wang Zheng, (Berkeley: University of California Press, 1992).

INTRODUCTION

1. Mo Meiquan, migrant worker, interview with author, August 25, 2000.
2. Mo Yukai, migrant worker, interview with author, August 25, 2000.
3. Mo Wenzhi and Mo Rubo, migrant workers, interview with author, November 1, 2000.
4. Mo Wenke, migrant worker, interview with author, October 28, 2000.
5. Mo Meiquan, interview with author, October 29, 2000.
6. Businessweek Editorial, "China's Homegrown Illegal Aliens," *Businessweek,* December 10, 2000, https://www.bloomberg.com/news/articles/2000 -12-10/chinas-homegrown-illegal-aliens-intl-edition (accessed September 24, 2019) and Dexter Roberts, "The Great Migration: Chinese peasants are fleeing their villages to chase big-city dreams," *Businessweek,* December 10, 2000, https://www.bloomberg.com/news/articles/2000-12-10/the-great -migration-intl-edition (accessed May 26, 2019).
7. Dominic Barton, Yougang Chen, and Amy Jin, "Mapping China's middle class," *McKinsey Quarterly,* June 2013, https://www.mckinsey.com/industries /retail/our-insights/mapping-chinas-middle-class (accessed August 13, 2019).
8. Barry Naughton, "Is China Socialist?," *Journal of Economic Perspectives* (Winter 2017): 18.

1. THE FACTORY

1. Mo Rubo, interview with author, April 19, 2017.
2. Mary Gallagher, "The Evolution of Workers' Rights in China," interview by Neysun Mahboubi, podcast of the University of Pennsylvania Center for the Study of Contemporary China, March 12, 2019, https://

cscc.sas.upenn.edu/podcasts/2019/03/12/ep-14-evolution-workers
-rights-china-mary-gallagher (accessed March 15, 2019).

3. Kam Wing Chan, *China's Hukou System at 60: Continuity and Reform*
https://www.researchgate.net/publication/324106192_China's_Hukou
_System_at_60_Continuity_and_Reform (accessed August 2, 2018).

4. Kam Wing Chan, professor at the University of Washington, interview
with author, March 9, 2012.

5. Kam Wing Chan, *China's Hukou System at 60: Continuity and Reform*
https://www.researchgate.net/publication/324106192_China's_Hukou
_System_at_60_Continuity_and_Reform (accessed August 2, 2018).

6. Ibid.

7. Dexter Roberts, "China: Wto or Bust?" *Businessweek,* November 22, 1999,
https://www.bloomberg.com/news/articles/1999-11-21/china-wto-or
-bust (accessed May 26, 2019).

8. Charlene Barshefsky, U.S. Trade Representative, interview by John
Bussey, *Wall Street Journal,* video, June 16, 2015, https://www.wsj.com
/video/negotiating-tips-the-only-word-for-no-is-no/BE3FF51D-B248
-46CB-A9A1-FA1BD81C2FAA.html (accessed May 26, 2019).

9. Alejandro Reyes, "Just a Start: The long WTO negotiations look easy
compared to what comes next," *Asiaweek,* November 26, 1999, http://
www.cnn.com/ASIANOW/asiaweek/magazine/99/1126/cover1.html
(accessed May 26, 2019).

10. Bob Davis, "When the World Opened the Gates of China," *Wall Street
Journal,* July 27, 2018, https://www.wsj.com/articles/when-the-world
-opened-the-gates-of-china-1532701482 (accessed May 26, 2019).

11. "The Opium War," National Army Museum, https://www.nam.ac.uk
/explore/opium-war-1839-1842 (accessed May 26, 2019).

12. Lee Khoon Choy, *Pioneers of Modern China: Understanding the Inscrutable
Chinese* (Singapore: World Scientific, 2005).
Juan Alejandro Forrest de Sloper, "First Opium War," *Book of Days Tales,*
June 3, 2015, http://www.bookofdaystales.com/first-opium-war/ (accessed
August 14, 2019).
Charles W. Hayford, "Lin Zexu," in *Encyclopaedia Britannica Online,* https://
www.britannica.com/biography/Lin-Zexu (accessed August 14, 2019).

13. Lin Zexu, "Lin Zexu (LinTse-hsu) writing to Britain's Queen Victoria
to Protest the Opium Trade, 1839," USC US-China Institute website,
2019, https://china.usc.edu/lin-zexu-lintse-hsu-writing-britains-queen
-victoria-protest-opium-trade-1839 (accessed September 26, 2019).

14. Huang Huiping, deputy chief of the Dongguan labor bureau, interview
with author, March 2005.

15. Dexter Roberts, "Inside a Chinese Sweatshop: 'A Life Of Fines And Beating,'" *Bloomberg Businessweek,* October 1, 2000, https://www.bloomberg
.com/news/articles/2000-10-01/inside-a-chinese-sweatshop-a-life-of
-fines-and-beating (accessed July 26, 2019).

16. Migrant worker, interview with author, September 1, 2000.

17. Selina Qing, factory manager, interview with author, August 23, 2000.

18. Anita Chan, *China's Workers Under Assault: The Exploitation of Labor in a Globalizing Economy* (Armonk, NY: M. E. Sharpe, 2001), 9.
19. Mo Meiquan and Mo Ruxian, migrant worker and father, interview with author, October 29, 2000.
20. Ibid.
21. Lei, factory director, interview with author, November 1, 2000.
22. Zhou Litai, worker rights lawyer, interview with author, November 2, 2000.
23. *Standing Up: The Workers Movement in China, 2000–2004*, China Labour Bulletin, July 8, 2007, http://www.clb.org.hk/en/content/standing -workers-movement-china-2000-2004 (accessed May 26, 2019).
24. Xu Zhiyong, "Sun Zhigang case: The Last Ten Years," *China Change*, June 5, 2013, https://chinachange.org/tag/sun-zhigang-case/ (accessed May 26, 2019).
25. "After the Detention and Death of Sun Zhigang: Prisons and Detention in China," Congressional-Executive Commission on China, October 27, 2003, https://www.cecc.gov/sites/chinacommission.house.gov/files/documents /roundtables/2003/CECC%20Roundtable%20-%20After%20Detention%20 Death%20Sun%20Zhigang%20Prisons%2C%20Detention%2C%20 Torture%20China%20-%2010.27.03.pdf (accessed May 26, 2019).
26. Teng Biao, "The Sun Zhigang Incident and the Future of Constitutionalism: Does the Chinese Constitution Have a Future?," Centre for Rights and Justice, Faculty of Law, the Chinese University of Hong Kong, December 30, 2013, https://www.law.cuhk.edu.hk/en/research/crj/download /papers/2013-tb-szg-constitutionalism.pdf (accessed May 26, 2019).

2. THE FAMILY

1. Confucius, *The Analects*, trans. William Edward Soothill (New York: Dover Publications, 1995).
2. Mo Rubo, interview with author, April 19, 2017.
3. Sanna Johnson, NGO director, interview with author, January 13, 2014.
4. Yang Dongping, 21st Century Institute president, interview with author, March 19, 2013.
5. Du Shuang, NGO director, interview with author, February 5, 2015.
6. Scott Rozelle, economist at Stanford University, interview with author, March 4, 2015.
7. Interview with boarding school principal, March 11, 2015.
8. Interview with boarding school student, March 11, 2015.
9. Heidi Ross, "China Country Study," UNESCO Digital Library, 2005, http://unesdoc.unesco.org/images/0014/001461/146108e.pdf (accessed May 26, 2019).
10. Arne Duncan, "Secretary Arne Duncan's Remarks at OECD's Release of the Program for International Student Assessment (PISA) 2009 Results," U.S. Department of Education, December 7, 2010, https://www .ed.gov/news/speeches/secretary-arne-duncans-remarks-oecds-release -program-international-student-assessment- (accessed May 26, 2019).
11. Christine Armario, "'Wake-up call': U.S. students trail global leaders,"

Associated Press, December 7, 2010, http://www.nbcnews.com/id/40544897/ns/us_news-life/t/wake-up-call-us-students-trail-global-leaders/#.W6c7uSN95DQ (accessed May 26, 2019).

12. Wu Xiaogang, professor at Hong Kong University of Science and Technology, interview with author, October 26, 2015.

13. Lynette Ong, professor at the University of Toronto, interview with author, February 10, 2013.

14. Hu Nan, "China Footprint: College entrance exam 40 years on," CGTN.com, September 16, 2017, https://news.cgtn.com/news/3259544d35557a6333566d54/share_p.html (accessed June 15, 2019).

15. Interview with boarding school principal, March 11, 2015.

16. Interview with dormitory monitor, March 11, 2015.

17. Interview with boarding school student, March 11, 2015.

18. Anita Koo, sociologist at Hong Kong Polytechnic University, interview with author, October 23, 2015.

19. Anita Koo, Holly Ming, and Bill Tsang, "The Doubly Disadvantaged: How Return Migrant Students Fail to Access and Deploy Capitals for Academic Success in Rural Schools," *Sociology*, January 13, 2014, https://www.researchgate.net/publication/274973248_The_Doubly_Disadvantaged_How_Return_Migrant_Students_Fail_to_Access_and_Deploy_Capitals_for_Academic_Success_in_Rural_Schools (accessed June 18, 2019).

20. Scott Rozelle, interview with author, March 4, 2015.

21. John Giles, World Bank, interview with author, August 18, 2019.

22. Interview with rural father and grandfather, March 11, 2015.

23. Chen Xueliang, restaurant cook, interview with author, March 12, 2015.

24. Zhao Yinan and Luo Wangshu, "'Reform needed' for vocational education," *China Daily*, June 24, 2014, http://www.chinadaily.com.cn/china/2014-06/24/content_17610342.htm (accessed June 14, 2019).

25. Ibid.

26. Interview with vocational student, March 12, 2015.

27. Interview with vocational school principal, March 12, 2015.

28. Mo Rubo, interview with author, February 18, 2018.

29. "Outline of China's National Plan for Medium and Long-term Education Reform and Development (2010–2020)," State Council, July 2010, http://ncee.org/wp-content/uploads/2016/12/Sha-non-AV-5-China-Education-Plan-2010-2020.pdf (accessed June 15, 2019).

30. Gerard Postiglione, director of University of Hong Kong Wah Ching Centre of Research on Education in China, interview with author, March 25, 2013.

31. Xu Zhiyong, "For Freedom, Justice and Love—My Closing Statement to the Court," *China Change*, January 22, 2014, https://chinachange.org/2014/01/23/for-freedom-justice-and-love-my-closing-statement-to-the-court/ (accessed May 26, 2019)

3. THE LAND

1. Fei Xiaotong, *From the Soil: The Foundations of Chinese Society. A Translation of Fei Xiaotong's* Xiangtu Zhongguo, *with an Introduction and Epilogue*

by Gary C. Hamilton and Wang Zheng. Translated and edited by Gary C. Hamilton and Wang Zheng, (Berkeley: University of California Press, 1992).

2. Aibida, *Qiannan shilue* (*A Handbook of Guizhou*). 1750. Reprint (Guiyang: Guizhou Renmin Chubanshe, 1992). Cited in Jodi L. Weinstein, *Empire and Identity in Guizhou: Local Resistance to Qing Expansion* (Seattle: University of Washington Press, 2014).

3. Joanna Waley-Cohen, "Expansion and Colonization in Early Modern Chinese History," *History Compass*, 2004, https://onlinelibrary.wiley .com/doi/pdf/10.1111/j.1478-0542.2004.00076.x (accessed June 15, 2019).

4. Jodi L. Weinstein, *Empire and Identity in Guizhou: Local Resistance to Qing Expansion* (Seattle, University of Washington Press: 2014).

5. Ibid.

6. Robert Darrah Jenks, *Insurgency and Social Disorder in Guizhou: The "Miao" Rebellion, 1854–1873* (Honolulu: University of Hawaii Press, 1994).

7. Chris Buckley, "Girl's Death Sparks Rioting in China," Reuters, June 28, 2008, https://uk.reuters.com/article/uk-china-riot/girls-death-sparks-rioting-in-china-idUKPEK27256220080628 (accessed August 7, 2019).

8. Fu Jing, "No officials' kin involved in girl's death in Guizhou," *China Daily,* July 2, 2008, http://www.chinadaily.com.cn/china/2008-07/02/content _6811162.htm (accessed August 7, 2019).

9. David M. Deal and Laura Hostetler, *The Art of Ethnography: A Chinese Miao Album* (Seattle: University of Washington Press, 2006), 159–60, 166–67.

10. Mike Dash, "Emperor Wang Mang: China's First Socialist?" Smithsonian .com, December 9, 2011, https://www.smithsonianmag.com/history /emperor-wang-mang-chinas-first-socialist-2402977/ (accessed June 14, 2019).

11. Wm. Theodore de Bary, *Sources of Chinese Tradition*, 2nd ed. (New York: Columbia University Press, 1999).

12. Karl Marx, "Revolution in China and In Europe," *New York Daily Tribune,* June 14, 1853, https://www.marxists.org/archive/marx/works/1853/06/14 .htm (accessed June 15, 2019).

13. Robert Darrah Jenks, *Insurgency and Social Disorder in Guizhou: The "Miao" Rebellion, 1854–1873* (Honolulu: University of Hawaii Press, 1994).

14. Ma Wenfeng, interview with author, March 12, 2014.

15. Head of U.S. agricultural trade association in China, interview with author, March 12, 2014.

16. Mao Zedong, "Report on an Investigation of the Peasant Movement in Hunan, March 1927," *Selected Works of Mao Tse-tung*, vol. 1 (Beijing: Foreign Languages Press, 1965), https://www.marxists.org/reference /archive/mao/selected-works/volume-1/mswv1_2.htm (accessed June 14, 2019).

17. "Land Reform Law," China.org.cn, September 16, 2009, http://www

.china.org.cn/features/60years/2009-09/16/content_18537591.htm (accessed June 15, 2019).

18. "'The Xiaogang village story," China.org.cn, May 30, 2018, http://www .china.org.cn/china/2018-05/30/content_51532371.htm (accessed June 15, 2019).

19. Xiao Guangfei, interview with author, April 4, 2016.

20. Cary Huang, "Xi Jinping hails China's reform and opening up policy in symbolic visit to its village 'birthplace,'" April 26, 2017, https://www .scmp.com/news/china/policies-politics/article/1938917/xi-jinping -hails-chinas-reform-and-opening-policy (accessed June 15, 2019).

21. "Xi calls for people-centric reform measures, stresses employment," Xinhua News Agency, April 28, 2016, http://en.people.cn/n3/2016/0428 /c90785-9050879-5.html (accessed June 15, 2019).

22. Cary Huang, "Xi Jinping hails China's reform and opening up policy in symbolic visit to its village 'birthplace,'" April 26, 2017, https://www .scmp.com/news/china/policies-politics/article/1938917/xi-jinping -hails-chinas-reform-and-opening-policy (accessed June 15, 2019).

23. Wang Ke, "Xiaogang Village, birthplace of rural reform, moves on," China .org.cn, December 15, 2008, http://www.china.org.cn/china/features /content_16955209_4.htm (accessed June 15, 2019).

24. Interview with Anhui farmers, April 4, 2016.

25. Liu Xiaobo, *No Enemies, No Hatred: Selected Essays and Poems*, ed. Perry Link (Cambridge, MA: Belknap Press of Harvard University Press, 2012).

26. Fu Shihuan, Hainan local party secretary, interview with author, March 20, 2001.

27. Orville Schell, author, interview with author, April 8, 2014.

28. David Barboza, "Contrarian Investor Sees Economic Crash in China," *New York Times*, January 7, 2010, https://www.nytimes.com/2010/01/08 /business/global/08chanos.html (accessed June 14, 2019).

29. Eric Lam, "China May Have $5.8 Trillion in Hidden Debt With 'Titanic' Risks," Bloomberg News, October 16, 2018, https://www.bloomberg .com/news/articles/2018-10-16/china-may-have-5-8-trillion-in-hidden -debt-with-titanic-risks (accessed June 14, 2019).

30. David Barboza, "Billions in Hidden Riches for Family of Chinese Leader," *New York Times*, October 25, 2012, https://www.nytimes.com /2012/10/26/business/global/family-of-wen-jiabao-holds-a-hidden -fortune-in-china.html (accessed August 7, 2019).

31. Shen Minggao, *China Macro View: Urbanization Revisited*, Citi Research, March 18, 2014.

32. Dexter Roberts, "A $6.8 Trillion Price Tag for China's Urbanization," Bloomberg News, March 25, 2014, https://www.bloomberg.com/news /articles/2014-03-25/a-6-dot-8-trillion-price-tag-for-chinas-urbanization (accessed June 14, 2019).

33. Interview with Chongqing farmer, June 3, 2013.

34. Interview with evicted Chongqing farmer, June 3, 2013.

35. Susan Whiting, "Property Rights and Economic Development in China," interview by Neysun Mahboubi, podcast of the University of Pennsylvania Center for the Study of Contemporary China Podcast, March 19, 2019, https://cscc.sas.upenn.edu/podcasts/2019/03/19/ep-15-property -rights-and-economic-development-china-susan-whiting (accessed June 14, 2019).

36. "Summary of 2011 17-Province Survey's Findings," Landesa Rural Development Institute, 2012, https://www.landesa.org/china-survey-6/ (accessed June 14, 2019).

37. Bert Hoffman, "How Urbanization Can Help the Poor," World Bank, April 17, 2014, http://www.worldbank.org/en/news/opinion/2014/04 /17/how-urbanization-can-help-the-poor (accessed June 15, 2019).

38. *Standing Their Ground: Thousands Face Violent Eviction in China,* Amnesty International, September 2012, https://www.amnestyusa.org/reports /standing-their-ground-thousands-face-violent-eviction-in-china/ (accessed June 15, 2019).

39. Kristin Aunan, Mette Halskov Hansen, and Shuxiao Wang, "Introduction: Air Pollution in China," *China Quarterly,* no. 234 (June 2018), https://www.cambridge.org/core/journals/china-quarterly/article/ introduction-air-pollution-in-china/8D36F205FEC68513BC45E2DEC0F 2AC26/core-reader (accessed June 15, 2019).

40. Dong Xiangzhu and Gao Chouni, interview with author, December 7, 2016, and Dexter Roberts, "China's Rural Poor Bear the Brunt of the Nation's Aging Crisis," *Bloomberg Businessweek,* January 5, 2017, https:// www.bloomberg.com/news/articles/2017-01-05/china-s-rural-poor -bear-the-brunt-of-the-nation-s-aging-crisis (accessed June 15, 2019).

41. Xiangming Fang, economist at China Agricultural University, interview with author, November 22, 2016.

42. Albert Park, economist at the Hong Kong University of Science and Technology, interview with author, November 16, 2016.

43. Xiangming Fang, interview with author, November 22, 2016.

4. THE PARTY

1. Dexter Roberts, "Waking Up To Their Rights," *Businessweek,* August 23, 2005, https://www.bloomberg.com/news/articles/2005-08-21/waking -up-to-their-rights (accessed June 15, 2019).

2. Zeng Feiyang, labor center director, interview with author, March 23, 2005.

3. Mao Zedong, "Analysis of the Classes in Chinese Society," March 1926 *Selected Works of Mao Tse-tung,* vol. 1 (Beijing: Foreign Languages Press, 1965), https://www.marxists.org/reference/archive/mao/selected-works /volume-1/mswv1_1.htm (accessed June 15, 2019).

4. Mao Zedong, "On the Correct Handling of Contradictions Among the People, February 27, 1957," *Selected Works of Mao Tse-tung,* vol. 5 (Beijing:

Foreign Languages Press, 1977), https://www.marxists.org/reference /archive/mao/selected-works/volume-5/mswv5_58.htm (accessed June 15, 2019).

5. Thomas Bird, "On the trail of Deng Xiaoping in the French town where he embraced Communism," *South China Morning Post Magazine,* November 17, 2018, https://www.scmp.com/magazines/post-magazine/long-reads/article/2173319/trail-deng-xiaoping-french-town-where-he -embraced (accessed June 14, 2019).

6. Dexter Roberts and Pete Engardio, "Secrets, Lies, and Sweatshops," *Bloomberg Businessweek,* November 26, 2006, https://www.bloomberg .com/news/articles/2006-11-26/secrets-lies-and-sweatshops (accessed June 15, 2019).

7. Ibid.

8. Ibid.

9. Mo Wenzhi, interview with author, August 25, 2000.

10. Qing Yongzhi, migrant worker, interview with author, April 24, 2014.

11. Wang Kan, professor at the China Institute of Industrial Relations, interview with author, October 26, 2016.

12. Adam Matthews, "Following Tiananmen's Tentative Torchbearers," *Globe and Mail,* June 2, 2012, https://www.theglobeandmail.com/news/ world/following-tiananmens-tentative-torchbearers/article4226137/ (accessed June 15, 2019).

13. Zhang Zhiru, labor activist, interview with author, February 22, 2012.

14. Martin Ma, NGO director, interview with author, February 16, 2012.

15. Dexter Roberts, "Why China's Factories Are Turning to Temp Workers: A law boosting full-time workers' rights also lowers their appeal," *Bloomberg Businessweek,* March 9, 2012, https://www.bloomberg.com /news/articles/2012-03-08/why-chinas-factories-are-turning-to-temp -workers (accessed June 15, 2019).

16. Ibid.

17. "Fears Arise over Health Situation of Imprisoned Liaoyang Labour Activists, Xiao Yunliang and Yao Fuxin, as Harsh Winter Conditions," *China Labour Bulletin,* December 21, 2004, https://clb.org.hk/content /fears-arise-over-health-situation-imprisoned-liaoyang-labour-activists -xiao-yunliang-and (accessed August 7, 2019).

18. Dexter Roberts, with Bruce Einhorn and Frederik Balfour, "China's Angry Workers: They're protesting over pay, layoffs and pensions. How far will Beijing go to stop them?," *Businessweek,* April 8, 2002, https:// www.bloomberg.com/news/articles/2002-04-07/chinas-angry-workers (accessed June 15, 2019).

19. Dexter Roberts, "Waking Up To Their Rights," *Businessweek,* August 21, 2005, https://www.bloomberg.com/news/articles/2005-08-21/waking-up -to-their-rights (accessed June 15, 2019).

20. Wang Kan, interview with author, October 26, 2016.

21. Wu Guijun, labor activist, interview with author, November 2, 2016.

22. Li Qian, "How Zhang Zhiru became one of China's top defenders of

labor rights," *Global Times,* September 19, 2014, http://www.globaltimes
.cn/content/882289.shtml (accessed June 15, 2019).

23. Zhang Zhiru, interview with author, April 24, 2014.

24. Interview with protesting worker, April 26, 2014.

25. V. I. Lenin, "The Trade Unions, the Present Situation and Trotsky's Mistakes," speech by V. I. Lenin on December 30, 1920, *Lenin's Collected Works,* 1st English ed. (Moscow: Progress Publishers, 1965), https://www.marxists.org/archive/lenin/works/1920/dec/30.htm (accessed June 15, 2019).

26. Elizabeth J. Perry, "Shanghai's Strike Wave of 1957," *China Quarterly,* no. 137 (March 1994): 1–27, https://www.jstor.org/stable/pdf/655685 .pdf?casa_token=aCp2L2-CuwkAAAAA:JJ5_sbN1f97pqPWQasZb _8eg42WlqvKAcad8jDTMdsVgWx9reV_JwLsMyjljawFlidQCqWXDD p4Q8piosStaUngS9si1f7ue5J42zXSqLP_LQ3cDHMe1 (accessed June 15, 2019).

27. Andrew G. Walder and Gong Xiaoxia, "Workers in the Tiananmen Protests: The Politics of the Beijing Workers' Autonomous Federation," *Australian Journal of Chinese Affairs,* no. 29 (January 1993), http://www .tsquare.tv/links/Walder.html (accessed June 15, 2019).

28. Han Dongfang, labor center director, interview with author, October 14, 2016.

29. Dexter Roberts, "Beijing Wants One Union to Rule Them All," *Bloomberg Businessweek,* November 10, 2016, https://www.bloomberg.com /news/articles/2016-11-10/beijing-wants-one-union-to-rule-them-all (accessed June 15, 2019).

30. Ibid.

31. Profile of Meng Han, *Chinese Human Rights Defenders,* September 6, 2016, https://www.nchrd.org/2016/09/meng-han/ (accessed June 15, 2019).

32. "Detained labour activist Meng Han unbowed and unrepentant," China Labour Bulletin, August 3, 2016, https://clb.org.hk/content/detained -labour-activist-meng-han-unbowed-and-unrepentant (accessed June 15, 2019).

33. Interview with worker organizer, May 29, 2016.

5. THE ROBOTS

1. "Ancient Building Complex in the Wudang Mountains," UNESCO World Heritage Centre, http://whc.unesco.org/en/list/705 (accessed June 15, 2019).

2. "Shennongjia Nature Reserve," China Travel China Guide, https:// www.travelchinaguide.com/attraction/hubei/shiyan/shennongjia .htm (accessed June 15, 2019).

3. Barry Naughton, "The Third Front: Defence Industrialization in the Chinese Interior," *China Quarterly,* no. 115 (September 1988): 351–386, https://www.jstor.org/stable/pdf/654862.pdf?refreqid=excelsior%3A14 630f44b6b99112cc33cbb70da218da (accessed June 15, 2019).

4. Ibid.

5. Qinhuangdao: Changli data, CEIC Data, https://www.ceicdata.com/en/china/population-rural-county-level-region/population-rural-hebei-qinhuangdao-changli (accessed June 15, 2019).

6. "Miao wei: yu guojiahua jiegui de renda daibiao" 苗圩：与国际化接轨的人大代表, Sina.com, March 8, 2005, http://news.sina.com.cn/c/2005-03-08/11235297920s.shtml (accessed June 15, 2019).

7. Miao Wei, general manager of Dongfeng, interview with author, July 25, 2003.

8. "Dongfeng, Nissan Sign Joint Venture Agreement," Xinhua News Agency, September 20, 2002, http://www.china.org.cn/english/features/44428.htm (accessed June 15, 2019).

9. Zhu Hansong, Goldman Sachs investment banker, interview with author, July 17, 2003.

10. Guan Suiqing, Dongfeng worker, interview with author, July 25, 2003.

11. Miao Wei, interview with author, July 25, 2003.

12. Lin Xiaozhao, "Shanghai Has Largest Migrant Population in China, but Shenzhen Has the Highest Ratio," *Yicai Global,* November 28, 2017, https://www.yicaiglobal.com/news/shanghai-has-largest-migrant-population-china-shenzhen-has-highest-ratio (accessed June 15, 2019).

13. Michael Bush, "Foxconn Crisis Proves Need For Global PR: 'Suicide Factory' Case Part of Growing Trend in Foreign Companies Seeking Image Counseling From U.S.," *AdAge,* November 8, 2010, https://adage.com/article/global-news/public-relations-foxconn-crisis-proves-global-pr/146932/ (accessed June 15, 2019).

14. Robin Kwong, "Terry Gou: Managing '1m animals' [updated with Foxconn statement]," *Financial Times,* January 19, 2012, https://www.ft.com/content/be3d2550-f9e6-34c0-91fb-afd639d3e750 (accessed June 15, 2019).

15. Interview with Foxconn worker counselor, April 25, 2014.

16. Dexter Roberts, "China's Young Men Act Out in Factories: Now a majority at many plants, males harass, strike, and quit," *Bloomberg Businessweek,* May 1, 2014, https://www.bloomberg.com/news/articles/2014-05-01/chinas-young-male-factory-workers-change-the-assembly-line (accessed June 15, 2019).

17. Louis Woo, assistant to the chairman of Foxconn, interview with author, April 25, 2014.

18. Eva Dou, "After Suicide, Foxconn Worker's Poems Strike a Chord," *Wall Street Journal,* November 7, 2014, https://blogs.wsj.com/chinarealtime/2014/11/07/after-suicide-foxconn-workers-poems-strike-a-chord/ (accessed June 15, 2019).

19. Barry Naughton, economist at University of California, San Diego, interview with author, September 1, 2016.

20. Wang Kan, interview with author, October 26, 2016.

21. "'Made in China 2025' plan unveiled," Xinhua News Agency, May 19, 2015,

http://www.chinadaily.com.cn/bizchina/2015-05/19/content_20760528 .htm (accessed June 15, 2019).

22. Ibid.

23. Dexter Roberts and Pete Engardio, "China's Economy: Behind All the Hype," *Bloomberg Businessweek*, October 22, 2009, https://www .bloomberg.com/news/articles/2009-10-22/chinas-economy-behind-all -the-hype (accessed June 15, 2019).

24. "Zhibo huifang: Guoqing 60 zhounian dahui zai Tiananmen Guangchang chenggong juxing" 直播回放：国庆60周年大会在天安门广 场成功举行, Zhongyang zhengfu menhu wangzhan 中央政府门户网站, October 1, 2009, http://www.gov.cn/60zn/content_1431280_2.htm (accessed August 14, 2019).

25. "34 floats forming 'Splendid China' in celebration parade," Xinhua News Agency, October 1, 2009, http://english.sina.com/china/p/2009 /1001/274807.html (accessed June 15, 2019).

26. Richard McGregor, "Forget Texas, China came out when Deng tipped his hat to Japan," *South China Morning Post,* December 1, 2018, https:// www.scmp.com/week-asia/opinion/article/2175446/forget-texas-china -came-out-when-deng-tipped-his-hat-japan (accessed June 15, 2019).

27. "Executive Summary World Robotics 2018 Industrial Robots," International Federation of Robotics, October 18, 2018, https://ifr.org /downloads/press2018/Executive_Summary_WR_2018_Industrial _Robots.pdf (accessed June 15, 2019).

28. "China Employer-Employee Survey Releases First Report," Hong Kong University of Science and Technology Institute for Emerging Market Studies, June 20, 2017, http://iems.ust.hk/updates/press-release/china -employer-employee-survey-releases-first-report (accessed June 15, 2019).

29. He Huifeng and Celia Chen, "'Made In China 2025': a peek at the robot revolution under way in the hub of the 'world's factory,'" *South China Morning Post,* September 18, 2018, https://www.scmp.com/economy /china-economy/article/2164103/made-china-2025-peek-robot -revolution-under-way-hub-worlds (accessed June 15, 2019).

30. "China Employer-Employee Survey Releases First Report," Hong Kong University of Science and Technology Institute for Emerging Market Studies, June 20, 2017, http://iems.ust.hk/updates/press-release/china -employer-employee-survey-releases-first-report (accessed June 15, 2019).

31. Hu Chengpeng, company CEO, interview with author, June 21, 2017, and Dexter Roberts, "China Robots Displace Workers as Wage Spiral Pressures Profits," Bloomberg News, July 2, 2017, https://www .bloomberg.com/news/articles/2017-07-02/china-robots-displace -workers-as-wage-spiral-pressures-profits (accessed June 15, 2019).

32. "GAC TRUMPCHI Electric Vehicles," wattEV2Buy, https://wattev2buy .com/electric-vehicles/guangzhou-automobile-group-electric-vehicles/ (accessed June 15, 2019).

33. Feng Xingya, president of GAC, interview with author, November 1, 2017, and Dexter Roberts, "Where 'Made in China' Means Flying Cars and Automated Pharmacies: Guangzhou, a major manufacturing hub, is doling out subsidies and free land as it sets out to retool its economy," *Bloomberg Businessweek*, November 21, 2017, https://www.bloomberg .com/news/articles/2017-11-21/where-made-in-china-means-flying-cars -and-automated-pharmacies (accessed June 15, 2019).

34. Dexter Roberts and Rachel Chang, with Thomas Black, "Inside China's Plans for World Robot Domination," Bloomberg News, April 24, 2017, https://www.bloomberg.com/news/articles/2017-04-24/resistance-is -futile-china-s-conquest-plan-for-robot-industry (accessed June 15, 2019).

35. Ibid.

36. Fang Hongbo, Midea chairman, interview with Bloomberg TV, October 30, 2017.

37. Dexter Roberts, "Kuka Plans for Robot Domination in China and Your Garage," Bloomberg News, December 25, 2017, https://www .bloomberg.com/news/articles/2017-12-25/kuka-s-ceo-plans-for-robot -domination-in-china-and-your-garage (accessed June 15, 2019).

38. Qiu Quanlin, "Midea, Kuka launch new smart park," *China Daily*, March 29, 2018, http://www.chinadaily.com.cn/a/201803/29/WS5abc6e6ea 3105cdcf6515125.html (accessed June 15, 2019).

39. Amanda Wang, Dexter Roberts, Daniela Wei, and Rachel Chang, "Chinese-Owned Robot Maker Is Gunning for No. 1 in Booming Market," Bloomberg News, March 8, 2017, https://www.bloomberg.com /news/articles/2017-03-08/midea-eyes-top-spot-for-kuka-in-china-s -booming-robot-market (accessed June 15, 2019).

40. Patrick McGee, "Till Reuter steps down as head of robotics group Kuka," *Financial Times*, November 26, 2018, https://www.ft.com/content /58be9d08-f16c-11e8-9623-d7f9881e729f (accessed June 15, 2019).

41. Arne Delfs and Patrick Donahue, "German Spy Chief Says China's Tech Takeovers Are a Security Risk," Bloomberg News, July 24, 2018, https:// www.bloomberg.com/news/articles/2018-07-24/german-spy-chief-says -china-s-tech-takeovers-are-security-risk (accessed June 15, 2019).

42. Dexter Roberts, "Where 'Made in China' Means Flying Cars and Automated Pharmacies: Guangzhou, a major manufacturing hub, is doling out subsidies and free land as it sets out to retool its economy," Bloomberg News, November 21, 2017, https://www.bloomberg.com /news/articles/2017-11-21/where-made-in-china-means-flying-cars-and -automated-pharmacies (accessed June 15, 2019).

43. Sidney Leng, "Beijing tries to play down 'Made in China 2025' as Trump escalates trade hostilities," *South China Morning Post*, June 26, 2018, https://www.politico.com/story/2018/06/26/beijing-made-in-china -2025-trump-trade-651852 (accessed June 15, 2019).

44. Ariana King, "Trump says trade war success can help 'heal' US divide," *Nikkei Asian Review*, November 8, 2018, https://asia.nikkei.com/Politics

/International-Relations/Trump-says-trade-war-success-can-help-heal
-US-divide (accessed June 15, 2019).

45. Jim Yong Kim, "Speech by World Bank President Jim Yong Kim: The
World Bank Group's Mission: To End Extreme Poverty," World Bank,
October 3, 2016, http://www.worldbank.org/en/news/speech/2016/10/03
/speech-by-world-bank-president-jim-yong-kim-the-world-bank-groups
-mission-to-end-extreme-poverty (accessed June 15, 2019).

46. Li Keqiang, "Full text: Premier Li's Dialogue with WEF Chief and International Business Leaders at the Annual Meeting of the New Champions 2017," Xinhua News Agency, June 30, 2017, http://www.xinhuanet
.com/english/2017-06/30/c_136404973.htm (accessed June 15, 2019).

47. Jane Cai, "Tax the terminator: Chinese adviser calls for levy to stop robots taking over the workplace: NPC delegate Cai Fang says it won't be
long before machines can do most things better than humans," *South
China Morning Post,* March 10, 2018, https://www.scmp.com/news/china
/economy/article/2136613/robots-set-overtake-humans-range-work
-tasks-10-20-years-top (accessed June 15, 2019).

48. Dee Lee, NGO director, interview with author, December 7, 2017.

6. GOING HOME

1. Mo Bochun, Binghuacun party organization chief, interview with author, June 21, 2016.

2. Mo Wangqing, returnee migrant, interview with author, June 21, 2016.

3. Mo Bochun, interview with author, June 21, 2016.

4. Li Xia, "China's migrant worker population growth slows down," Xinhua
News Agency, April 29, 2019, http://www.xinhuanet.com/english/2019
-04/29/c_138022474.htm (accessed August 13, 2019).

5. Wang Xiaodong, "Migrants shrink by 1.7 million," *China Daily,* November 11, 2017, http://www.chinadaily.com.cn/china/2017-11/11/content
_34390735.htm (accessed August 13, 2019).

6. David Stanway, "China's population set to peak at 1.44 billion in
2029—government report," Reuters, January 5, 2019, https://af.reuters
.com/article/worldNews/idAFKCN1OZ088 (accessed June 15, 2019).

7. "2017 Migrant Workers Survey Report" 年农民工监测调查报告, National
Bureau of Statistics 国家统计局, April 27, 2018, http://www.stats.gov.cn
/tjsj/zxfb/201804/t20180427_1596389.html (accessed June 15, 2019).

8. Dexter Roberts, "China's Consumers Need to Step Up: The leadership
is trying to refocus while resorting to old-fashioned stimulus," *Bloomberg Businessweek,* November 5, 2015, https://www.bloomberg.com
/news/articles/2015-11-05/china-s-consumers-need-to-step-up (accessed
June 17, 2019).

9. "2017 Migrant Workers Survey Report" 年农民工监测调查报告, National
Bureau of Statistics 国家统计局, April 27, 2018, http://www.stats.gov.cn
/tjsj/zxfb/201804/t20180427_1596389.html (accessed June 15, 2019).

10. "Number of Chinese Farmers Dropping," Xinhua News Agency, October 8,

2002, http://english.china.org.cn/english/BAT/45087.htm (accessed August 17, 2019).

11. Keegan Elmer, "A year after deadly Daxing fire, no let-up in campaign to marginalise migrant workers," *South China Morning Post,* November 18, 2018, https://www.scmp.com/news/china/society/article/2173745/year -after-deadly-daxing-fire-no-let-campaign-marginalise-migrant (accessed June 15, 2019).

12. Wong Lok-to, Hai Nan, and Yang Fan, "China Continues to Evict Migrants From Beijing As Temperatures Plummet," *Radio Free Asia,* November 27, 2017, https://www.rfa.org/english/news/china/evictions -11272017143549.html (accessed June 15, 2019).

13. Gabriele Battaglia, "Beijing Migrant Worker Evictions: The Four-Character Word You Can't Say Anymore," *South China Morning Post,* December 3, 2017, https://www.scmp.com/week-asia/society/article /2122496/beijing-migrant-worker-evictions-four-character-word-you -cant-say (accessed June 15, 2019).

14. Wong Lok-to, Hai Nan, and Yang Fan, "China Continues to Evict Migrants From Beijing As Temperatures Plummet," *Radio Free Asia,* November 27, 2017, https://www.rfa.org/english/news/china/evictions -11272017143549.html (accessed June 15, 2019).

15. Tang Ziyi, "Beijing's Population Falls Further," *Caixin Global,* January 23, 2019, https://www.caixinglobal.com/2019-01-23/beijings-population-falls -further-101373464.html (accessed June 15, 2019) and Bai Tiantian, "Beijing, Shanghai record first population decline in 40 years," *Global Times,* January 23, 2018, http://www.globaltimes.cn/content/1086195.shtml (accessed June 15, 2019).

16. Ernan Cui, Gavekal Dragonomics analyst, interview with author, February 16, 2017.

17. Mark Williams, chief Asia economist at Capital Economics, interview with author, June 11, 2016.

18. Chris Buckley and Keith Bradsher, "Xi Jinping's Marathon Speech: Five Takeaways," *New York Times,* October 18, 2017, https://www.nytimes .com/2017/10/18/world/asia/china-xi-jinping-party-congress.html (accessed June 15, 2019).
   Xi Jinping, "Secure a Decisive Victory in Building a Moderately Prosperous Society in All Respects and Strive for the Great Success of Socialism with Chinese Characteristics for a New Era: Delivered at the 19th National Congress of the Communist Party of China, October 18, 2017," Xinhua News Agency, November 3, 2017, 27–28, http://www .xinhuanet.com/english/special/2017-11/03/c_136725942.htm (accessed August 15, 2019).

19. Sit Tsui, Qiu Jiansheng, Yan Xiaohui, Erebus Wong, and Wen Tiejun, "Rural Communities and Economic Crises in Modern China," *Monthly Review,* September 1, 2018, https://monthlyreview.org/2018/09/01/rural -communities-and-economic-crises-in-modern-china/ (accessed June 15, 2019).

20. "Chinese premier lauds progress in mass entrepreneurship, innovation," Xinhua News Agency, June 27, 2017, http://news.xinhuanet.com/english/2017-06/27/c_136398203.htm (accessed June 15, 2019).

21. "China sees boom in rural e-commerce in 2017," Xinhua News Agency, January 25, 2018, http://www.xinhuanet.com/english/2018-01/25/c_136924446.htm (accessed June 15, 2019) and Frank Tong, "Online Retail Sales in China Soar Past $1 Trillion in 2017," *Digital Commerce 360*, February 8, 2018, https://www.digitalcommerce360.com/2018/02/08/online-retail-sales-china-soar-past-1-trillion-2017/ (accessed June 15, 2019).

22. Xuebei Lou, "In China's Taobao villages, e-commerce is one way to bring new jobs and business opportunities to rural areas," *East Asia & Pacific on the Rise* (blog), World Bank Blogs, November 22, 2018, http://blogs.worldbank.org/eastasiapacific/china-s-taobao-villages-e-commerce-one-way-bring-new-jobs-and-business-opportunities-rural-areas (accessed June 15, 2019).

23. Jim Yong Kim, World Bank president, Twitter, November 4, 2017, https://twitter.com/jimyongkim/status/1059149069984120832?s=12 (accessed June 15, 2019).

24. Xiao Xintian, official in local poverty alleviation bureau, interview with author, January 14, 2000.

25. Mo Ruxuan, deputy party chief, interview with author, October 27, 2000.

26. Mo Ruxuan, interview with author, October 28, 2000.

27. Official from Guizhou Provincial Government, email interview with author, May 15, 2018.

28. Viola Zhou, "How a poor rural province became the promised land for China's rising political stars," *South China Morning Post*, October 29, 2017, https://www.scmp.com/news/china/policies-politics/article/2117430/how-poor-rural-province-became-promised-land-chinas (accessed June 15, 2019).

29. Jane Cai, "Can China's poorest province achieve its dream of becoming the next big data hub? Mountainous Guizhou builds data centres but struggles to attract talent," *South China Morning Post*, February 1, 2018, https://www.scmp.com/news/china/article/2131158/will-poor-chinese-provinces-big-data-dreams-pay (accessed June 15, 2019).

30. Zhang Pinghui, "Why Xi Jinping cares so much about ending poverty in China: the political significance behind the campaign," *South China Morning Post*, September 4, 2017, https://amp.scmp.com/news/china/society/article/2109278/why-xi-jinping-cares-so-much-about-ending-poverty-china-political (accessed June 15, 2019).

31. Tan Xinyu, "War on poverty continues in 2019," *China Daily*, February, 22, 2019, http://www.chinadaily.com.cn/a/201902/22/WS5c6f86a5a3106c65c34ead2a.html (accessed August 13, 2019).

32. Viola Zhou, "How a poor rural province became the promised land for China's rising political stars," *South China Morning Post*, October 29, 2017,

https://www.scmp.com/news/china/policies-politics/article/2117430 /how-poor-rural-province-became-promised-land-chinas (accessed June 15, 2019).

33. Chris Buckley, "After Toiling in Rural China, Protégé of Xi Jinping Joins Party's Top Tiers," *New York Times,* September 12, 2017, https://www .nytimes.com/2017/09/12/world/asia/china-xi-jinping-successor-chen -miner.html (accessed August 17, 2019).

34. Paul Mozur, Daisuke Wakabayashi, and Nick Wingfield, "Apple Opening Data Center in China to Comply With Cybersecurity Law," *New York Times,* June 12, 2017, https://www.nytimes.com/2017/07/12/business /apple-china-data-center-cybersecurity.html (accessed August 17, 2019).

35. Tristan Kenderdine, " How China's Poorest Province Became a Political Kingmaker," *The Diplomat,* July 19, 2017, https://thediplomat.com /2017/07/how-chinas-poorest-province-became-a-political-kingmaker / (accessed August 17, 2019).

36. Tu Lei, "Guizhou, home of China's 'silicon village,' sees GDP surging on big data," *Global Times,* January 22, 2019, http://www.globaltimes.cn /content/1136685.shtml (accessed June 15, 2019).

37. Official from Guizhou Provincial Government, email interview with author, May 15, 2018.

38. Terry Gou, Foxconn chairman, press conference in Guiyang, Guizhou, July 10, 2014.

39. Official in employment department of Guizhou Province, email interview with author, June 24, 2016.

40. Ibid.

41. Official from Guizhou Provincial Government, email interview with author, May 15, 2018.

42. Sun Zhe, founder of Gohome, an online tourism agency, interview with author, July 20, 2016.

43. "Libo Ancient Town" 荔波古镇, *Baidu Baike,* https://baike.baidu.com/item /%E8%8D%94%E6%B3%A2%E5%8F%A4%E9%95%87 (accessed June 15, 2019).

44. Mo Rubo, interview with author, April 19, 2017.

45. Yang Meng, migrant worker, interview with author, May 29, 2016, and Dexter Roberts, "China's Factory Workers Head Home: Migrants from the interior return to set up businesses," *Bloomberg Businessweek,* July 13, 2016, https://www.bloomberg.com/features/2016-chinese-migrants/ (accessed June 15, 2019).

7. THE FUTURE

1. Shengxiao Li and Pengjun Zhao, "Restrained mobility in a high-accessible and migrant-rich area in downtown Beijing," *European Transport Research Review,* March 2018, https://link.springer.com/article/10 .1007/s12544-017-0278-0 (accessed February 10, 2019).

2. An Baijie, "President makes grassroots holiday visits in Beijing," *China Daily,* February 2, 2019, http://www.chinadaily.com.cn/a/201902

/02/WS5c54d034a3106c65c34e7db5.html (accessed on September 27, 2019).

3. Keegan Elmer, "At least five labour rights activists arrested across China," *South China Morning Post,* January 22, 2019, https://www.scmp.com /news/china/politics/article/2183209/least-five-labour-rights-activists -arrested-across-china (accessed February 11, 2019).

4. Lily Kuo, "50 student activists missing in China after police raid," *Guardian,* August 24, 2018, https://www.theguardian.com/world/2018 /aug/24/50-student-activists-missing-in-china-after-police-raid (accessed February 10, 2019).

5. "Police 'kidnap' 10 labour activists across China: Rights group," Agence France Presse, November 11, 2018, https://www.straitstimes.com/asia /east-asia/police-kidnap-10-labour-activists-across-china-rights-group (accessed February 17, 2019).

6. "The state of labour relations in China, 2018," China Labour Bulletin, January 9, 2019, https://clb.org.hk/content/state-labour-relations-china -2018 (accessed February 17, 2019).

7. Kate Taylor, "Black Friday and Cyber Monday set records—but combined, they still only made up half of Alibaba's Singles Day online sales," *Business Insider,* December 1, 2018, https://www.businessinsider .com/black-friday-cyber-monday-vs-singles-day-sales-2018-12 (accessed June 15, 2019).

8. Kate Taylor, "We went to Alibaba's 24-hour shopping extravaganza that is like nothing in America, featuring a Mariah Carey performance and an online-shopping-themed Cirque du Soleil act. Here's what it reveals about the future of retail," *Business Insider,* November 12, 2018, https:// www.businessinsider.com/alibabas-singles-day-2018-photos-2018-11 (accessed August 18, 2019).

9. Zen Soo and Li Tao, "Alibaba sets record US$30.8 billion for Singles' Day sales, underscoring resilience in consumer spending," *South China Morning Post,* November 11, 2018, https://www.scmp.com/tech/enterprises /article/2172523/alibabas-singles-day-sales-hit-1-bln-yuan-less-60-seconds (accessed June 15, 2019).

10. "Waimai xiaoge: Pingjun 2.5 Tian shangwang yige, bu shi song can shi songming" 外卖小哥: 平均2.5天伤亡一个, 不是送餐是送命Sohu.com, September 5, 2017, http://www.sohu.com/a/190094851_99916176 (accessed February 10, 2019).

11. "Shanghai mei 2.5 Tian jiu you 1 ming waimai xiaoge shangwang zhe gong-zuo za chengle gaowei" 上海每2.5天就有1名外卖小哥伤亡 这工作咋成了高危, CCTV.com, September 14, 2017, http://news.cctv.com/2017/09/14 /ARTIE7WENh6GehvE8fgiyDy0170914.shtml (accessed February 10, 2019).

12. "Behind the ecommerce boom: Exhausted delivery workers and rural poverty," China Labour Bulletin, November 22, 2018, https://clb.org.hk /content/behind-ecommerce-boom-exhausted-delivery-workers-and -rural-poverty (accessed February 10, 2019).

13. Albert Park, interview with author, January 22, 2016.

14. Dexter Roberts, "China Trumpets Its Service Economy: It accounts for half of GDP. The pay isn't great," *Bloomberg Businessweek*, January 28, 2016, https://www.bloomberg.com/news/articles/2016-01-28/china-trumpets-its-service-economy (accessed June 15, 2019).

15. Hu Yongqi, "Premier Li urges financial sector to better serve real economy," *China Daily*, January 5, 2019, https://www.chinadailyhk.com/articles/52/35/19/1546676230531.html (accessed February 10, 2019).

16. Xiaoqing Pi, Kevin Hamlin, James Mayger, Enda Curran, Miao Han, and Yinan Zhao, "China's Unlikely to Rebound From Its Slowdown Anytime Soon," Bloomberg News, January 20, 2019, https://www.bloomberg.com/news/articles/2019-01-21/china-s-economy-slows-to-weakest-pace-since-2009-amid-trade-war (accessed February 10, 2019).

17. Ernan Cui, "A Cold Winter In China's Job Market," Gavekal Dragonomics, January 9, 2019, https://research.gavekal.com/article/cold-winter-chinas-job-market (accessed February 10, 2019).

18. "Li Keqiang chaired a symposium of experts, scholars and business people," *China Hot News,* January 17, 2019, https://www.chinahotsnews.com/2019/01/17/li-keqiang-chaired-a-symposium-of-experts-scholars-and-business-people/ (accessed June 15, 2019).

19. Orange Wang, "China's gig economy losing ability to absorb laid off factory workers," *South China Morning Post,* February 13, 2019, https://www.scmp.com/economy/china-economy/article/2185789/chinas-grey-economy-losing-ability-be-employment-backstop-laid (accessed June 15, 2019).

20. Ernan Cui, "A Cold Winter In China's Job Market," Gavekal Dragonomics, January 9, 2019, https://research.gavekal.com/article/cold-winter-chinas-job-market (accessed February 10, 2019).

21. Lulu Yilun Chen, "Didi Starts Major Job Cuts as It Overhauls Business," Bloomberg News, February 14, 2019, https://www.bloomberg.com/news/articles/2019-02-15/didi-is-said-to-start-major-job-cuts-as-it-overhauls-business (accessed June 15, 2019).

22. Interview with factory owner, October 31, 2017.

23. Orange Wang, "China's wealth gap widens as more than half of its provinces missed growth targets last year," *South China Morning Post,* February 14, 2019, https://www.scmp.com/economy/china-economy/article/2185738/chinas-wealth-gap-widens-more-half-its-provinces-missed-growth (accessed June 15, 2019).

24. Thomas Piketty, Li Yang, and Gabriel Zucman, "Capital Accumulation, Private Property, and Rising Inequality in China, 1978–2015," NBER Working Paper 23368, National Bureau of Economic Research, April 2017, https://www.nber.org/papers/w23368 (accessed June 15, 2019).

25. Gabriel Zucman. "Global Wealth Inequality," NBER Working Paper 25462, National Bureau of Economic Research, January 2019, http://www.nber.org/papers/w25462 (accessed June 15, 2019).

26. Dexter Roberts, "The Controversial Chinese Economist Uncovering Tough Truths: 'What he found fundamentally changes the way we think,'"

Bloomberg Businessweek, March 23, 2017, https://www.bloomberg.com/ news/articles/2017-03-23/the-controversial-chinese-economist-uncovering-tough-truths (accessed June 15, 2019).

27. Martin Whyte and Teresa Wright, *Myth of the Social Volcano: Perceptions of Inequality and Distributive Injustice in Contemporary China; Accepting Authoritarianism: State-Society Relations in China's Reform Era,* (Stanford: Stanford University Press, 2010).

28. Richard Wike and Bridget Parker, "Corruption, Pollution, Inequality Are Top Concerns in China," Pew Research Center, September 24, 2015, http://www.pewglobal.org/2015/09/24/corruption-pollution-inequality -are-top-concerns-in-china/ (accessed June 15, 2019).

29. Yin Han, "Ethnic Han parents protest exam policy favoring minority students," *Global Times,* July 30, 2017, http://www.globaltimes.cn /content/1113091.shtml (accessed June 15, 2019).

30. Lynette H. Ong and Donglin Han, "What Drives People to Protest in an Authoritarian Country? Resources and Rewards vs Risks of Protests in Urban and Rural China," *Political Studies,* March 2018, https://journals .sagepub.com/doi/pdf/10.1177/0032321718763558 (accessed June 15, 2019).

31. Lynette H. Ong, Twitter interview with author, February 6, 2019.

32. John Knight and Ramani Gunatilaka, "Rural-Urban Migration and Happiness in China," *World Happiness Report 2018,* 2018, https://s3 .amazonaws.com/happiness-report/2018/CH4-WHR-lr.pdf (accessed June 15, 2019).

33. Dee Lee, interview with author, April 26, 2014.

34. Anita Chan and Kaxton Siu, "Chinese migrant workers: Factors constraining the emergence of class consciousness," *China's Peasants and Workers: Changing Class Identities* (2012): 79–101, https://www .researchgate.net/publication/295327631_Chinese_migrant_workers _Factors_constraining_the_emergence_of_class_consciousness (accessed June 15, 2019).

35. Wang Jiangsong, "The Significance of Crane Operators Across China Going on Strike," *China Change,* May 7, 2018, https://chinachange.org /2018/05/07/the-significance-of-crane-operators-across-china-going-on -strike/ (accessed June 15, 2019).

36. Mark Williams, interview with author, June 11, 2016.

37. Dexter Roberts, "This Is China's Real Economic Problem," *Bloomberg Businessweek,* July 13, 2017, https://www.bloomberg.com/news/articles /2017-07-13/this-is-china-s-real-economic-problem (accessed June 15, 2019).

38. Loren Brandt, economist at the University of Toronto, interview with author, June 30, 2017.

39. Andrew Batson, *Cyclically Fine, Structurally Well . . . ,* Gavekal Dragonomics, May 3, 2017, https://research.gavekal.com/article/cyclically -fine-structurally-well (accessed June 15, 2019).

40. James Liang, founder of Ctrip.com and the author of *The Demographics of Innovation,* interview with author, December 13, 2017.

41. Huang Yu, "Robot Threat or Robot Dividend? A Struggle between Two Lines," *Chinoiserie*, July 30, 2018, http://www.chinoiresie.info/robot -threat-robot-dividend/ (accessed February 6, 2019).

42. Fran Wang, "Trade War Fuels Majority of Export Manufacturers' Shift Out of China, Survey Shows," *Caixin*, January 8, 2019, https:// www.caixinglobal.com/2019-01-08/trade-war-fuels-majority-of-export -manufacturers-shift-out-of-china-survey-shows-101367788.html (accessed June 15, 2019).

43. Debby Wu, "Apple's Partners Quicken Shift From China as Trade Tensions Rise," Bloomberg News, January 27, 2019, https://www.bloomberg .com/news/articles/2019-01-27/pegatron-moves-some-china-production -to-indonesia-on-u-s-tariff (accessed June 15, 2019).

44. Debby Wu, "Apple iPhone Supplier Foxconn Planning Deep Cost Cuts," Bloomberg News, November 21, 2018, https://www.bloomberg.com /news/articles/2018-11-21/apple-s-biggest-iphone-assembler-is-said-to -plan-deep-cost-cuts (accessed June 15, 2019).

45. Austin Carr, "Foxconn Says It Will Build Wisconsin Plant After Trump Talks," Bloomberg News, February 1, 2019, https://www.bloomberg .com/news/articles/2019-02-01/foxconn-says-it-will-build-wisconsin -plant-after-trump-talks (accessed February 20, 2019).

46. Bryan M. Wolfe, "Wisconsin breaks ground on new Foxconn LCD panel facility," idownloadblog.com, June 29, 2018, https://www.idownloadblog .com/2018/06/29/wisconsin-foxconn-lcd/ (accessed June 15, 2019).

47. Anna Hensel, "Foxconn flip-flops on Wisconsin factory after meeting with President Trump," Venturebeat.com, February 1, 2019, https:// venturebeat.com/2019/02/01/foxconn-flip-flops-on-wisconsin-factory -after-meeting-with-president-trump/ (accessed June 15, 2019).

48. Terry Gou, CEO and chairman of Foxconn, speaking at the Fortune Global Forum in Guangzhou, December 6, 2017.

49. R. David Arkush, *Fei Xiaotong and Sociology in Revolutionary China* (Cambridge, MA: Harvard University Press, 1981), 67.

50. Fei Xiaotong, *From the Soil: The Foundations of Chinese Society. A Translation of Fei Xiaotong's Xiangtu Zhongguo, with an Introduction and Epilogue by Gary C. Hamilton and Wang Zheng.* Translated and edited by Gary C. Hamilton and Wang Zheng, (Berkeley: University of California Press, 1992).

51. Ibid.

52. R. David Arkush, *Fei Xiaotong and Sociology in Revolutionary China* (Cambridge, MA: Harvard University Press, 1981).

53. Fei Xiaotong, *From the Soil: The Foundations of Chinese Society. A Translation of Fei Xiaotong's Xiangtu Zhongguo, with an Introduction and Epilogue by Gary C. Hamilton and Wang Zheng.* Translated and edited by Gary C. Hamilton and Wang Zheng, (Berkeley: University of California Press, 1992).

54. Anne F. Thurston, "An Optimist's Life," *Wilson Quarterly,* Autumn 2005,

http://archive.wilsonquarterly.com/essays/optimists-life (accessed February 20, 2019).

55. CBNEditor, "Two Chinese Provinces See GDP's Exceed 9 Trillion Yuan in 2018," *China Banking News*, February 4, 2019, http://www .chinabankingnews.com/2019/02/04/guangdong-jiangsu-gdps-both -breach-9-trillion-yuan-in-2018/ (accessed February 21, 2019) and Caleb Silver, "Top 20 Economies in the World," Investopedia.com, June 7, 2019, https://www.investopedia.com/insights/worlds-top-economies/ (accessed February 21, 2019).

56. "The Trouble with China's Anti-Poverty Efforts," *Bloomberg Businessweek,* August 8, 2018, https://www.bloomberg.com/news/articles/2018 -08-08/the-trouble-with-china-s-anti-poverty-efforts (accessed on February 22, 2019).

57. Shuping Niu and Ken Wills, "World's Largest Water Diversion Plan Won't Quench China's Thirst," Bloomberg News, December 10, 2017, https://www.bloomberg.com/news/articles/2017-12-10/world-s-largest -water-diversion-plan-won-t-slake-china-s-thirst (accessed February 21, 2019).

58. Ross Anderson, "What Happens if China Makes First Contact?" *Atlantic,* December 2017, https://www.theatlantic.com/magazine/archive /2017/12/what-happens-if-china-makes-first-contact/544131/ (accessed February 22, 2019).

59. Edward Wong, "China Telescope to Displace 9,000 Villagers, in Hunt for Extraterrestrials," *New York Times,* February 17, 2016, https://www .nytimes.com/2016/02/18/world/asia/china-fast-telescope-guizhou -relocation.html (accessed February 22, 2019).

60. Sarah Rogers and Brooke Wilmsen, "Towards a critical geography of resettlement," *Progress in Human Geography* (January 2019), https:// journals.sagepub.com/doi/full/10.1177/0309132518824659 (accessed August 15, 2019).

61. Huang Yu, "Robot Threat or Robot Dividend? A Struggle between Two Lines," *Chinoiserie,* July 30, 2018, http://www.chinoiresie.info/robot -threat-robot-dividend/ (accessed February 6, 2019).

62. Xian Huang, "The Chinese dream: *hukou,* social mobility and regime support in China," unpublished paper (January 2019), http://dx.doi.org /doi:10.7282/t3-n1h0-f072 (accessed on February 20, 2019).

63. Dominic Barton, Yougang Chen, and Amy Jin, "Mapping China's middle class," *McKinsey Quarterly,* June 2013, https://www.mckinsey .com/industries/retail/our-insights/mapping-chinas-middle-class (accessed August 13, 2019).

64. Simon Kennedy, "China will overtake the U.S. economy in less than 15 years, says HSBC, challenging Trump's claim," Bloomberg News, September 25, 2018, https://www.bloomberg.com/news/articles/2018 -09-25/hsbc-sees-china-economy-set-to-pass-u-s-as-number-one-by-2030 (accessed February 22, 2019).

EPILOGUE

1. "CPC Q&A: What are China's two centennial goals and why do they matter?" Xinhua News Agency, October 17, 2017, http://www.xinhuanet.com//english/2017-10/17/c_136686770.htm (accessed July 22, 2019).

2. Manfred Elfstrom, "Video: Manfred Elfstrom Looks At Labor Unrest In China," USC U.S.-China Institute, video, April 18, 2019, https://china.usc.edu/video-manfred-elfstrom-looks-labor-unrest-china (accessed July 22, 2019).

3. Cheng Si, "Campaign to help migrant workers claim unpaid salaries," *China Daily*, July 18, 2019, http://www.chinadaily.com.cn/a/201907/18/WS5d30395da310d830563ffc63.html (accessed July 22, 2019).

4. "China: Police DNA Database Threatens Privacy: 40 Million Profiled Includes Dissidents, Migrants, Muslim Uyghurs," *Human Rights Watch*, May 15, 2017, https://www.hrw.org/news/2017/05/15/china-police-dna-database-threatens-privacy (accessed July 22, 2019).

5. Tan Weiping, "Chinese Approach to the Eradication of Poverty: Taking Targeted Measures to Lift People out of Poverty," speech at the Expert Panel on the Implementation of the Third UN Decade for the Eradication of Poverty (2018–2027), UN.org, April 18, 2018, https://www.un.org/development/desa/dspd/wp-content/uploads/sites/22/2018/05/15.pdf (accessed July 22, 2019).

6. Gao Qin, "Sinica Podcast: How China's Poverty Alleviation Program Works, Explained By Gao Qin," SupChina.com, March 15, 2018, https://supchina.com/2018/03/15/sinica-podcast-how-chinas-poverty-alleviation-program-works-explained-by-gao-qin/ (accessed August 15, 2019).

7. "China Focus: E-commerce sheds new light on China's poverty relief," Xinhua News Agency, October 17, 2017, http://www.xinhuanet.com/english/2017-10/17/c_136686845.htm (accessed July 22, 2019).

8. Lauly Li and Cheng Ting-Fang, "Apple weighs 15%-30% capacity shift out of China amid trade war," *Nikkei Asian Review*, June 19, 2019, https://asia.nikkei.com/Economy/Trade-war/Apple-weighs-15-30-capacity-shift-out-of-China-amid-trade-war (accessed July 22, 2019).

9. Debby Wu, "Apple iPhone Supplier Foxconn Planning Deep Cost Cuts," Bloomberg News, November 11, 2018, https://www.bloomberg.com/news/articles/2018-11-21/apple-s-biggest-iphone-assembler-is-said-to-plan-deep-cost-cuts (accessed July 22, 2019).

10. Daniela Wei and Jinshan Hong, "Walmart's Supplier Says Chinese Factories in 'Desperate' State," Bloomberg News, July 9, 2019, https://www.bloomberg.com/news/articles/2019-07-09/trade-war-threatens-chinese-factories-existence-li-fung-says (accessed July 22, 2019).

11. Neil Thomas, "Mao Redux: The Enduring Relevance of Self-Reliance in China," *MacroPolo*, April 25, 2019, https://macropolo.org/analysis/china-self-reliance-xi-jin-ping-mao/ (accessed July 22, 2019).

12. Chad P. Brown, "China Is Cutting Tariffs—For Everyone Else," *Atlantic*, June 18, 2019, https://www.theatlantic.com/ideas/archive/2019/06/chinas-two-pronged-trade-war/591877/ (accessed July 22, 2019).

Bibliography

Agence France Presse. "Police 'kidnap' 10 labour activists across China: Rights group." November 11, 2018. https://www.straitstimes.com/asia/east-asia/police-kidnap-10-labour-activists-across-china-rights-group (accessed February 17, 2019).

Aibida. *Qiannan shilue (A Handbook of Guizhou)*. 1750. Reprint. Guiyang: Guizhou Renmin Chubanshe, 1992. Cited in Jodi L. Weinstein, *Empire and Identity in Guizhou: Local Resistance to Qing Expansion*. Seattle: University of Washington Press, 2014.

Amnesty International. *Standing Their Ground: Thousands Face Violent Eviction in China*. September 2012. https://www.amnestyusa.org/reports/standing-their-ground-thousands-face-violent-eviction-in-china/ (accessed June 15, 2019).

An, Baijie. "President makes grassroots holiday visits in Beijing." *China Daily*, February 2, 2019. http://www.chinadaily.com.cn/a/201902/02/WS5c54d034a3106c65c34e7db5.html (accessed on September 27, 2019).

Anderson, Ross. "What Happens If China Makes First Contact?" *Atlantic*, December 2017. https://www.theatlantic.com/magazine/archive/2017/12/what-happens-if-china-makes-first-contact/544131/ (accessed February 22, 2019).

Arkush, R. David. *Fei Xiaotong and Sociology in Revolutionary China*. Cambridge, MA: Harvard University Press, 1981.

Armario, Christine. "'Wake-up call': U.S. students trail global leaders." Associated Press, December 7, 2010. http://www.nbcnews.com/id/40544897/ns/us_news-life/t/wake-up-call-us-students-trail-global-leaders/#.W6c7uSN95DQ (accessed May 26, 2019).

Aunan, Kristin, Mette Halskov Hansen, and Shuxiao Wang. "Introduction: Air Pollution in China." *China Quarterly*, no. 234 (June 2018). https://www.cambridge.org/core/journals/china-quarterly/article/introduction-air-pollution-in-china/8D36F205FEC68513BC45E2DEC0F2AC26/core-reader (accessed June 15, 2019).

Bai, Tiantian. "Beijing, Shanghai record first population decline in 40 years."

Global Times, January 23, 2018. http://www.globaltimes.cn/content/1086195 .shtml (accessed June 15, 2019).

Baidu Baike. "Libo Ancient Town" 荔波古镇. https://baike.baidu.com/item /%E8%8D%94%E6%B3%A2%E5%8F%A4%E9%95%87 (accessed June 15, 2019).

Barboza, David. "Billions in Hidden Riches for Family of Chinese Leader." *New York Times,* October 25, 2012. https://www.nytimes.com/2012/10/26 /business/global/family-of-wen-jiabao-holds-a-hidden-fortune-in-china .html (accessed August 7, 2019).

———. "Contrarian Investor Sees Economic Crash in China." *New York Times,* January 7, 2010. https://www.nytimes.com/2010/01/08/business /global/08chanos.html (accessed June 14, 2019).

Barshefsky, Charlene. Interview by John Bussey. *Wall Street Journal,* video, June 16, 2015. https://www.wsj.com/video/negotiating-tips-the-only-word -for-no-is-no/BE3FF51D-B248-46CB-A9A1-FA1BD81C2FAA.html (accessed May 26, 2019).

Barton, Dominique, Yougang Chen, and Amy Jin. "Mapping China's middle class." *McKinsey Quarterly,* June 2013. https://www.mckinsey.com /industries/retail/our-insights/mapping-chinas-middle-class (accessed August 13, 2019).

Batson, Andrew. "Cyclically Fine, Structurally Well . . ." Gavekal Dragonomics, May 3, 2017. https://research.gavekal.com/article/cyclically-fine -structurally-well (accessed June 15, 2019).

Battaglia, Gabriele. "Beijing Migrant Worker Evictions: The Four-Character Word You Can't Say Anymore." *South China Morning Post,* December 3, 2017. https://www.scmp.com/week-asia/society/article/2122496 /beijing-migrant-worker-evictions-four-character-word-you-cant-say (accessed June 15, 2019).

Bird, Thomas. "On the trail of Deng Xiaoping in the French town where he embraced Communism." *South China Morning Post,* November 17, 2018. https:// www.scmp.com/magazines/post-magazine/long-reads/article/2173319/trail -deng-xiaoping-french-town-where-he-embraced (accessed June 14, 2019).

Bloomberg News. "The Trouble With China's Anti-Poverty Efforts." *Bloomberg Businessweek,* August 8, 2018. https://www.bloomberg.com/news /articles/2018-08-08/the-trouble-with-china-s-anti-poverty-efforts (accessed on February 22, 2019).

Brandt, Loren, Luhan Wang, and Yifan Zhang. "Productivity in Chinese Industry: 1998–2013." China Development Research Centre–World Bank, 2017.

Brandt, Loren, Susan Whiting, Linxiu Zhang, and Tonglong Zhang. "Changing Property-Rights Regimes: A Study of Rural Land Tenure in China." *China Quarterly,* no. 232 (December 2017). https://www.cambridge.org/ core/journals/china-quarterly/article/changing-propertyrights-regimes -a-study-of-rural-land-tenure-in-china/A848DA88125B5ED3A7F7C6FBD CEE5160 (accessed June 19, 2019).

Buckley, Chris. "After Toiling in Rural China, Protégé of Xi Jinping Joins Party's Top Tiers." *New York Times,* September 12, 2017. https://www

.nytimes.com/2017/09/12/world/asia/china-xi-jinping-successor-chen
-miner.html (accessed June 15, 2019).

———. "Girl's Death Sparks Rioting in China." Reuters, June 28, 2008.
https://uk.reuters.com/article/uk-china-riot/girls-death-sparks-rioting
-in-china-idUKPEK27256220080628 (accessed August 14, 2019).

Buckley, Chris, and Keith Bradsher. "Xi Jinping's Marathon Speech: Five Takeaways." *New York Times*, October 18, 2017. https://www.nytimes.com/2017
/10/18/world/asia/china-xi-jinping-party-congress.html (accessed June 15,
2019).

Bush, Michael. "Foxconn Crisis Proves Need For Global PR: 'Suicide Factory' Case Part of Growing Trend in Foreign Companies Seeking Image Counseling From U.S." *AdAge*, November 8, 2010. https://adage.com
/article/global-news/public-relations-foxconn-crisis-proves-global-pr
/146932/ (accessed June 15, 2019).

Businessweek Editorial. "China's Homegrown Illegal Aliens." *Businessweek*,
December 10, 2000. https://www.bloomberg.com/news/articles/2000-12-10
/chinas-homegrown-illegal-aliens-intl-edition (accessed September 24, 2019).

Cai, Fang, Yaohui Zhao, and Albert Park. "The Chinese Labor Market in the
Reform Era." In *China's Economic Transition: Origins, Mechanism, and Consequences*, edited by Loren Brandt and Thomas Rawski, 167–214. Cambridge University Press, 2008.

Cai, Jane. "Can China's poorest province achieve its dream of becoming
the next big data hub? Mountainous Guizhou builds data centres but
struggles to attract talent." *South China Morning Post*, February 1, 2018.
https://www.scmp.com/news/china/article/2131158/will-poor-chinese
-provinces-big-data-dreams-pay (accessed June 15, 2019).

———. "Tax the terminator: Chinese adviser calls for levy to stop robots taking over the workplace: NPC delegate Cai Fang says it won't be long before
machines can do most things better than humans." *South China Morning Post*, March 10, 2018. https://www.scmp.com/news/china/economy
/article/2136613/robots-set-overtake-humans-range-work-tasks-10-20
-years-top (accessed June 15, 2019).

Carr, Austin. "Foxconn Says It Will Build Wisconsin Plant After Trump
Talks." Bloomberg News, February 1, 2019. https://www.bloomberg.com
/news/articles/2019-02-01/foxconn-says-it-will-build-wisconsin-plant-after
-trump-talks (accessed February 20, 2019).

CBNEditor. "Two Chinese Provinces See GDP's Exceed 9 Trillion Yuan in 2018."
China Banking News, February 4, 2019. http://www.chinabankingnews.com
/2019/02/04/guangdong-jiangsu-gdps-both-breach-9-trillion-yuan-in-2018/
(accessed February 21, 2019).

CCTV News. "Shanghai mei 2.5 Tian jiu you 1 ming waimai xiaoge shangwang zhe gongzuo za chengle gaowei" 上海每2.5天就有1名外卖小哥伤亡
这工作咋成了高危. September 14, 2017. http://news.cctv.com/2017/09/14
/ARTIE7WENh6GehvE8fgiyDy0170914.shtml (accessed February 10, 2019).

Chan, Anita. *China's Workers Under Assault: the Exploitation of Labor in a Globalizing Economy*. Armonk, NY: M. E. Sharpe, 2001.

Chan, Anita, Richard Madsen, and Jonathan Unger. *Chen Village Under Mao and Deng*, 2nd ed. Berkeley: University of California Press, 1992.

Chan, Anita, and Kaxton Siu. "Chinese migrant workers: Factors constraining the emergence of class consciousness." *China's Peasants and Workers: Changing Class Identities*, January 2012. https://www.researchgate.net/publication /295327631_Chinese_migrant_workers_Factors_constraining_the _emergence_of_class_consciousness (accessed June 15, 2019).

Chan, Kam Wing. "Achieving Comprehensive *Hukou* Reform in China." *Paulson Policy Memorandum*, December 2014.

———. "China's Hukou System at 60: Continuity and Reform." In *Handbook on Urban Development in China*, edited by Ray Yep, Jun Wang, Thomas Johnson, 59–79. Cheltenham: Edward Elgar, 2019.

Chang, Leslie. *Factory Girls: From Village to City in a Changing China*. New York: Spiegel & Grau, 2007.

Chen, Guidi, and Wu Chuntao. *Will the Boat Sink the Water: The Life of China's Peasants*. New York: Public Affairs, 2006.

Chen, Lulu Yilun. "Didi Starts Major Job Cuts as It Overhauls Business." Bloomberg News, February 14, 2019. https://www.bloomberg.com/news /articles/2019-02-15/didi-is-said-to-start-major-job-cuts-as-it-overhauls -business (accessed June 15, 2019).

China Hot News. "Li Keqiang chaired a symposium of experts, scholars and business people." January 17, 2019. https://www.chinahotsnews.com /2019/01/17/li-keqiang-chaired-a-symposium-of-experts-scholars-and -business-people/ (accessed June 15, 2019).

China Labour Bulletin. "Behind the ecommerce boom: Exhausted delivery workers and rural poverty." November 22, 2018. https://clb.org.hk /content/behind-ecommerce-boom-exhausted-delivery-workers-and -rural-poverty (accessed February 10, 2019).

———. "Detained labour activist Meng Han unbowed and unrepentant." August 3, 2016. https://clb.org.hk/content/detained-labour-activist-meng -han-unbowed-and-unrepentant (accessed June 15, 2019).

———. "Fears Arise over Health Situation of Imprisoned Liaoyang Labour Activists, Xiao Yunliang and Yao Fuxin." December 21, 2004. https://clb .org.hk/content/fears-arise-over-health-situation-imprisoned-liaoyang -labour-activists-xiao-yunliang-and (accessed August 7, 2019).

———. "Standing Up: The Workers Movement in China, 2000–2004." July 8, 2007. http://www.clb.org.hk/en/content/standing-workers-movement -china-2000-2004 (accessed May 26, 2019).

———. "The State of Labour Relations in China, 2018." January 9, 2019. https:// clb.org.hk/content/state-labour-relations-china-2018 (accessed February 17, 2019).

China.org.cn. "Land Reform Law." September 16, 2009. http://www.china.org .cn/features/60years/2009-09/16/content_18537591.htm (accessed June 15, 2019).

———. "The Xiaogang village story." May 30, 2018. http://www.china.org .cn/china/2018-05/30/content_51532371.htm (accessed June 15, 2019).

Clark, Duncan. *Alibaba: The House That Jack Ma Built.* New York: Ecco, 2016.

Confucius. *The Analects.* Translated by William Edward Soothill. New York: Dover Publications, 1995.

Congressional-Executive Commission on China. "After the Detention and Death of Sun Zhigang: Prisons and Detention in China." October 27, 2003. https://www.cecc.gov/sites/chinacommission.house.gov /files/documents/roundtables/2003/CECC%20Roundtable%20-%20 After%20Detention%20Death%20Sun%20Zhigang%20Prisons%2C%20 Detention%2C%20Torture%20China%20-%2010.27.03.pdf (accessed May 26, 2019).

Cui, Ernan. "A Cold Winter In China's Job Market." Gavekal Dragonomics, January 9, 2019. https://research.gavekal.com/article/cold-winter-chinas -job-market (accessed February 10, 2019).

———. "The Lost Promise of Urbanization." Gavekal Dragonomics, February 1, 2017. https://research.gavekal.com/article/lost-promise-urbanization (accessed June 19, 2019).

Davis, Bob. "When the World Opened the Gates of China." *Wall Street Journal,* July 27, 2018. https://www.wsj.com/articles/when-the-world-opened -the-gates-of-china-1532701482 (accessed May 26, 2019).

Dash, Mike. "Emperor Wang Mang: China's First Socialist?" Smithsonian.com, December 9, 2011. https://www.smithsonianmag.com/history/emperor -wang-mang-chinas-first-socialist-2402977/.

de Bary, Wm. Theodore. *Sources of Chinese Tradition,* 2nd ed. New York: Columbia University Press, 1999.

de Brauw, Alan, and John Giles. "Migrant Opportunity and the Educational Attainment of Youth in Rural China." *Journal of Human Resources,* 2017.

Deal, David M., and Laura Hostetler. *The Art of Ethnography: A Chinese Miao Album.* Seattle: University of Washington Press, 2006.

Delfs, Arne, and Patrick Donahue. "German Spy Chief Says China's Tech Takeovers Are a Security Risk." Bloomberg News, July 24, 2018. https:// www.bloomberg.com/news/articles/2018-07-24/german-spy-chief-says -china-s-tech-takeovers-are-security-risk (accessed June 15, 2019).

Dikotter, Frank. *The Tragedy of Liberation: A History of the Chinese Revolution, 1945–57.* London: Bloomsbury, 2013.

Dou, Eva. "After Suicide, Foxconn Worker's Poems Strike a Chord." *Wall Street Journal,* November 7, 2014. https://blogs.wsj.com/chinarealtime /2014/11/07/after-suicide-foxconn-workers-poems-strike-a-chord/ (accessed June 15, 2019).

Duncan, Arne. "Secretary Arne Duncan's Remarks at OECD's Release of the Program for International Student Assessment (PISA) 2009 Results." U.S. Department of Education, December 7, 2010. https://www .ed.gov/news/speeches/secretary-arne-duncans-remarks-oecds-release -program-international-student-assessment- (accessed May 26, 2019).

EastSouthWestNorth (blog). "The Weng'an Mass Incident." July 1, 2008. http:// zonaeuropa.com/20080701_1.htm (accessed June 15, 2019).

Elmer, Keegan. "A year after deadly Daxing fire, no let-up in campaign to marginalise migrant workers." *South China Morning Post,* November 18, 2018. https://www.scmp.com/news/china/society/article/2173745/year-after-deadly-daxing-fire-no-let-campaign-marginalise-migrant (accessed June 15, 2019).

———. "At least five labour rights activists arrested across China." *South China Morning Post,* January 22, 2019. https://www.scmp.com/news/china/politics/article/2183209/least-five-labour-rights-activists-arrested-across-china (accessed February 11, 2019).

Engardio, Pete, and Dexter Roberts, with Brian Bremner. "The China Price." *Businessweek,* December 5, 2004. https://www.bloomberg.com/news/articles/2004-12-05/the-china-price (accessed September 24, 2019).

Fallows, James. *Postcards from Tomorrow Square: Reports from China.* New York: Vintage, 2008.

Fang, Hongbo. Midea chairman. Interview with Bloomberg TV. October 30, 2017.

Fang, Xiangming. "Does New Rural Social Pension Insurance Relieve Depression of the Elderly in Rural China? Evidence from the China Health and Retirement Longitudinal Study." China Agricultural University. Powerpoint presentation from author. 2016.

Fei Xiaotong, *From the Soil: The Foundations of Chinese Society. A Translation of Fei Xiaotong's* Xiangtu Zhongguo, *with an Introduction and Epilogue by Gary C. Hamilton and Wang Zheng.* Translated and edited by Gary C. Hamilton and Wang Zheng. (Berkeley: University of California Press, 1992).

Fincher, Leta Hong. *Betraying Big Brother: The Feminist Awakening in China.* New York: Verso, 2018.

Fong, Mei. *One Child: The Story of China's Most Radical Experiment.* New York: Houghton Mifflin Harcourt, 2016.

Forrest de Sloper, Juan Alejandro. "First Opium War." *Book of Days Tales,* June 3, 2015. http://www.bookofdaystales.com/first-opium-war/ (accessed May 26, 2019).

Gallagher, Mary. "The Evolution of Workers' Rights in China—Mary Gallagher." Interview by Neysun Mahboubi. Podcast of the University of Pennsylvania Center for the Study of Contemporary China, March 12, 2019. https://cscc.sas.upenn.edu/podcasts/2019/03/12/ep-14-evolution-workers-rights-china-mary-gallagher (accessed March 15, 2019).

Gan, Li 甘犁. "Nongcun tudi liuchuande xiankuang jijie yinxiang" 农村土地流转的现状及其影响. xinan caijing daxue 西南财经大学 zhongguo jiating jinrong diaocha yu yanjiu zhongxin 中国家庭金融调查与研究 中心. 2016.

———. "Urbanization and the Housing Market in China." China Household Finance Survey, Texas A&M University and Southwestern University of Finance and Economics, China Household Finance, November 6, 2014. http://people.tamu.edu/~ganli/Urbanization-Nov-6-2014.pdf (accessed June 20, 2019).

Gan, Li, and Guan Gong. "Estimating Interdependence between Health and Education in a Dynamic Model." NBER Working Paper No. 12830.

National Bureau of Economic Research. Issued in January 2007. https://www.nber.org/papers/w12830 (accessed June 17, 2019).

Giles, John, and Ren Mu. "Village Political Economy, Land Tenure Insecurity, and the Rural to Urban Migration Decision: Evidence from China." *American Journal of Agricultural Economy,* 2017.

Giles, John and Yang Huang. "Migration and Human Capital in China," IZA World of Labor (*in press*). Bonn: IZA Institute of Labor Economics, 2019.

Gou, Terry, CEO and chairman of Foxconn. Press conference in Guiyang, Guizhou. July 10, 2014.

———. Speech at the Fortune Global Forum in Guangzhou. December 6, 2017.

Halegua, Aaron. "Who Will Represent China's Workers?: Lawyers, Legal Aid, and the Enforcement of Labor Rights." U.S.-Asia Law Institute, New York University School of Law, October 2016. https://www.aaronhalegua.com/chinasworkers (accessed June 20, 2019).

Harney, Alexandra. *The China Price: The True Cost of Chinese Competitive Advantage.* New York: Penguin, 2008.

Hayford, Charles W. "Lin Zexu." In *Encyclopaedia Britannica Online.* https://www.britannica.com/biography/Lin-Zexu) (https://www.britannica.com/topic/opium-trade (accessed May 26, 2019).

He, Huifeng, and Celia Chen. "'Made In China 2025': a peek at the robot revolution under way in the hub of the 'world's factory.'" *South China Morning Post,* September 18, 2018. https://www.scmp.com/economy/china-economy/article/2164103/made-china-2025-peek-robot-revolution-under-way-hub-worlds (accessed June 15, 2019).

Hensel, Anna. "Foxconn flip-flops on Wisconsin factory after meeting with President Trump." Venturebeat.com, February 1, 2019. https://venturebeat.com/2019/02/01/foxconn-flip-flops-on-wisconsin-factory-after-meeting-with-president-trump/ (accessed June 15, 2019).

Hessler, Peter. *River Town: Two Years on the Yangtze.* New York: Harper, 2001.

Hoffman, Bert. "How Urbanization Can Help the Poor." World Bank, April 17, 2014. http://www.worldbank.org/en/news/opinion/2014/04/17/how-urbanization-can-help-the-poor (accessed June 15, 2019).

Hong Kong University of Science and Technology Institute for Emerging Market Studies. "China Employer-Employee Survey Releases First Report." Press release. June 20, 2017. http://iems.ust.hk/updates/press-release/china-employer-employee-survey-releases-first-report (accessed June 15, 2019).

Hu, Nan. "China Footprint: College entrance exam 40 years on." CGTN.com, September 16, 2017. https://news.cgtn.com/news/3259544d35557a6333566d54/share_p.html (accessed June 15, 2019).

Hu, Yongqi. "Premier Li urges financial sector to better serve real economy." *China Daily,* January 5, 2019. https://www.chinadailyhk.com/articles/52/35/19/1546676230531.html (accessed February 10, 2019).

Huang, Cary. "Xi Jinping hails China's reform and opening up policy in symbolic visit to its village 'birthplace.'" *South China Morning Post,* April 26, 2017.

https://www.scmp.com/news/china/policies-politics/article/1938917
/xi-jinping-hails-chinas-reform-and-opening-policy (accessed June 15,
2019).

Huang, Xian. "The Chinese dream: *hukou*, social mobility and regime support in China." Unpublished paper, January 2019. http://dx.doi.org/doi:10
.7282/t3-n1h0-f072 (accessed on February 20, 2019).

Huang, Yasheng. *Capitalism with Chinese Characteristics: Entrepreneurship and
the State.* New York: Cambridge University Press, 2008.

Huang, Yu. "Robot Threat or Robot Dividend? A Struggle between Two
Lines." *Chinoiserie,* July 30, 2018. http://www.chinoiresie.info/robot-threat
-robot-dividend/ (accessed February 6, 2019).

Huang, Yukon. *Cracking the China Conundrum.* Oxford: Oxford University
Press, 2017.

International Federation of Robotics. "Executive Summary World Robotics 2018 Industrial Robots." October 18, 2018. https://ifr.org/downloads
/press2018/Executive_Summary_WR_2018_Industrial_Robots.pdf (accessed June 15, 2019).

Jenks, Robert D. *Insurgency and Social Disorder in Guizhou: The "Miao" Rebellion. 1854–1873.* Honolulu: University of Hawaii Press, 1994.

Johnson, Ian. *The Souls of China: The Return of Religion After Mao.* New York:
Pantheon, 2017.

Kenderdine, Tristan. "How China's Poorest Province Became a Political
Kingmaker." *The Diplomat,* July 19, 2017. https://thediplomat.com/2017
/07/how-chinas-poorest-province-became-a-political-kingmaker/ (accessed
August 17, 2019).

Kennedy, Simon. "China will overtake the U.S. economy in less than
15 years, says HSBC, challenging Trump's claim." Bloomberg News,
September 25, 2018. https://www.bloomberg.com/news/articles/2018-09
-25/hsbc-sees-china-economy-set-to-pass-u-s-as-number-one-by-2030 (accessed February 22, 2019).

Kim, Jim Yong. "Speech by World Bank President Jim Yong Kim: The World
Bank Group's Mission: To End Extreme Poverty." World Bank, October 3,
2016. http://www.worldbank.org/en/news/speech/2016/10/03/speech
-by-world-bank-president-jim-yong-kim-the-world-bank-groups-mission
-to-end-extreme-poverty (accessed June 15, 2019).

———. "The world can learn a lot from Guizhou, one of the poorest
provinces of #China." Twitter, November 4, 2017. https://twitter.com
/jimyongkim/status/1059149069984120832?s=12 (accessed June 15, 2019).

King, Ariana. "Trump says trade war success can help 'heal' US divide."
Nikkei Asian Review, November 8, 2018. https://asia.nikkei.com/Politics
/International-Relations/Trump-says-trade-war-success-can-help-heal
-US-divide (accessed June 15, 2019).

Knight, John, and Ramani Gunatilaka. "Rural-Urban Migration and Happiness in China." *World Happiness Report 2018,* 2018. https://s3.amazonaws
.com/happiness-report/2018/CH4-WHR-lr.pdf (accessed June 15, 2019).

Knight, John, Deng Qucheng, and Li Shi. "The Puzzle of Migrant Labor

Shortage and Rural Labor Surplus in China." *China Economic Review,* November 2011. https://www.researchgate.net/publication/251637514_The _Puzzle_of_Migrant_Labor_Shortage_and_Rural_Labor_Surplus_in _China (accessed June 20, 2019).

Koo, Anita, Holly Ming, and Bill Tsang. "The Doubly Disadvantaged: How Return Migrant Students Fail to Access and Deploy Capitals for Academic Success in Rural Schools." *Sociology,* January 13, 2014. https://www .researchgate.net/publication/274973248_The_Doubly_Disadvantaged _How_Return_Migrant_Students_Fail_to_Access_and_Deploy _Capitals_for_Academic_Success_in_Rural_Schools (accessed June 18, 2019).

Kroeber, Arthur. *China's Economy: What Everyone Needs to Know.* Oxford: Oxford University Press, 2016.

Kuijs, Louis. "China's labor market—softer but still resilient." *Oxford Economics,* October 12, 2016.

Kuo, Lily. "50 student activists missing in China after police raid." *Guardian,* August 24, 2018. https://www.theguardian.com/world/2018/aug/24 /50-student-activists-missing-in-china-after-police-raid (accessed February 10, 2019).

Kwong, Robin. "Terry Gou: Managing '1m animals' [updated with Foxconn statement]." *Financial Times,* January 19, 2012. https://www.ft.com /content/be3d2550-f9e6-34c0-91fb-afd639d3e750 (accessed June 15, 2019).

Kynge, James. *China Shakes the World: The Rise of a Hungry Nation.* London: Weidenfeld & Nicolson, 2006.

Lam, Eric. "China May Have $5.8 Trillion in Hidden Debt With 'Titanic' Risks." Bloomberg News, October 16, 2018. https://www.bloomberg .com/news/articles/2018-10-16/china-may-have-5-8-trillion-in-hidden -debt-with-titanic-risks (accessed June 14, 2019).

Landesa Rural Development Institute. "Summary of 2011 17-Province Survey's Findings." 2012. https://www.landesa.org/china-survey-6/ (accessed June 14, 2019).

Lardy, Nicholas. *Markets over Mao: The Rise of Private Business in China.* Washington D.C.: Peterson Institute for International Economics, 2014.

———. *The State Strikes Back: The End of Economic Reform in China?* Washington D.C.: Peterson Institute for International Economics, 2019.

Lee, Khoon Choy. *Pioneers of Modern China: Understanding the Inscrutable Chinese.* Singapore: World Scientific, 2005.

Leng, Sidney. "Beijing tries to play down 'Made in China 2025' as Trump escalates trade hostilities." *South China Morning Post,* June 26, 2018. https:// www.politico.com/story/2018/06/26/beijing-made-in-china-2025-trump -trade-651852 (accessed June 15, 2019).

Lenin, V. I. "The Trade Unions, the Present Situation and Trotsky's Mistakes." Speech by V. I. Lenin on December 30, 1920. *Lenin's Collected Works.* 1st English ed. Moscow: Progress Publishers, 1965. https://www.marxists.org /archive/lenin/works/1920/dec/30.htm (accessed June 15, 2019).

Li, Keqiang. "Full text: Premier Li's Dialogue with WEF Chief and International Business Leaders at the Annual Meeting of the New Champions 2017." Xinhua News Agency, June 30, 2017. http://www.xinhuanet.com /english/2017-06/30/c_136404973.htm (accessed June 15, 2019).

Li, Qian. "How Zhang Zhiru became one of China's top defenders of labor rights." *Global Times,* September 19, 2014. http://www.globaltimes.cn /content/882289.shtml (accessed June 15, 2019).

Li, Shengxiao, and Pengjun Zhao. "Restrained mobility in a high-accessible and migrant-rich area in downtown Beijing." *European Transport Research Review,* March 2018. https://link.springer.com/article/10.1007/s12544-017 -0278-0 (accessed February 10, 2019).

Li, Xia. "China's migrant worker population growth slows down." Xinhua News Agency, April 29, 2019. http://www.xinhuanet.com/english/2019 -04/29/c_138022474.htm (accessed August 13, 2019).

Liang, James. *The Demographics of Innovation: Why Demographics Is a Key to the Innovation Race.* Hoboken: Wiley, 2018.

Lin, Xiaozhao. "Shanghai Has Largest Migrant Population in China, but Shenzhen Has the Highest Ratio." *Yicai Global,* November 28, 2017. https://www.yicaiglobal.com/news/shanghai-has-largest-migrant -population-china-shenzhen-has-highest-ratio (accessed June 15, 2019).

Liu, Xiaobo. *No Enemies, No Hatred: Selected Essays and Poems.* Edited by Perry Link. Cambridge, MA: Belknap Press of Harvard University Press, 2012.

Lin, Zexu. "Lin Zexu (LinTse-hsu) writing to Britain's Queen Victoria to Protest the Opium Trade, 1839." USC US-China Institute website, 2019. https://china.usc.edu/lin-zexu-lintse-hsu-writing-britains-queen-victoria -protest-opium-trade-1839 (accessed September 26, 2019).

Lou, Xuebei. "In China's Taobao villages, e-commerce is one way to bring new jobs and business opportunities to rural areas." *East Asia & Pacific on the Rise* (blog). World Bank Blogs, November 22, 2018. http://blogs.worldbank .org/eastasiapacific/china-s-taobao-villages-e-commerce-one-way-bring -new-jobs-and-business-opportunities-rural-areas (accessed June 15, 2019).

Luethje, Boy. "How Will China's Industrial Modernization Plan Affect Workers?" *East-West Wire,* October 16, 2017.

Ma, Damien, and William Adams. *In Line Behind a Billion People.* Upper Saddle River, NJ: FT Press, 2014.

Mao Zedong. "An Analysis of the Classes in Chinese Society." March 1926. *Selected Works of Mao Tse-tung.* Vol. 1. Beijing: Foreign Languages Press, 1965. https://www.marxists.org/reference/archive/mao/selected-works /volume-1/mswv1_1.htm (accessed June 15, 2019).

———. "On the Correct Handling of Contradictions Among the People, February 27, 1957." *Selected Works of Mao Tse-tung.* Vol. 5. Beijing: Foreign Languages Press, 1977. https://www.marxists.org/reference/archive/mao /selected-works/volume-5/mswv5_58.htm (accessed June 15, 2019).

———. "Report on an Investigation of the Peasant Movement in Hunan, March 1927." *Selected Works of Mao Tse-tung.* Vol. 1. Beijing: Foreign Languages Press, 1965. https://www.marxists.org/reference/archive/mao /selected-works/volume-1/mswv1_2.htm (accessed June 14, 2019).

Marx, Karl. "Revolution in China and in Europe." *New York Daily Tribune,* June 14, 1853. https://www.marxists.org/archive/marx/works/1853/06 /14.htm (accessed June 15, 2019).

Matthews, Adam. "Following Tiananmen's Tentative Torchbearers." *Globe and Mail,* June 2, 2012. https://www.theglobeandmail.com/news/world /following-tiananmens-tentative-torchbearers/article4226137/ (accessed June 15, 2019).

McGee, Patrick. "Till Reuter steps down as head of robotics group Kuka." *Financial Times,* November 26, 2018. https://www.ft.com/content/58be9d08 -f16c-11e8-9623-d7f9881e729f (accessed June 15, 2019).

McGregor, James. *One Billion Customers: Lessons from the Front Lines of Doing Business in China.* New York: Free Press, 2005.

McGregor, Richard. "Forget Texas, China came out when Deng tipped his hat to Japan." *South China Morning Post,* December 1, 2018. https://www .scmp.com/week-asia/opinion/article/2175446/forget-texas-china-came -out-when-deng-tipped-his-hat-japan (accessed June 15, 2019).

———. *The Party: The Secret World of China's Communist Rulers.* New York: Harper, 2010.

Meng Han profile. Chinese Human Rights Defenders. September 6, 2016. https://www.nchrd.org/2016/09/meng-han/ (accessed June 15, 2019).

Miller, Tom. *China's Urban Billion: The Story behind the Biggest Migration in Human History.* London: Zed Books, 2012.

Mozur, Paul, Daisuke Wakabayashi, and Nick Wingfield. "Apple Opening Data Center in China to Comply With Cybersecurity Law." *New York Times,* June 12, 2017. https://www.nytimes.com/2017/07/12/business /apple-china-data-center-cybersecurity.html (accessed August 17, 2019).

National Army Museum. "The Opium War." https://www.nam.ac.uk/explore/ opium-war-1839-1842 (accessed May 26, 2019).

National Bureau of Statistics 国家统计局. "2017 Migrant Workers Survey Report" 年农民工监测调查报告. April 27, 2018. http://www.stats.gov.cn/tjsj /zxfb/201804/t20180427_1596389.html (accessed June 15, 2019).

Naughton, Barry. "Is China Socialist?" *Journal of Economic Perspectives,* Winter 2017.

———. "Supply-Side Structural Reform: Policy-makers Look For a Way Out." *China Leadership Monitor,* March 1, 2016. https://www.hoover.org/sites /default/files/research/docs/clm49bn.pdf (accessed August 17, 2019).

———. "The Third Front: Defence Industrialization in the Chinese Interior." *China Quarterly,* no. 115 (September 1988). https://www.jstor.org /stable/pdf/654862.pdf?refreqid=excelsior%3A14630f44b6b99112cc33cbb 70da218da (accessed June 15, 2019).

———. "Two Trains Running: Supply-Side Reform, SOE Reform and the Authoritative Personage." *China Leadership Monitor,* July 19, 2016. https://www.hoover.org/sites/default/files/research/docs/clm50bn .pdf#overlay-context=publications/china-leadership-monitor (accessed August 17, 2019).

Ngai, Pun, and Anita Koo. "A 'World-Class' (Labor) Camp/us: Foxconn and China's New Generation of Labor Migrants." *Positions: East Asia Cultures Critique,* July 2015. https://www.researchgate.net/publication /283798241_A_World-Class_Labor_Campus_Foxconn_and_China's _New_Generation_of_Labor_Migrants (accessed June 18, 2019).

Niu, Shuping, and Ken Wills. "World's Largest Water Diversion Plan Won't Quench China's Thirst." Bloomberg News, December 10, 2017. https:// www.bloomberg.com/news/articles/2017-12-10/world-s-largest-water -diversion-plan-won-t-slake-china-s-thirst (accessed February 21, 2019).

Ong, Lynette H., and Donglin Han. "What Drives People to Protest in an Authoritarian Country? Resources and Rewards vs Risks of Protests in Urban and Rural China." *Political Studies,* March 2018. https://journals .sagepub.com/doi/pdf/10.1177/0032321718763558 (accessed June 15, 2019).

Osnos, Evan. *Age of Ambition: Chasing Fortune, Truth, and Faith in the New China.* New York: Farrar, Straus & Giroux, 2014.

Pan, Philip P. *Out of Mao's Shadow: The Struggle for the Soul of a New China.* New York: Simon & Schuster, 2008.

Pantsov, Alexander V., and Steven I. Levine. *Deng Xiaoping: A Revolutionary Life.* Oxford: Oxford University Press, 2015.

———. *Mao: The Real Story.* New York: Simon & Schuster, 2013.

Perry, Elizabeth J. "Shanghai's Strike Wave of 1957." *China Quarterly,* no. 137 (March 1994). https://www.jstor.org/stable/pdf/655685.pdf?casa_token =aCp2L2-CuwkAAAAA:JJ5_sbN1f97pqPWQasZb_8eg42WlqvKAcad- 8jDTMdsVgWx9reV_JwLsMyjljawFlidQCqWXDDp4Q8piosStaUngS9si1 f7ue5J42zXSqLP_LQ3cDHMe1 (accessed June 15, 2019).

Pi, Xiaoqing, Kevin Hamlin, James Mayger, Enda Curran, Miao Han, and Yinan Zhao. "China's Unlikely to Rebound From Its Slowdown Anytime Soon." Bloomberg News, January 20, 2019. https://www.bloomberg.com /news/articles/2019-01-21/china-s-economy-slows-to-weakest-pace-since -2009-amid-trade-war (accessed February 10, 2019).

Piketty, Thomas, Li Yang, and Gabriel Zucman. "Capital Accumulation, Private Property, and Rising Inequality in China, 1978–2015." *NBER Working Paper 23368,* National Bureau of Economic Research, April 2017. https://www.nber.org/papers/w23368 (accessed June 15, 2019).

Pomfret, John. *Chinese Lessons: Five Classmates and the Story of the New China.* New York: Henry Holt, 2006.

Qinhuangdao: Changli data, CEIC Data. https://www.ceicdata.com/en/china /population-rural-county-level-region/population-rural-hebei-qinhuangdao -changli (accessed June 15, 2019).

Qiu, Quanlin. "Midea, Kuka launch new smart park." *China Daily,* March 29, 2018. http://www.chinadaily.com.cn/a/201803/29/WS5abc6e6ea3105 cdcf6515125.html (accessed June 15, 2019).

Reyes, Alejandro. "Just A Start: The long WTO negotiations look easy com- pared to what comes next." *Asiaweek,* November 26, 1999. http://www.cnn .com/ASIANOW/asiaweek/magazine/99/1126/cover1.html (accessed May 26, 2019).

Roberts, Dexter. "A $6.8 Trillion Price Tag for China's Urbanization."

Bloomberg News, March 25, 2014. https://www.bloomberg.com/news /articles/2014-03-25/a-6-dot-8-trillion-price-tag-for-chinas-urbanization (accessed June 14, 2019).

———. "Beijing Wants One Union to Rule Them All." *Bloomberg Businessweek,* November 10, 2016. https://www.bloomberg.com/news/articles/2016-11 -10/beijing-wants-one-union-to-rule-them-all (accessed June 15, 2019).

———. "China Robots Displace Workers as Wage Spiral Pressures Profits." Bloomberg News, July 2, 2017. https://www.bloomberg.com/news /articles/2017-07-02/china-robots-displace-workers-as-wage-spiral -pressures-profits (accessed June 15, 2019).

———. "China Trumpets Its Service Economy: It accounts for half of GDP. The pay isn't great." *Bloomberg Businessweek,* January 28, 2016. https:// www.bloomberg.com/news/articles/2016-01-28/china-trumpets-its -service-economy (accessed June 15, 2019).

———. "China: Wto or Bust?" *Businessweek,* November 22, 1999. https:// www.bloomberg.com/news/articles/1999-11-21/china-wto-or-bust (accessed May 26, 2019).

———. "China's Consumers Need to Step Up: The leadership is trying to refocus while resorting to old-fashioned stimulus." *Bloomberg Businessweek,* November 5, 2015. https://www.bloomberg.com/news/articles/2015-11 -05/china-s-consumers-need-to-step-up (accessed June 17, 2019).

———. "China's Factory Workers Head Home: Migrants from the interior return to set up businesses." *Bloomberg Businessweek,* July 13, 2016. https:// www.bloomberg.com/features/2016-chinese-migrants/ (accessed June 15, 2019).

———. "China's Rural Poor Bear the Brunt of the Nation's Aging Crisis." *Bloomberg Businessweek,* January 5, 2017. https://www.bloomberg.com /news/articles/2017-01-05/china-s-rural-poor-bear-the-brunt-of-the -nation-s-aging-crisis (accessed June 15, 2019).

———. "China's Young Men Act Out in Factories: Now a majority at many plants, males harass, strike, and quit." *Bloomberg Businessweek,* May 1, 2014. https://www.bloomberg.com/news/articles/2014-05-01/chinas-young -male-factory-workers-change-the-assembly-line (accessed June 15, 2019).

———. "Inside a Chinese Sweatshop: 'A Life of Fines and Beating.'" *Bloomberg Businessweek,* October 1, 2000. https://www.bloomberg.com/news /articles/2000-10-01/inside-a-chinese-sweatshop-a-life-of-fines-and -beating (accessed July 26, 2019).

———. "Kuka Plans for Robot Domination in China and Your Garage." Bloomberg News, December 25, 2017. https://www.bloomberg.com /news/articles/2017-12-25/kuka-s-ceo-plans-for-robot-domination-in -china-and-your-garage (accessed June 15, 2019).

———. "The Controversial Chinese Economist Uncovering Tough Truths: 'What he found fundamentally changes the way we think.'" *Bloomberg Businessweek,* March 23, 2017. https://www.bloomberg.com/news /articles/2017-03-23/the-controversial-chinese-economist-uncovering -tough-truths (accessed June 15, 2019).

———. "The Great Migration: Chinese peasants are fleeing their villages to chase big-city dreams." *Businessweek*, December 10, 2000. https://www.bloomberg.com/news/articles/2000-12-10/the-great-migration-intl-edition (accessed May 26, 2019).

———. "This Is China's Real Economic Problem." *Bloomberg Businessweek*, July 13, 2017. https://www.bloomberg.com/news/articles/2017-07-13/this-is-china-s-real-economic-problem (accessed June 15, 2019).

———. "Waking Up To Their Rights." *Businessweek*, August 23, 2005. https://www.bloomberg.com/news/articles/2005-08-21/waking-up-to-their-rights (accessed June 15, 2019).

———. "Where 'Made in China' Means Flying Cars and Automated Pharmacies: Guangzhou, a major manufacturing hub, is doling out subsidies and free land as it sets out to retool its economy." Bloomberg News, November 21, 2017. https://www.bloomberg.com/news/articles/2017-11-21/where-made-in-china-means-flying-cars-and-automated-pharmacies (accessed June 15, 2019).

———. "Why China's Factories Are Turning to Temp Workers: A law boosting full-time workers' rights also lowers their appeal." *Bloomberg Businessweek*, March 9, 2012. https://www.bloomberg.com/news/articles/2012-03-08/why-chinas-factories-are-turning-to-temp-workers (accessed June 15, 2019).

Roberts, Dexter, and Rachel Chang, with Thomas Black. "Inside China's Plans for World Robot Domination." Bloomberg News, April 24, 2017. https://www.bloomberg.com/news/articles/2017-04-24/resistance-is-futile-china-s-conquest-plan-for-robot-industry (accessed June 15, 2019).

Roberts, Dexter, with Bruce Einhorn and Frederik Balfour. "China's Angry Workers: They're protesting over pay, layoffs and pensions. How far will Beijing go to stop them?" *Businessweek*, April 8, 2002. https://www.bloomberg.com/news/articles/2002-04-07/chinas-angry-workers (accessed June 15, 2019).

Roberts, Dexter, and Pete Engardio. "China's Economy: Behind All the Hype." *Bloomberg Businessweek*, October 22, 2009. https://www.bloomberg.com/news/articles/2009-10-22/chinas-economy-behind-all-the-hype (accessed June 15, 2019).

———. "Secrets, Lies, and Sweatshops." *Bloomberg Businessweek*, November 17, 2006. https://www.bloomberg.com/news/articles/2006-11-26/secrets-lies-and-sweatshops (accessed June 15, 2019).

Rogers, Sarah, and Brooke Wilmsen. "Towards a critical geography of resettlement." *Progress in Human Geography* (January 2019). https://journals.sagepub.com/doi/full/10.1177/0309132518824659 (accessed February 22, 2019).

Ross, Heidi. "China Country Study." UNESCO Digital Library, 2005. http://unesdoc.unesco.org/images/0014/001461/146108e.pdf (accessed May 26, 2019).

Rozelle, Scott, and Natalie Johnson. *China's Invisible Crisis: The Growing Urban-Rural Divide and What It Means for the World Economy.* London: Oneworld Publications, 2019.

Schell, Orville, and John Delury. *Wealth and Power*. New York: Random House, 2013.

Schell, Orville, and David Shambaugh. *The China Reader*. New York: Vintage, 1999.

Shen, Minggao. *China Macro View: Urbanization Revisited*. Citi Research, March 18, 2014.

Silver, Caleb. "Top 20 Economies in the World." *Investopedia.com*, June 7, 2019. https://www.investopedia.com/insights/worlds-top-economies/ (accessed February 21, 2019).

Sina.com. "Miao wei: yu guojiahua jiegui de renda daibiao" 苗圩: 与国际化接轨的人大代表. March 8, 2005. http://news.sina.com.cn/c/2005-03-08/11235297920s.shtml (accessed June 15, 2019).

Sohu.com. "Waimai xiaoge: Pingjun 2.5 Tian shangwang yige, bu shi song can shi songming" 外卖小哥: 平均2.5天伤亡一个, 不是送餐是送命. September 5, 2017. http://www.sohu.com/a/190094851_99916176 (accessed February 10, 2019).

Solinger, Dorothy J. *Contesting Citizenship in Urban China: Peasants, Migrants, the State, and the Logic of the Market*. Berkeley: University of California Press, 1999.

Soo, Zen, and Li Tao. "Alibaba sets record US$30.8 billion for Singles' Day sales, underscoring resilience in consumer spending." *South China Morning Post*, November 11, 2018. https://www.scmp.com/tech/enterprises/article/2172523/alibabas-singles-day-sales-hit-1-bln-yuan-less-60-seconds (accessed June 15, 2019).

Stanway, David. "China's population set to peak at 1.44 billion in 2029—government report." Reuters, January 5, 2019. https://af.reuters.com/article/worldNews/idAFKCN1OZ088 (accessed June 15, 2019).

State Council. "Outline of China's National Plan for Medium and Long-term Education Reform and Development (2010–2020)." July 2010. http://ncee.org/wp-content/uploads/2016/12/Sha-non-AV-5-China-Education-Plan-2010-2020.pdf (accessed June 15, 2019).

Studwell, Joe. *How Asia Works: Success and Failure in the World's Most Dynamic Region*. London: Profile Books, 2014.

Su, Fubing, and Ran Tao. "The China model withering? Institutional roots of China's local developmentalism." *Urban Studies*, 2017.

Tan, Xinyu. "War on poverty continues in 2019." *China Daily*, February, 22, 2019. http://www.chinadaily.com.cn/a/201902/22/WS5c6f86a5a3106c65c34ead2a.html (accessed August 13, 2019).

Tang, Ziyi. "Beijing's Population Falls Further." *Caixin Global*, January 23, 2019. https://www.caixinglobal.com/2019-01-23/beijings-population-falls-further-101373464.html (accessed June 15, 2019).

Taylor, Kate. "Black Friday and Cyber Monday set records—but combined, they still only made up half of Alibaba's Singles Day online sales." *Business Insider*, December 1, 2018. https://www.businessinsider.com/black-friday-cyber-monday-vs-singles-day-sales-2018-12 (accessed June 15, 2019).

———. "We went to Alibaba's 24-hour shopping extravaganza that is like nothing in America, featuring a Mariah Carey performance and an online-shopping-themed Cirque du Soleil act. Here's what it reveals about the future of retail." *Business Insider,* November 12, 2018. https://www.businessinsider.com/alibabas-singles-day-2018-photos-2018-11 (accessed August 18, 2019).

Teng, Biao. "The Sun Zhigang Incident and the Future of Constitutionalism: Does the Chinese Constitution Have a Future?" Centre for Rights and Justice, Faculty of Law, the Chinese University of Hong Kong, December 30, 2013. https://www.law.cuhk.edu.hk/en/research/crj/download/papers/2013-tb-szg-constitutionalism.pdf (accessed May 26, 2019).

Thurston, Anne F. "An Optimist's Life." *Wilson Quarterly,* Autumn 2005. http://archive.wilsonquarterly.com/essays/optimists-life (accessed February 20, 2019).

Tong, Frank. "Online Retail Sales in China Soar Past $1 Trillion in 2017." *Digital Commerce 360,* February 8, 2018. https://www.digitalcommerce360.com/2018/02/08/online-retail-sales-china-soar-past-1-trillion-2017/ (accessed June 15, 2019).

TravelChinaGuide.com. "Shennongjia Nature Reserve." https://www.travelchinaguide.com/attraction/hubei/shiyan/shennongjia.htm (accessed June 15, 2019).

Tsui, Sit, Qiu Jianshen, Yan Xiaohui, Erebus Wong, and Wen Tiejun. "Rural Communities and Economic Crises in Modern China." *Monthly Review,* September 1, 2018. https://monthlyreview.org/2018/09/01/rural-communities-and-economic-crises-in-modern-china/ (accessed June 15, 2019).

Tu, Lei. "Guizhou, home of China's 'silicon village,' sees GDP surging on big data." *Global Times,* January 22, 2019. http://www.globaltimes.cn/content/1136685.shtml (accessed June 15, 2019).

UNESCO World Heritage Centre. "Ancient Building Complex in the Wudang Mountains." http://whc.unesco.org/en/list/705 (accessed June 15, 2019).

Walder, Andrew G. *China Under Mao: A Revolution Derailed.* Cambridge, MA: Harvard University Press, 2015.

Walder, Andrew G., and Gong Xiaoxia. "Workers in the Tiananmen Protests: The Politics of the Beijing Workers' Autonomous Federation." *Australian Journal of Chinese Affairs,* no. 29, January 1993. http://www.tsquare.tv/links/Walder.html (accessed June 15, 2019).

Waley-Cohen, Joanna. "Expansion and Colonization in Early Modern Chinese History." *History Compass,* 2004. https://onlinelibrary.wiley.com/doi/pdf/10.1111/j.1478-0542.2004.00076.x. (accessed October 2, 2019).

Wang, Amanda, Dexter Roberts, Daniela Wei, and Rachel Chang. "Chinese-Owned Robot Maker Is Gunning for No. 1 in Booming Market." Bloomberg News, March 8, 2017. https://www.bloomberg.com/news/articles/2017-03-08/midea-eyes-top-spot-for-kuka-in-china-s-booming-robot-market (accessed June 15, 2019).

Wang, Fran. "Trade War Fuels Majority of Export Manufacturers' Shift

Out of China, Survey Shows." *Caixin*, January 8, 2019. https://www
.caixinglobal.com/2019-01-08/trade-war-fuels-majority-of-export
-manufacturers-shift-out-of-china-survey-shows-101367788.html (accessed
June 15, 2019).

Wang, Jiangsong. "The Significance of Crane Operators Across China
Going on Strike." *China Change*, May 7, 2018. https://chinachange.org
/2018/05/07/the-significance-of-crane-operators-across-china-going-on
-strike/ (accessed June 15, 2019).

Wang, Ke. "Xiaogang Village, birthplace of rural reform, moves on." *China.org
.cn*, December 15, 2008. http://www.china.org.cn/china/features/content
_16955209_4.htm (accessed June 15, 2019).

Wang, Orange. "China's gig economy losing ability to absorb laid off factory
workers." *South China Morning Post*, February 13, 2019. https://www.scmp
.com/economy/china-economy/article/2185789/chinas-grey-economy
-losing-ability-be-employment-backstop-laid (accessed June 15, 2019).

———. "China's wealth gap widens as more than half of its provinces
missed growth targets last year." *South China Morning Post*, February 14,
2019. https://www.scmp.com/economy/china-economy/article/2185738
/chinas-wealth-gap-widens-more-half-its-provinces-missed-growth (accessed June 15, 2019).

Wang, Xiaodong. "Migrants shrink by 1.7 million." *China Daily*, November 11,
2017.http://www.chinadaily.com.cn/china/2017-11/11/content_34390735.htm
(accessed August 13, 2019).

wattEV2Buy. "GAC TRUMPCHI Electric Vehicles." https://wattev2buy.com/
electric-vehicles/guangzhou-automobile-group-electric-vehicles/ (accessed
June 15, 2019).

Watts, Jonathan. *When a Billion Chinese Jump: How China Will Save Mankind—
Or Destroy It*. New York: Scribner, 2010.

Weinstein, Jodi L. *Empire and Identity in Guizhou: Local Resistance to Qing Expansion*. Seattle: University of Washington Press, 2014.

Whiting, Susan. "Property Rights and Economic Development in China."
Interview by Neysun Mahboubi. Podcast of the University of Pennsylvania Center for the Study of Contemporary China, March 19, 2019. https://
cscc.sas.upenn.edu/podcasts/2019/03/19/ep-15-property-rights-and
-economic-development-china-susan-whiting (accessed June 14, 2019).

Whyte, Martin and Teresa Wright. *Myth of the Social Volcano: Perceptions of
Inequality and Distributive Injustice in Contemporary China; Accepting Authoritarianism: State-Society Relations in China's Reform Era*. Stanford: Stanford University Press, 2010.

Wike, Richard, and Bridget Parker. "Corruption, Pollution, Inequality Are
Top Concerns in China." Pew Research Center, September 24, 2015.
http://www.pewglobal.org/2015/09/24/corruption-pollution-inequality
-are-top-concerns-in-china/ (accessed June 15, 2019).

Wolfe, Bryan M. "Wisconsin breaks ground on new Foxconn LCD panel
facility." *idownloadblog.com*, June 29, 2018. https://www.idownloadblog
.com/2018/06/29/wisconsin-foxconn-lcd/ (accessed June 15, 2019).

Wong, Edward. "China Telescope to Displace 9,000 Villagers, in Hunt for Extraterrestrials." *New York Times,* February 17, 2016. https://www.nytimes.com/2016/02/18/world/asia/china-fast-telescope-guizhou-relocation.html (accessed February 22, 2019).

Wong, Lok-to, Hai Nan, and Yang Fan. "China Continues to Evict Migrants From Beijing As Temperatures Plummet." *Radio Free Asia,* November 27, 2017. https://www.rfa.org/english/news/china/evictions-11272017143549.html (accessed June 15, 2019).

Wu, Debby. "Apple iPhone Supplier Foxconn Planning Deep Cost Cuts." Bloomberg News, November 21, 2018. https://www.bloomberg.com/news/articles/2018-11-21/apple-s-biggest-iphone-assembler-is-said-to-plan-deep-cost-cuts (accessed June 15, 2019).

———. "Apple's Partners Quicken Shift From China as Trade Tensions Rise." Bloomberg News, January 27, 2019. https://www.bloomberg.com/news/articles/2019-01-27/pegatron-moves-some-china-production-to-indonesia-on-u-s-tariff (accessed June 15, 2019).

Xi, Jinping. "Secure a Decisive Victory in Building a Moderately Prosperous Society in All Respects and Strive for the Great Success of Socialism with Chinese Characteristics for a New Era: Delivered at the 19th National Congress of the Communist Party of China, October 18, 2017." Xinhua News Agency, November 3, 2017. http://www.xinhuanet.com/english/special/2017-11/03/c_136725942.htm,

Xinhua News Agency. "China sees boom in rural e-commerce in 2017." January 25, 2018. http://www.xinhuanet.com/english/2018-01/25/c_136924446.htm (accessed June 15, 2019).

———. "Chinese premier lauds progress in mass entrepreneurship, innovation." June 27, 2017. http://news.xinhuanet.com/english/2017-06/27/c_136398203.htm (accessed June 15, 2019).

———. "Dongfeng, Nissan Sign Joint Venture Agreement." September 20, 2002. http://www.china.org.cn/english/features/44428.htm (accessed June 15, 2019).

———. "'Made in China 2025' plan unveiled." May 19, 2015. http://www.chinadaily.com.cn/bizchina/2015-05/19/content_20760528.htm (accessed June 15, 2019).

———. "Number of Chinese Farmers Dropping." October 8, 2002. http://english.china.org.cn/english/BAT/45087.htm (accessed August 17, 2019).

———. "34 floats forming 'Splendid China' in celebration parade." October 1, 2009. http://english.sina.com/china/p/2009/1001/274807.html (accessed June 15, 2019).

———. "Xi calls for people-centric reform measures, stresses employment." April 28, 2016. http://en.people.cn/n3/2016/0428/c90785-9050879-5.html (accessed June 15, 2019).

Yin, Han. "Ethnic Han parents protest exam policy favoring minority students." *Global Times,* July 30, 2017. http://www.globaltimes.cn/content/1113091.shtml (accessed June 15, 2019).

Young, Michael W. *Malinowski: Odyssey of an Anthropologist 1884–1920.* New Haven: Yale University Press, 2004.

Zhang, Pinghui. "Why Xi Jinping cares so much about ending poverty in China: the political significance behind the campaign." *South China Morning Post,* September 4, 2017. https://amp.scmp.com/news/china/society /article/2109278/why-xi-jinping-cares-so-much-about-ending-poverty -china-political (accessed June 15, 2019).

Zhang, Zhenzhen, and Ge Yang. "Internal Migration in China: Changes and Trends." In *Contemporary Demographic Transformations in China, India, and Indonesia,* edited by C. Z. Guilmoto and G. W. Jones. Switzerland: Springer, 2016.

Zhao, Yinan, and Luo Wangshu. "'Reform needed' for vocational education." *China Daily,* June 24, 2014, http://www.chinadaily.com.cn/china /2014-06/24/content_17610342.htm (accessed June 14, 2019).

Xu, Zhiyong. "For Freedom, Justice and Love—My Closing Statement to the Court." *China Change,* January 22, 2014. https://chinachange.org/2014 /01/23/for-freedom-justice-and-love-my-closing-statement-to-the-court/ (accessed May 26, 2019).

———. "Sun Zhigang case: The Last Ten Years." *China Change,* June 5, 2013, https://chinachange.org/tag/sun-zhigang-case/ (accessed May 26, 2019).

Zhongyang zhengfu menhu wangzhan 中央政府门户网站. "Zhibo huifang: Guoqing 60 zhounian dahui zai Tiananmen Guangchang chenggong juxing" 直播回放：国庆60周年大会在天安门广场成功举行. October 1, 2009. www.gov.cn/60zn/content_1431280_2.htm (accessed August 15, 2019).

Zhou, Viola. "How a poor rural province became the promised land for China's rising political stars." *South China Morning Post,* October 29, 2017. https://www.scmp.com/news/china/policies-politics/article/2117430/how -poor-rural-province-became-promised-land-chinas (accessed June 15, 2019).

Zucman, Gabriel. "Global Wealth Inequality." NBER Working Paper 25462, *National Bureau of Economic Research,* January 2019. http://www.nber.org /papers/w25462 (accessed June 15, 2019).

Index